The Last Trumpet

A Comp~~~~
Christian-Is~~~~ ~~~~ology

Samuel Shahid, Ph.D.

The Last Trumpet:
A Comparative Study in Christian-Islamic Eschatology
by Samuel Shahid

Printed in the United States of America

ISBN 1-597810-32-0

First printing 2005

www.xulonpress.com

With Deep Affection and
Appreciation
I Dedicate This Book to
My Beloved Wife Ellen

Acknowledgements

This study is the fruit of tedious uninterrupted research that required several years of scholarship under duress, patience, and perseverance. I made every effort to produce a literary work for the benefit of both Muslims and Christians with great integrity and objectivity. As I embarked on my research, I was amazed at the scope of the dependence of Islamic eschatology on Zoroastrian literature, the Bible, and the apocryphal and Christian legendary material. That incited me to look more thoroughly into as many sources as available that existed before and during Muhammad's life and era, especially in the Neareast. The puzzling question that continued to confront me was, how Muhammad was able to compre-hend this material, which was written in Syriac, Persian or Greek languages and even Latin, if he was functionally illiterate. It was not easy to come up with concrete answers. However, as I examined the sources and tried to trace the development of the relationship between the Islamic community in Arabia and Christians and Jews who lived at that time in history, it became obvious that much information must have been related to Muhammad orally. Yet, there is strong tangible evidence that the transmitters of these information have occasionally relied on written documents. Thus, it is not far from the truth to say that Muhammad's views of the apocalyptic events were basically derived from various un-related sources that lacked accuracy and chronological order.

Furthermore, when examining the corpus of Tradition, it is difficult to sort out the authentic *Hadith* from the spurious. This fact created serious problems for this writer since he had to rely on those traditions Muslim scholars frequently cite.

This having been said, I would like now to express my deep appreciation to all those who contributed, in one way or another, to make this project possible. I am grateful to my colleague Dr. Bruce Corley, who read some portions of this manuscript and proposed invaluable suggestions; to Dr. Justice Anderson who proof-read some chapters and suggested changes; to Dr. E. Earle Ellis who assisted me in discovering important sources, to Dr. Edwin Yamauchi professor of ancient history at Miami University, Oxford, Ohio, who provided me with a list of sources and references of which I was not aware, and to Southwestern Baptist Theological Seminary library officials who helped me to obtain some documents that were not available to me, and to my co-worker Greg Self who sacrificially spent long hours in editing the manuscript and helping me to clarify some ambiguous points. I am also grateful to Dr. Ken Hemphill who graciously wrote the Forward for this book.

Last and not least, I would like to express my deep gratitude to my wife Ellen, who did not only endure long hours of loneliness while I was writing this book, but she was also the encouraging force behind this project from the moment I began.

S. S.

Table of Contents

Forward

It is a distinct honor to be invited to write the forward for Dr. Shahid's monumental new book, *The Last Trumpet*. This interesting book is well researched, thoroughly documented, and an invaluable resource for all readers who are serious to discover and understand the elements that shape the Islamic eschatology and their effect on their relationship with God, salvation and future destiny. While the book makes no apology for being a serious academic work, it is nonetheless highly readable.

As the title would indicate, this comparative study focuses primarily on the eschatology of both the Christian and Islamic faiths. However, it raises a number of issues concerning the concept of revelation, redemption, salvation and eternity.

This study also demonstrates that many of the Islamic documents are mutually contradictory. This is not surprising since most Islamic eschatological information is borrowed from eclectic sources and most probably orally related. The author was objectively able to trace the original documents of these Islamic eschatological materials as they are recounted in Zoroastrianism, Christian apocryphal sources, apocalyptic studies, ancient Christian legends and the Bible, that are incorporated in the Qur'an or Islamic Tradition. It is so difficult for any Muslim scholar in any Islamic society to objectively study the Qur'an and question its veracity without being subject to the retribution of the Islamic law. Those who have dared to criticize the Qur'an, even on a scholarly level, were considered as the enemy of Islam. This stands in stark constract to the academic, but faithful study of the Bible, encouraged by the

9

evangelical community. This insight places in greater focus the necessity for a clear understanding of the doctrine of revelation and the uniqueness of the inerrancy of God's Word.

Through the study of the eschatology of these two world religions, Dr. Shahid points out that the basic difference between the Christian and Islamic faiths start with their revelatory and eschatological viewpoints. "In Christianity the crucifixion of Jesus and His resurrection are the focal points in systematic theology, including the events of the end of time. The redemptive act of Christ on the cross that reconciled man and creation with God and recovered the lost relationship, restored also the eschatological hope of all the redeemed." In contrast, Islam has a theology of deeds and not of redemption. "Their salvation depends on their deeds and the Mercy of God. Actually, Islamic theology advocates a reward-based eschatology where man's eternal life is determined by his human effort."

Dr. Shahid's study of the Islamic concept of heaven will actually help the reader to understand current world events, and perhaps better explain the concept of reward in the hereafter. For example, Dr. Shahid indicates that the suicidal activities of radical Muslims are inspired by the rewards that Islamic paradise offers that are not available to them in this life. The tragedy is that most Muslims do not realize that these images of paradise are mere reflections of the Zoroastrian paradise. The appeal of the sensual pleasures of paradise inflames their desire to die for the cause of Allah. The author asks a penetrating question any suicidal radical in particular and Muslims in general should contemplate: What might occur if Muslims are made aware that their view of paradise is just an echo of the Zoroastrian

10

paradise? "Would they sacrifice their lives for a mirage or an illusion?"

This book is indespensable for anyone who has the desire to understand in-depth the forces that motivate sincere Muslims to adhere to their faith. It also unveils the eschatological differences between Christianity and Islam. It is essential for anyone who wants to comprehend the complicated implications of the extremists' worldviews based on their eschatological and religious ideologies.

This study also, is a necessary source for whoever is interested to be effective in sharing the plan of salvation and the Good News of redemption in heaven with a Muslim neighbor, for only through Jesus Christ and His atoning sacrifice one can attain his eternal life.

Kenneth Hemphill

Kenneth S. Hemphill is the national strategist for the Southern Baptist Convention's Empowering Kingdom Growth, and former president of Southwestern Baptist Theological Seminary.

Introduction

Since man has harbored in his heart a deep desire for immortality, eschatology has become a vibrant part of the great world religions. It is difficult to study the mythologies of ancient religions without encountering some aspects of eschatological emphasis. Greek, Egyptian, the Babylonian epic of Gilgamesh, and many other cultures and traditions recount briefly or in thorough details, the existence of the paradisiacal world and eternal torment.[1] Primitive millenarian and messianic myths and legends are "found in the tribal cultures in Africa, South America, and Melanesia."[2] Among World's Living Religions, Judaism, Christianity, and Islam, the concept of hereafter constitutes a fundamental creed in their systematic theology. Before then, Zoroastrianism developed an intricate dogma of the end of time.[3]

Examining great world's living religions however, Christianity has provided humanity with the most detailed and elaborate biblical scripture of the end of time. Some aspects of eschatological texts are written in prophetical and allegorical style. These features create interpretative problems for those who are not familiar with the biblical language. In fact, this is the dilemma for much of the eschatological material found in these religions. In case of Christianity and Islam, such difficulty does not preclude that, a common agreement exists among the majority of the theologians of the two faiths about the second coming of Christ.

The word eschatology is derived from the Greek words *eschatos* and *logos*, which literally means the study of the times of the end, or the last things, or end times.

Zoroastrianism, Christianity and Islam, all believe that world history is indeed oriented towards an end, creating or recreating a new holy and complete world. All believe this world is temporary, incomplete, and imperfect but as it pursues its historical course it will achieve its completion and perfection, devoid of evil and conflict at the end of time.

Thus, this study focuses on the second coming of Christ and life after death in Islam. But since Christ is the focal point of these eschatological and glorious events, it is impossible to eschew examining the impact of Christianity on Islamic eschatological thought. Islamic sources made it conspicuous that Christian data has been incorporated into the Islamic episodes of the end of time. Most of this data is diluted with fairy tales like the incident of the Jassasa.[4] Consequently, a section of this study will be set apart to discuss the corpus of material Islam borrowed from Christianity. Some of the Islamic narratives are based on ambiguous characters that will play a vital part in the historical events before the coming of the Hour (the resurrection and the Day of Judgment), such as the Antichrist, Gog and Magog, the Beast, etc. Though they represent the powers of evil and destruction and soon would perish, these evil forces are transformed into deformed characters in the Islamic account. Even the role Jesus Christ would assume in this world event is perverted to fit the Islamic concept of Isa (the Qur'anic name for Jesus) as a mere prophet who will return to proclaim to the entire world that Islam is the true religion of God.[5] Thus, before the end of the world, only the faith of Islam will prevail and no other religion will survive.

It is appropriate here to indicate that the Shi'ites also anticipate the second coming of Christ. However, they

14

view this event from a rather different perspective. The second advent of Christ synchronizes with the advent of the Mahdi (the rightly guided Imam) from his occultation,[6] or soon after his return. The Mahdi will join forces with Christ in His final battle against the powers of the Antichrist. In the Shi'ite traditions the relationship between these two super beings is rather veiled with obscurity (this issue will be discussed in chapter six).

Most Islamic data that explored the role of these supernatural characters that would appear on the stage of world history to unfold the prophetic events, is ascribed to Muhammad. This reality creates an enigmatic problem to the researcher of this study. Since the authenticity of a large body of Islamic Traditions is questionable, the possibility that many spurious traditions are falsely attributed to Muhammad is high. On the other hand, many of these traditions are handed down through different sets of chain of authorities that mostly were Muhammad's companions. If by evidence of these chains of authorities Muhammad did really relate to his followers the story of the Jassasa and the episode of the Antichrist who was imprisoned, fettered in chains in an island when roving Muslim or (Arab) sailors visited with him, then we are faced with a series of complicated questions: When and where was this fiend born? If he was already an adult during Muhammad's epoch, he must be by now over 1400 years old. How did it happen that he was at that island? What was the name of the island? Which sea did they navigate? Was it so close to Arabia or down by the great sea? Is the Jassasa the same Beast mentioned in the Qur'an? And most importantly to this study, did the prophet of the Arabs really transmit these incidents to his audience? If so, then why?

It is also necessary to briefly mention in this vein that Sufism, represented in the person of Ibn Arabic, who in spite of his mystical views and beliefs did not attempt to subvert the Islamic eschatological dogma or spiritualize it,

> "Far from rejecting such articles of faith as the two angels who question the soul in the grave, the blast on Seraphiel's trumpet that awakens the dead, the Balance set up to weigh human deeds at the Resurrection, and the division of human beings into the inhabitants of paradise and hell, Ibn Arabi maintains that anyone who attempts to turn these doctrines into allegories through 'rational hermeneutics' only proves that his intelligence is corrupt and his faith is imperfect.[7]

In Ibn 'Arabi's opinion there is no reason to interpret or explain the Qur'anic verses and the *hadith* "to fit into a rational system of thought"[8] and cannot be comprehended literally.

Lastly, it is an arduous task to find an entire scholarly book in English dealing with Christian-Islamic eschatological literature.[9] The few precious articles that searched the Islamic anecdotes of the second coming of Christ and contrasted them with Christian and apocalyptic material were brief and very rare.[10] But recently the Arab world has witnessed an invasion of several hundred of new modern Islamic apocalyptic resources and references in Arabic, inspired by the political events and the struggle between Arabs and Israel.[11] The Muslim writers who benefited from, and exploited the Christian apocalyptic interpretations and expectations, found in their views and

16

writings inexhaustible sources of information.[12] Neverthe-less if these modern books were mainly proliferated as the result of the political struggle, the majority of ancient Islamic studies are collections or compendiums from the books of the *Hadith* (books of Islamic Traditions), which, in most cases, concerned themselves with the prophetical future events on a religious basis. This does not mean at all that the political elements were absent from the ancient Islamic perspectives. However, these ancient materials have failed to respond to the current political situations and world events that relentlessly created successive crises to the Islamic Middle East. The following is a selective list of bibliographies of these resources and references:[13]

- Muhammad al-Barzanji, *al-Isha'at li Ashrat al-Sa'at,* (no place: al-Sa'adah,1356 *H./*1939 A.D..).
- Siddiq Hasan Khan, *al-Idha'ah lima kana wa Yakunu* Bayn *Yadayi al-Sa'at,* (Egypt: Namakani press, 1379 H./1959 A.D.)
- Al-Suyuti, *Al-I'lam bi Hukm 'Isa fi Akhir al-Zaman,* (no place: al-Muniriyya ed., 1352 H./1933 A.D.)
- Al-Ghumari, *Iqamat al-Burhan fi Nuzul 'Isa fi Akhir al-Zaman,* (Egypt: no publisher, no date)
- _____ *'Aqidat al_islam fi Nuzul 'Isa 'Alayhi al-Salam,* (No place: `Atif ed., no date)
- Al-Kashmiry, *'Aqidat al-Islam fi Hayat 'Isa 'Alayhi al-Salam,* (India: Qasimi Ed., no date)
- Ibn Hajar al-'Asqalani, *Fath al-Bari bi Sharh al-Bukhari* (Egypt: Bulaq ed., 1300 H./1911 A.D.)
- Muhammad Anwar Shah al-Kaskmiri, *(Al-Tasrih bima Tawatara fi Nuzul al-Masih,* (Aleppo: Maktabat al-Matbu'at al-Islamiya, (1385 H./1965 A.D.).

- Ragnar Eklund, *Life Between Death and Resurrection According to Islam,* (Uppsala: Almquist and Wiksells, 1941).
- Abu Hamid Muhammad al-Ghazali, *The Remembrance of Death and the Afterlife;* Translated by T. J. Winter, (Cambridge: The Islamic Texts Society), 1989.
- Christopher C. Hong, *A History of the Future: A Study of the Four Major Eschatologies,* (Washington D. C.: University Press of America), 1981.
- Salih Tuq, "Death and Immortality in Islamic Thought," *In Death and Immortality in the Religions of the World;* ed. Paul and Linda Badham, 86-92; (New York, NY: Paragon House), 1987.
- Sulayman S. Nyang, "The Teaching of the Qur'an Concerning Life after Death", in *Death and Immortality in the Religions of the World,* ed. Paul and Linda Badham, 71-85, (New York, NY: Paragon House), 1989.
- Jan Knappert, "The Concept of Death and the Afterlife in Islam", in *Perspectives on Death and Dying;* ed. Arthur Berger and Others, 55-65, (philadephia, PA: Charles Press), 1989.
- Ahmad Anisuzzaman Muwahidi, "The Concept of Death and the Afterlife in Islam", in *Perspectives on Death and Dying,* ed. Arthur Berger and Others, 38-54, (Philadelphia, PA: Charles Press), 1989.
- Ahmad H. Sakr, *Death and Dying,* (Lombard, IL.: Foudation for Islamic Knowledge), 1995.

In addition to the Shi'ite Hadith collections, below is selective list of books appertained to the topic under discussion:

- Kamel Sulayman, *Yawm al-Khalas,* (Beirut: Dar Al-Kitab al-Lubnani, 7th ed., 1991).
- Sa'id Ayyub, *'Aqidat al-Masih al-Dajjal fi al-Adyan* (Beirut, Lebanon: Dar al-Hadi, 1st ed. 1991).
- Most compilers of the Islamic Hadith earmarked in their collections, a section or more to the episode of the second coming of Christ.
- W. C. Chittick, (Ed. & trsl.), *A Shi'ite Anthology,* (Albany, New York: Suny Press, 1981).
- D.M. Donaldson, *The Shi'ite Religion,* (London, 1942).
- J. M. Hussain, *The Occultation of the Twelfth Imam,* (London: The Muhammadi Trust, 1982).
- Mojan Momen, *Shi'ite Islam,* New Haven: Yale University Press, 1985).
- A. Sachedina, *Islamic Messianism,* (Albany, New York: Suny Press, 1981).
- M. Husayn al-Tabataba'i, *Shi'ite Islam,* Transl. by Seyyed Hossein Nasr, (State University of New York Press, 1977).
- H.A.R. Gibb & J.H. Kramer, *Shorter Encyclopedia of Islam,* (Leiden: E. J. Brill, 1974).

More resources and references, in both Arabic and English, are listed in the general bibliography of this study.

Biblical quotations are cited from New American Standard, 1995 update, with the expanded edition of Ryrie Study Bible. The Qur'anic citations are quoted from The Meaning of the Holy Qur'an, Abdullah Yusuf 'Ali's translation, Arberry translation and M. H. Shakir translation, unless it is indicated that the translation is mine. Furthermore, whenever the term *Hadith* is capitalized it alludes to the entire compendiums of Islamic traditions,

19

whereas when is used with lower case it denotes one or several individual *hadiths*. This also applies to the term tradition. When the upper case is used, it points to the corpus of Islamic Tradition; but when the lower case is used as in tradition(s), it implies that one or more of the individual traditions is intended.

It is also necessary for some Arabic quotations to be literally translated into English. Thus, the actual translation may not follow the correct English literary expression otherwise losing some important and valuable shades of its meaning.

Most of the Hadith quotations are cited from the CD ROM 'Alim' produced by ISL Software Corporation, 6th edition, 1986-1999, unless specified otherwise.

CHAPTER ONE

The Hour is Imminent

Muslims, both Sunnis and Shi'ites, adhere to the concept of the second coming of Christ. But the two sects are incongruent in their perspectives of this future eschatological event. As they embrace two far-reaching contrasting perspectives of world-views, their interpretations of the meanings and the sequences of the phenomenon of the end of times are incompatible. Thus, it is incumbent on the students of the Islamic eschatology to address both views for such a study to be adequate and valuable.

Any scholar who endeavors to examine the eschatological Islamic data of the second coming of Christ has to resort to the *Hadith*[1] and not to the Qur'anic scriptures. The Qur'an is surprisingly silent about this significant event and does not reveal any information except what it is recorded in chapter 43:61,

> And (Jesus) shall be a sign (for the coming of) the Hour (of Judgment)): therefore have no doubt about the (Hour) but follow ye me: this is a Straight Way.

وَإِنَّهُ (عِيسى) لَعِلْمٌ لِلسَّاعَةِ فلا تَمْتَرُنَّ بها وَاتَّبِعون هذا صِرَاطٌ مُسْتَقِيمٌ

There is no indication in this verse that the word "*Innahu*" which means "it is" or "he is," refers to Jesus.

Muslims adopted the popular interpretation on the basis of the *Hadith's* allusion as it attributed to Muhammad. Others hint that the context of the Qur'anic verses suggests, "it is" implies Jesus. However, some former scholars claim that there is a different reading to the word *'ilm'*. It was recited as *'alam*[2], which means: indication, insignia, emblem, mark or guidepost.

The roots of the Islamic eschaton originated from the Holy Qur'an, but that doctrine "was expanded in the Traditions and then worked out in detail in every (sic) numerous little popular eschatological tractates."[3] The Qur'an, however, refers frequently to the Hour of Judgment in number of various *suras* (or, chapters). The scene is very terrifying and macabre. It aims at creating a sense of awe in the hearts of the disbelievers. In this context, the return of Christ is one of the major signs that signal the approach of the Hour. The Qur'an made the Hour an evitable event that would afflict all God's creation. For "to Allah belongs the dominion of the heavens and the earth and the Day that the Hour of Judgment is established."[4] "The Hour is surely coming" (15:85) and "the Hour is certain" (15:99) whether it is the hour of death or the Hour of the Day of Judgment. When it dreadfully occurs "The decision of the Hour is as the twinkling of the eye or even quicker" (16:77) and the "convulsion of the Hour of Judgment will be a thing terrible" (22:1). The vivid picture of the anguish of the sudden Hour delineated by the Qur'an, is full of horrors (22:2, 11 and 55). In Sura 81:1-14 the Qur'an says:

> When the sun (with its spacious light) is folded up; when the stars fall, losing their luster; when the mountains vanish (like a mirage); when the she-camels, ten month with young, are left untended; when the wild beasts are herded together (in human habi-

tations); when the oceans boil over with a swell; when the souls are sorted out, (being joined, like with like); when the female (infant) is questioned for what crime she was killed; when the scrolls are laid open; when the world on high is unveiled; when the blazing fire is kindled to fierce heat; when the Garden is brought near; (then) shall each soul know what it has put forward.

إِذَا الشَّمْسُ كُوِّرَتْ؛ وَإِذَا النُّجُومُ انْكَدَرَتْ؛ وَإِذَا الْجِبَالُ سُيِّرَتْ؛ وَإِذَاالْعِشَارُ عُطِّلَتْ؛ وَإِذَا الْوُحُوشُ حُشِرَتْ؛ وَإِذَا الْبِحَارُ سُجِّرَتْ؛ وَإِذَا النُّفُوسُ زُوِّجَتْ ؛ وَإِذَا الْمَوْءُدةُ سُئِلَتْ؛ بِأَي ذَنْبٍ قُتِلَتْ؛ وَإِذَا الصُّحُفُ نُشِرَتْ؛ وَإِذَا السَّمَاءُ كُشِطَتْ؛ وَإِذَا الْجَحِيمُ سُعِّرَتْ؛ وَإِذَا الْجَنَّةُ أُزْلِفَتْ؛ عَلِمَتْ نَفْسٌ مَا أَحْضَرَتْ.

In that Day "all men shall be sorted out" (30:14) "the guilty will be struck dumb with despair" (30:12) and "the dealers in falsehood will perish."[5]

So the Hour is surely coming[6] "all of a sudden while they (people) perceive not" (22:55)[7] and feel secured, but there is no security from the final Hour (12:107).

The Qur'an also asserts that no father can protect his son nor a son can intercede for his father to shelter him from the wrath of God and His condemnation. The Hour is a day in which every person is accountable for his deeds.[8] But there is hope or reward for the righteous who believe in the veracity of the Hour and the Day of Judgment[9] and retribution for those who violate God's laws and disbelieve in the day of reckoning. Muhammad actually made the belief in the Day of Judgment as one of the fundamentals of

23

Islam.[10] Obviously, Islam teaches that man's acts, good or bad, are observable by God.

But who has the knowledge of the Hour?

The Qur'an clearly demonstrates that only God possesses the knowledge of the hour[11] and if He delays the coming of this terrible day, He does that in order to punish the disbelievers and the wicked.[12] Obviously, Muhammad was acquainted with Jesus' allusion to the day of resurrection and His emphasis that only the Father knows the day and the Hour. In comparison, we read in Matthew 24: 36, *"No one knows about that day or hour, not even the angels in heaven, nor the Son, but only the Father"*.[13] This concept fits well with the Islamic doctrine of the sovereign-ty of God.

In his call, Muhammad had continuously warned both the believers and the polytheists of Mecca, to watch for the signs of the Hour. It is certainly impending and if they observe carefully the signs of time, they will recognize that the end is at hand. On the authority of 'Abdullah b. Hawala al-Azdi, one of Muhammad's intimate companions, he related a hadith ascribed to Muhammad concerning the nearness of the dooms day. He said:

> ...he placed his hand on my head and said,
> 'Ibn Hawala, when you see the caliphate has
> settled in the holy land, earthquake, sorrows,
> and serious matters will have drawn near,
> (and) on that day the last Hour will be nearer
> to mankind than the hand of mine is to your
> head'.[14]

What did Muhammad mean by the "holy land"? If he meant Arabia and the establishment of the caliphate in

24

Yathrib (al-Madina), that took place over 1400 years ago and the Hour has yet to come. If Palestine was the intended holy land, no seat of a caliph had been founded in Jerusalem. The Qur'an, however, like the Bible, does not specify the exact appointed time of the Hour. It only refers to events that will signal its arrival. Apparently, Muham-mad firmly embraced the teaching or the expectation of the early Christians who anticipated the second coming of Christ during their lifetime.[15] Based on some historical events, some Muslim scholars endeavored to suggest various dates for the coming of the Hour.[16] Despite that, why did the Qur'an fail to elaborate on the second coming of Christ? One question that surely begs for an answer is: Why is there only one orphan ambiguous verse about the center figure that is going to play a dramatic role in the world events?

Muslims agree that Sura 43 was revealed during the Meccan period when Muhammad was still striving to survive the vehement attack of his vicious enemies. It seems that Muhammad encountered in Mecca a situation similar to that of the apostle Paul among the Athenians and Epicurean philosophers.[17] The people of Mecca derided the whole concept of the resurrection of the dead and the Hour of God's doomsday. The Athenians' elites reflected the same sarcastic attitude of the Meccans when they heard Paul's thesis on the resurrection of the dead. It is also certain that Muhammad acquired bits of information about the Second coming of Christ from the heretical Christians he met in his first twelve years of his mission. Some pseudo-canonical literature and Gnostic books were in vogue among the learned Arab Christians.[18] These Chris-tians, it seems, related verbally to Muhammad some aspects of Christian eschatology as is interpreted by non-orthodox Christian sects. That does not negate that they incorporated into their narratives various biblical perspectives. It is difficult to believe otherwise, since a thorough study of the Islamic data reveals these discrepancies.[19]

As we thoroughly compare the concept of the Hour (the day of resurrection) with that of Christianity, we encounter a number of major discords between the two. It seems that the Bible points to two types of resurrections.[20] **The first** occurs in the second coming of Christ to assemble the believers, both the dead and the living. It will be a glorious moment in the life of the church. The dead in Christ are the first to rise and soon those who are still alive and have been left, will be caught up together with them in the clouds to meet the Lord forever (1 Thessalonians 4: 16-17). There is a sequence for this supernatural event: (a) Jesus will come in a majestic visible way and with a great shout, (b) a voice of an angel will echo, recognizable by everyone, (c) a call of the trumpet of the Lord will be heard everywhere, (d) the dead in Christ will rise from the graves and (e) the living believers will be raptured and join the rising dead in the cloud to meet the Lord in the air. **The second resurrection** is the resurrection for the Day of Judgment. This is a general resurrection. The prophetic language suggests that in this resurrection only the condemned will be resurrected (Revelation 20:6). However, some biblical scholars indicate that the believers of the Old Testament will also be resurrected in this second event,[21] or the martyrs who shed their blood for the sake of Christ during the tribulation.

In Islam, there is only one resurrection. According to the *Hadith,* after the demise of Christ, in His second coming, all Muslim believers will miraculously die. The resurrection will come upon the wicked that are still alive. It is true that all humankind will be resurrected for the Day of Judgment, but the believers who died by a divine 'pleasant wind that soothes (people) even under their armpits, will be spared the agony that will afflict the wicked before the Hour.'[22] Thus, Muhammad was obsessed with the concept of the day of resurrection and judgment as he strove to win the Meccan to the new faith.[23]

In the Qur'anic eschatology, the wrath of God and the Day of Judgment were two effective weapons Muhammad utilized in his strategy. This strategy had two dimensions. On one hand, it was a fortified front of defense against his persecutors who physically tortured him and the few adherents he won. At the time, he had no military power to rely on in defending himself against the terrorism of his foes. In his weakness, he had no choice but to constantly threatening them with the wrath of God. Though the Qurayshites (Muhammad's tribe) were a polytheistic tribe, they acknowledged the existence of a supreme inactive God. They were more concerned in propitiating the idols of the ka'ba than worshipping this supreme God. The Qur'an reactivated and restored the power of this "secluded" God and His sovereignty over the entire universe. He is not only the supreme God, but he is the only God. Thus, whoever harms Allah's messenger will incur upon himself the wrath of God. On the other hand, Muhammad had to warn them of the consequences of their defiance against Allah the Creator and the Judge, and His messenger. The rejection of the prophethood of Muhammad and his mission entails the rejection of Allah's ordination and revelation. To reinforce this intimate relationship between Allah and His messenger Muhammad, it became incumbent on every Muslim whenever he uttered the Confession of Faith الشّهادة, to associate the name of Muhammad with the name of Allah. It is not sufficient to acknowledge Allah and to worship Him in order to be a Muslim. Muhammad has to be acknowledged, as well, as the last messenger of Allah. This confession of faith makes a person a Muslim and an adherent of Islam. Defying this peremptory command would result in eternal excruciation in hell. It was not difficult for the people of Mecca to comprehend the ideology of God's condemnation, but their main problem was to believe in the concept of resurrection and in Muhammad's prophethood. It was very critical for Muhammad to be recognized as a prophet. In his book *Fi al-Shi'r al-Jahili* (In Pre-Islamic Poetry), the Egyptian scholar Taha Husein indicated that at the inception of Islam in Mecca, Muhammad and his followers were weak and, thus, the only method to which he resorted was the pure ideological debate on the basis of the Qur'anic revelation.[24]

Though Islam claims there is no preference among Allah's prophets,[25] a closer look at the creeds of the faith impels the reader to admit that Islam bestows a distinctive status on Muhammad as the seal of the prophets and as the only prophet that was sent as a mercy to the entire world.[26] Thus, Muhammad's threat to the disbelievers bears the stamp of personal antagonism against the skeptics.

In Yathrib, the City of the Prophet, Muhammad was more exposed to the Jews, the Christians, and Zoroastrians, or former adherents of these religions who were converted to Islam. But the impact of Christianity and Zoroastrianism on the Islamic eschatology was far more dominant than Judaism.[27] In this eschatological realm the Jews, in the person of the Antichrist, manifested the forces of evil.[28] In most cases, Muhammad's eschatological knowledge he acquired from these different sources was not authentic because they were related to him verbally. The originality of Muhammad was in his brilliant ability in molding and formulating such knowledge in an Arabic context appealing to the understanding and the mood of the Arabs in general, and the Meccans and Madinites in particular. It is not difficult to infer from the above that Muhammad could not have received valid information about the Second Coming

28

of Christ from Orthodox *Nasara*.[29] Obviously, the picture did not change too much between the two cities. Both the Meccan and the Madinite Suras lacked any allusion to the Second Coming of Christ, with the exception of the above-mentioned verse. So, the puzzling question why has the Qur'an failed to clarify the significant role of Jesus in this world drama, continued to be unanswered.

For this study, the major source for the Islamic Second Coming of Christ is the *Hadith*. But the *Hadith* is subject to incredulity. Though most information reiterated in this study is quoted from the most reliable collections of *Hadith*, there is no assurance or guarantee that all the information cited here is accurate and trustworthy. Muslim scholars admit that a sizeable volume of the *Hadith* is spurious, despite the meticulous and tremendous efforts of the famous compilers of the Islamic Tradition to sift the sound from the falsified. Many *hadiths* are repeated more than once in the same collection. Naturally, most of these *hadiths* are ascribed to Muhammad. This is why both Sunnis and Shi'ites rely heavily on the *Hadith* in this regard as their second most important source. Certainly, they do not have any other comprehensive source to which they can resort to obtain their information about the Islamic Second Coming of Christ.

CHAPTER TWO
The Minor Signs
ألعلامات الصُّغرى

M uslims have divided the signs that herald the end of time into two categories: minor signs and major signs.

Minor Signs العلامات الصغرى

In Islam, minor signs of the end of time are the signs that take place seriatim (in continuous series over time). They are normal events that characterize any society that undergoes cultural changes as the result of social, religious, political, economical or technical evolution. Primitive societies are prone to be more stable, simplistic and homogeneous, while developed countries are subject to perpetual changes, for good or for bad. Through this changing process in which drastic transformation, modified modes, values and social classification may significantly affect all aspects of the daily life of people. What was considered a taboo in the past may not be currently regarded as a taboo. In other words, the worldview of a given society becomes more materialistic, individualistic and irreligious.

Such societies experience moral disorder, spiritual decadence, and fierce struggle between liberalism and conservatism. Thus, according to Islamic ethics, Islamic societies have suffered from these social maladies since the inception of the reign of the Umayyad epoch. This trend continued to underscore the daily life of the Islamic communities in urban areas throughout the reign of the Abbasid dynasty. The spiritual life became very bleak despite the efforts of Muslim religious leaders to contain the tide of depravity and immorality. All attempts to re-generate a righteous society after the model of the Islamic community of the Madinites as it was during the life of Muhammad, have failed. The Islamic civilization was not the only or the first civilization to sustain such moral decay. Great civilizations before: Greek, Roman, Persian, Egyptian and others, were subject to fatal moral degeneration that corroded their societies in spite of their highly developed civilizations.

By examining the nature of the minor signs we realize that some of them are normal events that plague any society at any given point in its historical course. While other signs are categorized as normal events, they are, in reality, extraordinary. They would baffle the mind if they ever actually happened.

The Normal Minor Signs

a. The increase of ignorance.[1] Ignorance of the funda-mentals of Islamic religion. The ordinances of Islam will cease to be an integral part of the daily religious life of Muslim communities. There will be a lack of Imams and spiritual guidance, and mosques will be deserted.[2] Corporal tantalizations become the idols worshipped by people. It is a tragic return to the era of ignorance of the pre-Islamic time but in different form. One reason for such ignorance is the death of religious learned men. The Hajj journey (pilgrimage) to the Ka'ba will be abandoned[3]. Furthermore, the Hour will not be established until the women of the tribe of Dus resume their dancing around the idol *Dhi*

31

al-khulasa.[4] It is a religious inversion in defiance to Islam, and a return to polytheism.

b. The prevalence of drinking alcohol and the practice of open illegal sexual intercourse.[5] This is a violation of the Islamic moral code. In this case, the Islamic Law becomes dysfunctional since its religious custodians are powerless or already deceased. The breakdown of the socio-religious values will create a chaotic, unrestrained society that indulges openly in mundane pleasures.

These immoral practices are vibrantly depicted in the New Testament. It seems that Muslim traditionalists or even Muhammad himself, were aware of the biblical teachings about the evil that would embroil the society in the last days. Matthew 24:12 indicates that because of increase of wickedness, the love of God will grow cold in the hearts of many believers, '*There will be terrible times in the last days. People will be lovers of themselves, lovers of money, boastful, proud, abusive, disobedient to their parents, ungrateful, unholy, without love, unforgiving, slanderous, without self-control, brutal, not lovers of good, treacherous, rash, conceited, lovers of pleasure rather than lovers of God - having a form of godliness but denying its power'.*[6] Such abominable society reflects not only the secular world but also alludes to the corruption that would permeate the spiritual life of many of so-called Christians. In reality, a large segment of the traditional Christian world will relinquish its faith and defy all the biblical values.

d. Apostasy.[7] The Hour of the end of time will not be established until some Muslim believers are enticed by the *Dajjal* (Anti-Christ) and follow him. They will be deceived by the temporary power he enjoys and the miracles he performs.

Jesus predicted that *'many false prophets will arise and will mislead many'* (Matthew 24:11). These false prophets are *the avant-garde* who would pave the way for the dramatic appearance of the Antichrist. In another place, Jesus warned the believers that *"false christs and false prophets will arise and will show great signs and wonders, so as to mislead, if possible, even the elect"* (Matthew 24:24).

Evidently Muhammad heard of the Antichrist and other false prophets that would entice and mislead entire communities from Christians. Those Christians were zealously anticipating the second coming of Christ like their predecessors.They watched for the signs of which Jesus prophesized, and endeavored to read the future. Most probably their preachers, orators, and hermits such as "Umayya bin Abi al-Salt (d. 624),[8] who was a contemporary of Muhammad, Quss bin Sa'ida al-Ayadi (d.600),[9] whom Muhammad as a youth heard him preaching in the literary assembly of Suq of 'Ukaz and quoted a portion of his sermon, and, Waraqa bin Nawfal,[10] who was the most knowledgeable Christian religious scholar in Mecca, and Muhammad's first wife's cousin;[11] all reflected in their sermons images the Qur'an later echoed about the Hour of the resurrection.

e. The end of time will come when earthquakes will be more frequent, plagues will be widespread so that no Arab house will escape, murder crimes will increase, money will overflow among Muslims and time will pass very quickly. The wealth will be in abundance so that one will become worried, for no one will accept his Almsgiving (Zakat), and the person to whom the charity is offered will reply, *'I am not in need of it'*.[12] These calamities will afflict the world.

f. The Hour will approach when women outnumber men so that one man will look after fifty women.[13] There is no reason given for this imbalance between men and women. Most probably Muslim traditionalists anticipated that a large number of men will be killed in wars and leave behind a large crowd of widows and orphans.

g. The Hour will come when the power of authority is entrusted to the hand of unfit or unqualified people.[14] Among these people who lack honesty, corruption will prevail. In another *hadith,* it is stated: 'when bare footed naked people become the chiefs of the people'.[15] Moreover, 'the last Hour will not come until the most fortunate of men in the world will be baseborn, son of a baseborn'.[16]

h. The Hour will come when people boast of building luxurious mosques.[17] Al-Bukhari remarks that the Hour will come when 'the shepherds of black camels start boasting and competing with each other in the construction of higher buildings'.[18] Some Muslim expounders found in the profound change of the Saudi Arabia nomadic society that transformed it into unprecedented sophisticated sedentary life, a fulfillment of this tradition.

i The Hour will not be established until a "man passes by the grave of another man and says, 'If I were in his place.'"[19] Some Muslim expositors remark that death becomes the desire of many devout Muslims who suffer from the blights and wickedness of the society, or to spare themselves the wrath of the sovereign God. In Revelation 6:16-17 we read *"And they said to the mountains and the rocks, 'Fall on us and hide us from the presence of Him who sits on the throne, and from the wrath of the Lamb; for the great day of their wrath has come and who is able to stand'?"* One

34

wonders if these Muslim traditionalists had been acquainted with Christian eschatological phenomenon..

j. The Hour will not be established till Muslims "copy the deeds of the previous nations and follow them very closely." When Muhammad was asked if he meant by those (nations) the Persians and the Byzantines, he said, "Who can it be other than they?"[20] This is a tenuous claim since these two empires -especially the Persian Empire - impacted culturally, administratessly and politically the structure of the new Islamic empire and the end of time has not yet come.

k. The Hour will not be established until:

> There is a war between two groups among whom there will be a great number of casualties, though the claims (or religion) of both of them will be the same.[21]

It is possible that this was the tradition that suggested to the Muslim commentators that women would outnumber men one to fifty. Most probably, these two groups are two Muslim sects who, for political or ideological reasons, will wage war against each other.

l. The Hour will not come untill a man from Qahtan appears who would drive the people with his staff.[22] According to South Arabia traditions this Qahtanid man is regarded as the Mahdi of the pre-Islamic Himyarite era "whose duty is that of herding his people together preparatory to the resurrection and Day of Judgment, Perhaps through the re-institution of the pre-Islamic monarchy and its supposed rule of Justice.[23] His rise will usher the end of time.

m. The Last Hour will not come before thirty (or thirty-one) false prophets, among them four women, would come forth;[24] each one claims that he is the apostle of Allah,[25] or lying on Allah and His apostle. Muhammad made it clear that those alleged prophets would emerge from among the Arabs *my community,* who would relate to the Muslims innovative traditions of which they and their forefathers have never heard.[26] It seemed that Muhammad was acquainted with the teaching of Jesus, who warned His followers against the false prophets who would propagate their heresies, claiming that they were the Messiah. This account is found in the Gospel of Matthew 24:23-24. Church history has affirmed that innumerable false prophets have appeared among the Jews who were expecting the coming of the Messiah, as well as the Christendom even to the present time. On the authority of Muhammad, Ibn Kathir indicates that before the coming of the Hour, over 70 propagandists from among *my community,* would lead people to hell with their heresies and if '*I wish I would have foretold you their names and the names of their tribes.*'[27] Why did Muhammad abstain from predicting their names and the name of their tribes? That would have guarded the Muslims against their perfidy. That was not the only time in which Muhammad reiterated such a remark. In the context of his relating to his audience the episode of the future massacre between Muslims and the Byzantines, he alluded to the ten horsemen who were sent as a military vanguard to investigate a rumor about the Antichrist. He said, '*And indeed I know their names, the names of their fathers and the color of their horses. They are the best horsemen of the time on the surface of the earth.*'[28]

إنِّي لأعْرِفُ أسْماءَهُم وأسْماءَ آبائهِم وَألوانَ خيولِهِم. هُم خَيْرُ فوارسَ على
ظَهْرِ الأرْض يَوْمَئذٍ

36

It is an effete attempt to justify Muhammad's reluctance to foretell their names since he claimed that he had an intimate knowledge of them. It is the belief of this writer that disclosing their names would make Muhammad vulnerable in case it was proven that his prediction was a false prognosis. There is a precedent in the Qur'an in which Muhammad was challenged by the people of Mecca to perform a miracle. He rejected their request claiming that even if he complied with their demand they would not believe. The Qur'an also made it clear that God did not allow Muhammad to make a prodigy (chapter 30:59). The inmitability of the Qur'an as the inspired word of God is sufficient for Muslims to regard it as the irrefutable miracle. Thus, we do not have any record in the Qur'an of any miracle made by Muhammad, though in the view of the community, miracles were *sine qua non* as a definite peremptory proof of prophethood. All what is recorded in the Islamic Traditions and later biographies about Muhammad's miracles defy the prescribed verses of the Qur'an and are mere inventions of the imagination of Muslims who ascribed to Muhammad these miracles following the example of the former prophets. To both Christians and Muslims, miracles are tangible evidence to the authenticity of a prophet.

n. The last Hour does not come until Muslims murder their leader, fight among themselves with their swords and the worst of the people will inherit all their worldly possessions.[29] The history of Arab Islamic empire dynasties is a belligerent history. Since its inception, several caliphs have been assassinated, such as 'Umar bin al-Khattab 'Uthman bin Affan, 'Ali bin abi Talib and his two sons, the fight among the companions, the wars between the Shi'its and the

37

Sunnis, the 'Umayyad and the 'Abbasids, even among the members of the household of the caliphs. Despite this sanguinary history, the last Hour is still hidden in the obscure future and never materialized.

o. The Hour does not arrive until there will be commotions like bits of a dark night in which a man who would be a believer in the morning would turn into an infidel in the evening, or who had been an infidel in the evening would turn into a believer in the morning.[30] This fluctuation between faith and skepticism reflects the state of chaos that stigmatized the degenerated society especially during the disintegration of the declined Arab empire.[31]

p. The Hour will not come upon people until the caliphate has been established in the holy land, and earthquakes, calamities and serious matters are drawn near.[32]

q. One of the signs of the approach of the last Hour will be the destruction of the Arabs.[33]

History recounts that the destruction of the Arabs was simultaneous with the collapse of the political system of the empire. Foreign powers such as the Mamluks, the Buwayhids and the Suljuks ripped apart the Arab empire. Later Hulago the Tatar conquered and looted the city of Baghdad and destroyed other diminutive kingdoms. Soon the Ottoman Empire annexed to its domain the entire Middle East with the exception of Persia. For over four hundred years, Arab countries have continued to be subjugated to this formidable super power. In the twentieth century however, Arab countries, against all odds, regained their sovereignty, independence, freedom and survived the vicissitudes of life. Evidently, the Arabs have not been eradicated and presently they are impacting the world history as

38

they try to revive the past glory of Islam. Still the Hour has not come yet.

r. The last Hour would not come until the habitations of Medina would extend to *Ihab* or *Yahab*.[34] It is rather difficult to comprehend why the expansion of Madina to these suburbs is a sign of the coming of the Hour. It is natural for a city in which the tomb of Muhammad is located and regarded as the second sacred shrine in Islam to expand. Pilgrimage to Mecca and Madina is one of the pillars of Islam. Consequently, there is a need for expansion, prosperity and cultural development.

s. The Hour will come when people believe in the stars and reject their preordained fate (the Divine Decree of destiny).[35] There was no time in the history of the Arabs in which a large segment of the society has refrained from practicing divination and astrology. Such pursuit was part of their conventional life. Fear of the unknown, superstition and the anxiety of the future made people to resort to such invisible powers to ward off evil.

t. The Hour will not come until Muslims will fight people whose shoes are made of hair and until they fight the Turks whose eyes are small, their faces are red, the tips of their noses are flat, and their faces as stricken shields.[36] It is not clear here whether these traditions appertain to the Turks or the Tatars or both of them. Historically, however, the Arabs fought against both peoples and lost, yet the Hour did not come.

u. The Hour does not come...until the best of the Muslims, the people of Hijaz, who do not fear in God the reproach of the disgruntled, will march against the Byzantine and they will conquer Constantinople with *praises and the call: God is Greater*.[37] This same tradition was related in *Sahih of Muslim* as a sound

39

hadith in which the compiler presented a different version. On the authority of Muhammad, Abu Hurayra related that the Hour would not come until seventy thousands of the children of Isaac (the Jews) invade Constantinople without employing any type of arms. All its fortified walls will fall by *praises and the call of God is Greater.* Based on the historical account, Constantinople was conquered by the Otto-man dynasty (Turks) in the fifteenth century and not by the Arabs. Secondly, the contradiction between the two traditions is obvious since the Children of Isaac has nothing to do with the conquest of Constan-tinople. Thirdly, it seems that the narrator of this tradition was historically confused that he failed to differentiate between the episodes of the fall of Jericho as it is recorded in chapter six of the book of Joshua and the myth of the conquest of Constantino-ple. Such contradiction and confusion suggest that this tradition was a late fabrication by the narrators who sought to amaze their audience. Most probably, they heard the biblical story from some Jewish friends and weaved it into the fabric of their tradition. It also aimed at proving that Muhammad, like other prophets of the Old Testament, did prophesy about future events, specially the end of time. Thus, to lend authen-ticity to these claims they ascribed these traditions to Muhammad. Otherwise, if Muhammad is the source of this information, then his prophecies lack the veracity of the true prophets of God. Besides, Cons-tantinople of today, which is now called Istanbul, is the capital of an Islamic country. In another tradition, it is alleged that the believers of al-Hijaz will also capture Rome by the power *of praises* and the call of *God is Greater.*[38] Indeed, it is believed that such events will take place under the banner of a caliph who will restore the glory of Islam.

40

v. The Hour will not come until God will cause the believers of the time to die peacefully and gracefully and leave the wicked alive to indulge in their lust *pro tem* until the appointed hour of resurrection.[39] This image reflects the biblical account of the rapture in which the living believers are taken away from the earth and the ungodly are left to face their destiny after the second resurrection. Since Islamic theology does not accommodate for the concept of rapture, the miraculous death of the believers replaces the supernatural event of the rapture.

x. The Hour will not come until the city of Mecca is turned into ruins.[40] The Islamic tradition implies that an obscure Ethiopian man, whose surname is Thu al-Suwayqatayn, will ravage the city of Mecca, which would be inhabited by wild animals and predacious birds.[41] There is not a definite explanation for the tragic end of the most sacred city in the Islamic world except that he sought to plunder the treasures of the Ka'ba. Other traditions indicate that both the Ka'ba [42] and the Madinat of the Prophet[43] are going to be subject to permanent destruction and desolation, and will never be rebuilt again.

The Extraordinary Minor Signs

- The last Hour will not arrive till people come forth who eat with their tongues as cows do.[44] There is no explanation of the origin of these people and their role in the historical events unless these are the people of Gog and Magog.[45]

- The last Hour will not come before time contracts, a year being like a month, a month like a week, a week like a day, a day like an hour and an hour like the kindling of the fire.[46] Such statement echoes what Jesus has taught in Matthew 24:22, '*Unless those days had been cut short, no life have been saved; but for the sake of the elect those days will be cut short.'* Though Jesus was referring to different circumstances in which either the elects will suffer, during the destruction of Jerusalem in the year 70 A.D. or in the midst of the terrible tribulation, or in both, Muhammad borrowed the notion of the contraction of time as a sign that the end of the world is nigh.

- The last Hour will not arrive before wild beasts speak to men, the end of a man's whip and the thong of his sandals would talk to him, and his thigh would inform him about what his family has done since he left them.[47] What is the significance of this sign? Does this apply to the departing husband only? What about the spouse who is left behind? Does her thigh inform her about the behavior and activity of her husband? Empirically, how does, this sign contribute to the end of time?

- The Euphrates uncovers a mountain of gold. People will fight to death to possess it. Ninety-nine out of one hundred will die as they fight with each other hoping that one of them will survive and possess it.[48] But the tradition warns whosoever will be present at that time must abstain from taking from it.[49] It is evident that this sign will create a state of sedition, causing blood shed among the people and reflecting their mundane nature. People's lives will be absorbed with materialism and distracted from the spiritual precepts. It is also possible that the notion of the drying up of the water of the river Euphrates is borrowed from Revelation 16:12, *"The sixth angel poured out his bowl on the great river, the Euphrates; and its water was dried up, so that the way would be prepared for the kings from the east."*[50]

Conclusion

When the major source of such a study is based on the oral tradition that is handed down from one generation to another, it becomes very difficult for the researcher to discern between the spurious and the authentic heritage. Thus, the citation of all these traditions is based, not on their authenticity, but rather on the acceptance of Muslim scholars of these traditions.

The minor signs reflect the reality of the daily life in any society that becomes indifferent to the restrictions of the religious laws and obligations. Islam, in general, is subject to the ceremonial rituals imposed on the Muslims, whether they perform the five Pillars of Islam or other aspects of their creeds. This does not mean that Islam lacks faith. But Muslims, in general, are judged by their conspicuous religious behavior. The profile of the religious zeal in the history of Islam reveals that these minor signs are an indication of the deterioration of the social moral life during the Abbasid period and even during the last decades of the Umayyad regime. The rapid Islamic conquest of the Levant, Egypt, Persia, Mesopotamia, and other parts of Africa and Europe, provided an opulence of wealth of which the Arabs never dreamt before. Gradually they distanced themselves from the ascetic age of the first four caliphs and they vigorously indulged in life of pleasure and bawdiness. This moral depravity prompted the pious religious leaders, the self-denying Sufis and the ascetics to caution their societies against the wrath of God, Who would mercilessly punish them for their violation of His law. They claimed that the mundane life and the moral corruption of the community are among the signs of the end of time. Therefore, the author believes that these traditions, or at least large fragments of them, are the creation of the pietistic sect to restore the moral life of the declining society. In order to reinforce their points of view, they ascribed these traditions to Muhammad; otherwise, their preaching and warning will fail to have any impact on the people. If it is assumed, as most Muslims are convinced, that these traditions are really uttered by Muhammad himself, then, there is nothing prodigious about them. They are normal events in the life of any society that is suddenly exposed to unprecedented wealth and power, and lost its original enthusiasm in what is empyrean.

On the other hand, some traditionalists and narrators found in this exciting future drama a fertile ground to fabricate some amazing stories or traditions to capture the imagination of their audience and to generate some remuneration. In his book, *al-Fitan wa al-Malahim,* Ibn Kathir provides us with a striking paradigm.[51] This episode addressed in this book is attributed to Muhammad, yet any objective critic of the text recognizes the fanciful creation permeating its events that exposes the innovation of the storytellers. It is difficult to epitomize this story, but the reader gets the impression that he is reliving a scene from a mythical world where God the almighty is the main actor and the producer of a formidable melodrama. This author does not attempt to present an acrimonious criticism against the Islamic eschatology but rather to recapitulate the problems that face the researcher who endeavors to represent a scholarly study when he is forced to rely on doubtful resources or references.

CHAPTER THREE

The Antichrist المسيح الدجَّال

T he Islamic Tradition confers on this ambiguous figure several titles among them the liar christ and the christ of deception.[1] But before we examine the epic of the Antichrist as it is unfolded in Islamic eschatology there are number of questions that will be discussed within the context of this chapter.

Major Signs العلامات الكبرى

Islamic eschatology lists ten major signs that precede the Hour يوم القيامة. These ten signs are not listed in sequential order but rather arbitrarily. Since it is difficult to rearrange them, the author will try to examine them according to their significance to this study.

In a tradition ascribed to Muhammad, he remarks that the ten major signs are: **The smoke, the appearance of the Anti-Christ, the beast, The rising of the sun from the West, the descent of Jesus son of Mary, the invasion of Gog and Magog, three landslides in three different places: one in the East, one in the West, and one in Arabia and a fire that would blaze from the bottom of Yemen and would drive people to their assembly place.**[2]

The first sign is the concept of the Antichrist as it is reflected in Islamic Tradition, Biblical sources and other apocryphal materials.

45

The Antichrist المسيح الدَّجال

Linguistically, the term *Dajjal* implies several meanings.These meanings mirror the perceptions of Muslims of the role and the characteristics of the Antichrist. The term *Dajjal* means the one who is constantly lying, who is coating or concealing the truth, or who is covering up and distorting the facts, and or the one who has the ability to traverse long distances of the land in a very short period. These traits apply to the Islamic Antichrist because upon his inception he will try to deceive people through his hypocritical piety at first, and then through his delusive miracles. He is also a character who will be able to roam around the world with incomprehensible speed. Thus, who is the Antichrist?

There are several conflicting stories about the origin of the Islamic Antichrist. Most Muslims agree that he is a human being created by God and possesses a super power to be a trial and allurement to many. It is alleged that his surname is *Abu Yusuf* (father of Joseph).[3] Muhammad is claimed to have said that the *Dajjal's* parents will be childless for thirty years; then a one eyed son, who is good for nothing, will be born to them 'whose eyes slumber but his heart does not';[4] then he describes the *Dajjal's* father as a tall man with a flabby body and a long nose like a beak, while his mother has a dark skin and two huge breasts.[5] He will appear first in Isbahan (a city in Iran) in a quarter called the Quarter of the Jews. He will be supported by seventy thousand Jews armored with weaponry and wearing crowns and green palliums. Another tradition indicates that the number is ninety thousand.[6] Then seventy thousand of the Tatar will side with him as well as a large crowd of the people of Khurasan.[7] Among his followers will be numerous women. At the beginning of his reign, he will act like one of the mighty kings and will demonstrate a

46

great piety. Many will be deceived by his godliness. Soon, in *Kufa* he will claim the prophethood, then the deity. The ignorant and the lowly from among the common people and the mob will believe in him. The pious and the worshippers of God will defy him. Gradually he will 'vanquish country by country and fort by fort, region by region, vicinity by vicinity so that there would not be a land that he did not tread over with his horses and his infantry except Mecca and Madina.'[8] He will last on this earth for forty days. One day is like a year, another day is like a month and a third day is like a week. The rest of his days are similar to the days of the ordinary people.[9] God will allow him to perform miracles to misguide those He wills from among His creation and to steadfast the believers so their faith will be strengthened and their guidance will increase.[10]

But this is not the entire story of the Antichrist. Islamic traditions provide more information about this ambiguous creature characterized with contradictions and illusions. A number of the *hadiths* indicate that the word infidel كافر is written between the eyes of the Antichrist. But Ibn 'Abbas[11] who was known as the interpreter of the Qur'an asserted that he did not hear Muhammad saying that the *Dajjal* will come with the word infidel written in between his eyes.[12] Actually, there is a corpus of *hadiths* in which Muhammad gave a description of the Antichrist without alluding to this mark on the forehead of the *Dajjal*. In most cases, Muhammad used to say to his audience:

> All prophets from the time of Noah warned their own people against the Dajjal…but I tell you about him something of which no prophet told his nation before; you should know that he is one-eyed, and Allah is not one-eyed.[13]

47

One *hadith* portrayed him as a man whose right eye is blind and protruding, while his left eye looks like a shining planet.[14] In addition, one of his eyes is described as a green glass.[15]

In other instances, Muhammad described him as a young man with curly cropped hair and a blind eye. He also compared him with 'Abdul 'Uzza ibn Qatan.[16] Another *hadith* depicted him as 'a short man, hen-toed, woolly haired, one-eyed, an eye-sightless, and neither protruding nor deep-seated.[17] He is a Jew and childless.[18] He will also emerge from the East.[19]

An examination of the books of the Bible will show that none of the prophets from the time of Noah warned their own people against the *'Dajjal*. With the exception of the book of Daniel, a few indirect remarks in another one or two Old Testaments books and what it is recorded in the New Testament scriptures, Christians do not possess any direct reference to the Antichrist. Moreover, how did it happen that among all the divine references about him, Muhammad alone described him in the *Hadith* only (not in the Qur'an) as a one-eyed man? Did he borrow that from one of the extant folkloric myth or apocryphal books?[20]

As these various conflicting traditions are critically examined, an interpretation is needed to clarify the inscrutability that shrouded these *hadiths*. This writer tends to believe that either the word *Kafir* (infidel) was a late addition to the *Hadith* by the narrators who heard about the Christian Antichrist and the mark of the Beast,[21] or that Muhammad at an early stage of his mission in Madina, did not obtain the right information about the Christian Antichrist from those who orally related to him a distorted story of the Beast. Thus, he failed at the beginning to mention the mark of the Islamic Antichrist. But at a later time he became familiar with this event and included this bit of information in his description of his Antichrist. This very fact becomes obvious when we read the story of the Jassasa as it is related in *Sahih of Muslim*. This episode is fascinating because of its setting and the occasion in which presumably, Muhammad himself related it publicly. The story states that after the time of prayer, Muhammad asked the congregation to remain seated in the mosque because he had something to share with them. He detained the people because "Tamim al-Dari, a former Christian who came and accepted Islam, told me something which agrees with what I was telling you about the *Dajjal*..."[22] What Tamim had confided to him was virtually either a creation of Tamim's imagination, or the work of the fantasy of the story-tellers. However, at this time we are not intending to confute the authenticity of this anecdote or to reject it, but rather to accept it at its face value. Muhammad **himself** said,

> He (Tamim) narrated to me that **he** had sailed in a ship with thirty men of Banu Lakhm and Banu Judham (Two Arab tribes) and had been tossed by waves in the ocean for a month. Then these (waves) took them (near) the land within the ocean (island) at the time of the sunset. They sat in a small rowing- boat and landed on that island. There was a beast with a long thick hair (and because of this) they could not distinguish his face from his back. They said: Woe to you, who can you be? Thereupon it said, I am al-Jassasa... It said: O, people, go to this person in the monastery, as he is very much eager to know about you. He (Tamim) said: When it named a person for us we were afraid of it (the Jassasa) lest it should be the

49

Devil. Then we hurried on until we came to that monastery[23] and found a well-built person there with his hand tied to his neck and iron shackles gripping his legs by the ankles.[24] We said, Woe to you, who are you? He said, ...I am the *Dajjal*...[25]

سرد محمد نفسه هذا الحديث:

حدَّثَني (تميم الدَّاري) أنه ركِبَ في سَفينةٍ بحريَّةٍ مع ثلاثين رَجُلاً من لَخَم وجُذامٍ، فلعبَ بهم الموجُ شهراً في البحر ثم أرْفَوا إلى جزيرةٍ في البحر حتى مَغرِب الشَّمس فجلَسُوا في أقرُبِ السَّفينةِ فدخَلوا الجزيرة فلَقِيَتْهُم دابّة أهْلَبُ كثيرُ الشَّعَر لا يَدرونَ ما قُبْلُهُ من دُبُرِه من كَثْرةِ الشعَر، فقالوا : ويلكِ ما أنتِ؟ فقالت أنا الجسَّاسة... أيها القومُ انطلِقوا إلى هذا الرجلِ في الدَّيرِ فإنه إلى خَبَرِكُمْ بالأشْواقِ. قال (تميم) لما سمَّتْ لنا رجلاً فرِقنا منها أن تكونَ شيطانةً. قال (تميم) فانطلقنا سِراعاً حتى دَخَلْنا الدَّيْرَ فإذا فيه أعْظَمُ إنسانٍ رأيْناهُ قطُّ خَلْقاً وأشدُّهُ وِثاقاً مَجموعَةٌ يَداهُ إلى عُنُقِهِ ما بين رُكْبَتَيْهِ إلى كَعْبَيْهِ بالحديد. قُلنا ويلكَ ما أنتَ؟ ...إني أنا المسيحُ (الدجَّال)*

It is apt here to underscore two significant points; we aver first, that Muhammad at this stage was not aware of the mark of the Beast. The description of the *Dajjal* delineated in the story does not mention the word *Kafir* or even that the *Dajjal* was a one eyed man. It did not seem that there was any disfigurement in the face of the *Dajjal,* which drew the sailors' attention. This tradition was repeated several times in the collection of the books of *Hadith* through different chains of authorities without referring to the word infidel. Faced with this problem, another tradition attempted to explain this dilemma by alleging that The *Dajjal* will suffer from deformation after he proclaims that he is god. At that moment his right eye will become blind, his ears will be chopped off, and will be written between his two eyes infidel, ...and his followers

50

will be the Majians, the Jews, the *Nasara* and these non-Arabs from among the polytheists.[26]

فتعمش عينه اليمنى، وتقطع أذناه، ويكتب بين عينيه كافر،
فلا يُخفى على كل مسلم ... ويكون أصحابه المجوس
واليهود والنصارى وهذه الأعاجم من المشركين.

It seems that this *hadith* endeavors to explain that the *Dajjal* before he apotheosizes himself would look like any ordinary man. He will be afflicted with these deformations after his claim of deity. But that does not explain why the *Dajjal* was not called infidel, and it does not convey why, in various other traditions, he was described as a one-eyed man only.

The second interesting point is that other *hadiths* negate that Tamim al-Dari did sail with his relatives. Actually Fatima Bint Qays (the same lady who originally related the previous *Hadith*) *reiterated this time this very same account*, remarking that **Muhammad himself** indicated that *the cousins of Tamim were the ones who had sailed in the sea* and Tamim only related to him the story he heard from them.[27] In this case, it was obvious that Tamim was not an eyewitness but rather a reporter who related a story he heard from the sailors. There is even an obscure *hadith* ascribed to Muhammad in which he asked Tamim himself to narrate this incident to the congregation in the mosque.[28]

In addition, other details compel this author to question the story's validity. On the authority of Fatima, Tamim claimed that he sailed in a ship in an ocean, but his ship lost its way and thus, landed at an island. He walked around looking for water...[29] In another tradition, Fatima said that 'Allah's Messenger ...said: 'O people, Tamim Al-Dari has reported to me that **some persons of his tribe sailed in the ocean** in a boat and it capsized and some of

51

them traveled on one of the planks of the boat and they went to an island in the ocean..."[30]

A different story reports that Muhammad said, "Tamim ad-Dari...transmitted to me **from a man** who was on the island of the sea. All of a sudden, he found a woman who was trailing her hair. He asked, Who are you? She said: I am the Jassasa..."[31] It should be noted here that an anonymous person who happened to find himself on an unknown island somewhere in the ocean reports this story to Tamim. Tamim and Muhammad accepted his report without questioning the veracity of the story.

The perplexing question we encounter here is which of these stories should we accept as authentic? It would not be of any surprise if the traditionalists would attempt to forcibly reconcile between the conflicting *hadiths* by far-fetched interpretations to eliminate any disharmony that may shed doubts on the entire episode. This myth was, undoubtedly, the creation of the imagination of Tamim, unless it was the fabrication of later storytellers.

But these contrasting reports are not the only problematic issues that engulf the person of the *Dajjal*. One of the enigmas that encompassed this character was the title 'christ' the Hadith bestowed on him. Why was he called *christ*? The Bible never called the beast or the dragon *christ*. The beast is called the Antichrist. It is true that Muslims had added certain epithets to that name such as 'liar' or 'of deception' to distinguish him from the true Christ. Muslims have recognized this problem and have tried to speculate without success. Many claim that he is called Christ because his right eye is flattened or because he is a one-eyed man and maybe because he will traverse مسح the land in a short period with great speed.[32] All these speculations have failed to explain why he is given the title

52

Christ. Muslims allude to the fact that the *Dajjal* has called himself Christ. However, that tradition is susceptible to doubt. Why did he choose to call himself Christ while the *Hadith* indicated that he deified himself and proclaimed that he was god?

It is the opinion of the writer that the Islamic Antichrist is called Christ in the Islamic Hadith because he made every effort to imitate Christ in His miracles, power over nature, quickening the dead, providing food for the people and even in riding a donkey instead of a horse. Besides, since in the Islamic view, Christians embrace the blasphemous creed of Christ as the Son of God, the *Dajjal* who would deify himself resembles the Christian image of Jesus Christ that is rejected by Islamic theology. He is the counterfeit of Christ.

Another major problem appertain to the ambiguity of the Islamic discourse is that the Qur'an has never mentioned any minute detail about the *Dajjal*. How could it be that such an infamous figure of this stature, which would possess the power to disturb the world order and create unparallel tribulation in world history, be disregarded by the Qur'an! He will be imbued with a super-power to misguide the faithful and mislead the believers. How can Muslim scholars significantly explain the existence of a large corpus of the Traditions about the *Dajjal*, his trial that will afflict the world and the destruction he will incur and no trace of intimation is found about him in the Qur'an? A question Muslims have constantly struggled to answer. Ibn Kathir recognizes the legality of this question and strives to provide a response. He attempts to present a three-fold answer[33]:

> a He believes that the Qur'an has mentioned the
> *Dajjal* in chapter 6:15:

...The day that certain of the signs thy Lord do come, no good will it do to soul to believe in them if it believed not before, nor earned righteousness through its faith...

...يَوْمَ يَأْتِي بَعْضُ آيَاتِ رَبِّكَ لا يَنْفَعُ نَفْساً إِيمَانُهَا لم تَكُنْ آمَنَتْ مِنْ قَبْلُ أَوْ كَسَبَتْ فِي إِيمَانِهَا خَيْراً...

Then he cites a tradition attributed to Muhammad that these 'some signs' are the *Dajjal*, the Beast and the rise of the sun from the West.[34] After the appearance of these signs, repentance and faith are of no avail. But there are some indications that some unbelieving people will revert to faith for one reason or another during the era of the *Dajjal*.[35] Also, this verse is quoted out of context, since the first part of it deals with those who refuse to believe until they see signs of God. Besides, some Muslim scholars interpreted this verse differently. In his footnote on this verse, Abdullah Yusuf Ali, the translator of the Qur'an, remarks, "Faith is belief in things you do not see with your eyes but you understand with your spiritual sense: If your whole will consents to it, it results in deeds of righteousness, which are the evidence of your faith."[36]

> b. The second coming of the Messiah, Jesus Son of Mary, is indirectly necessitated the mentioning of the imposter christ or the christ of deception who is the Antichrist of the true Christ of Guidance الهدى . By using the antidote, the Arabs find it sufficient to mention one of the two opposite names only and the other will be indirectly implicit.

This explanation does not persuade the inquisitive mind since it does not show why the name of the *Dajjal* is not recorded in the Qur'an in spite of his notorious role in the Islamic eschatology. It is claimed also that,

54

c. He was not lucidly mentioned in the Qur'an as an expression of contempt for him since he deified himself and equated his person with God almighty. Thus, he was despised in the eyes of God and was not mentioned in the Qur'an. God has entrusted this responsibility to the prophets to reveal his real color because God with His glory and majesty would not concern Himself with such a vile person.

This reasoning lacks the logical acumen because it fails to recognize that the Antichrist was mentioned in other revealed scriptures acknowledged by the Qur'an itself. Significant portion of the New Testament is designated to the theme of the Antichrist.[37] Some Books of the Old Testament implicitly allude to it.[38] God's contempt to the Antichrist does not prohibit Him from revealing the characters of the sinful behavior of the one who is bent on challenging God's plan for the salvation of the human race. Besides, the fulfillment of the predictions of the emergence of the Antichrist and his fervent endeavor to corrupt the world as detailed in the scriptures would be a proof of the authenticity of the revealed word of God.

But when will the *Dajjal* appear on the world stage? Due to the confusion that permeates the Islamic Traditions, the reader finds himself striving to discern between what is falsified and what is valid. In view of the contradictory collected datum he finds himself a prey for precarious conclusions. Some *hadiths* indicate that the *Dajjal* will appear in the seventh year after the Great War between the Muslims and the Byzantine Army and the subsequent fall of Constantinople.[39] Another sound *hadith* reports that the conquest of Constantinople and the coming of the *Dajjal* will take place within a period of six months.[40] A third *hadith* accounts that "The Antichrist will come when the community of Islam will be divided into two camps: the camp of faith...and the camp of hypocrisy. When that happens expect the Antichrist that day or the next."[41]

Muhammad was so much concerned about the tribulation of the *Dajjal* that he used to pray and taught his followers to pray to seek refuge with Allah from four trials. He urged them to say, "O Allah I seek refuge with thee from the torment of the hell, from the torment of the grave, from the trial of life and death and from the evil of the trial of *Masih ad-Dajjal* (the Antichrist)."[42]

Muhammad himself was accustomed to say: "Allah I seek refuge in You from the torment of hell and I seek refuge in You from the trial of the *Dajjal*."[43] In another place he declared that the trial of the grave is "like or near the trial of the *Dajjal*."[44]

But how does the *Dajjal* attempt to accomplish his goals?

Islamic Traditions provide a list of paradigms of the ways and the methods the *Dajjal* would employ to mislead the people away from God and the teaching of the Qur'an. It is necessary here to hint that the information acquired from the *Hadith* may not always appeal to the critical mind. But since the *Hadith* is the only available document of information we possess, it becomes the only source on which we rely.

The image of the *Dajjal* as it is depicted in the *Hadith*, is of a person characterized with cruelty, godliness and deceit. In order to corroborate his claim of deity, he would substantiate that claim with the performance of miracles. Miracles would be the most effective approach to convince the skeptic and the hesitant. Muhammad realized that the eminence of miracles was very critical to the adherents of Islam. There was a need for an explanation to justify how an impostor like the *Dajjal* would be able to perform miracles. That was not difficult to answer. The *Dajjal* would not be able to perform these miracles by his own power. God almighty will allow him to demonstrate such power for a while to test the faith of the believers and to expose the hypocrites.[45] Muhammad warned Muslims to obviate any contact with the *Dajjal*. He said,

> Let him who hears about the *Dajjal* stay away from him for I swear by Allah that a man will come to him thinking that he is a believer (but would) follow him because of confused idea roused in him by the *Dajjal*.[46]

The *Dajjal* will have with him two flowing rivers: one will look like pure water while the other will appear like flaming fire. The believer should choose the river that looks like fire and drink from it, for it will be cold water, while the river that looks like pure water is fire.[47] This ploy is one of the *Dajjal's* stratagems to ambush people. Two angels, one at his right and the other at his left, will also accompany him. That would be a trial for the people. He would say, *"Am I not your lord? Do not I quicken people and cause them to die? One of the angles would answer: you are a liar. But no body would hear him except the other angel who would respond: you are right; and everybody will hear him and they will believe that he is affirming the claim of the Dajjal."*[48] Muhammad indicated that these two angels resemble two prophets and *"If I wish I would reveal their names and the names of their fathers."*[49] Again Muhammad had failed to mention their names.

Unlike Jesus, the miracles the *Dajjal* employs to deceive both the faithful and the hypocrites, are limited in nature. Yet there are similarities in their function. He will attempt to demonstrate his power in three areas: raising the dead, feeding the people and bringing down the rain. There is nothing about miracles of healings, compassion, love and redemption. His sole purpose is to be deified, worshiped and to reign. In his militaristic mentality, he aims at conquering the world and replacing God in the hearts of people. Muhammad claimed that he is going to stay on earth for forty days, "one day like a year, one day like a month and one day like a week, and the rest of his days will be like your days."[50] In other places, these two rivers are called hell and paradise.[51]

During this period, he endeavors to embark on establishing his kingdom and solidifying his power. He will be met with fierce resistance, but his adversaries will be defeated and some of them will take refuge in the mountains.[52] But he will be given power over one person only whom he will kill, and then resurrect him. An anonymous believer will be taken to the *Dajjal*, and as soon as the believer sees him, he would say:

> I testify that you are the *Dajjal* of whom the Apostle of God told us. The *Dajjal* would say (to the people): If I kill him and then I raise him would you have any doubt about this matter? They will say, 'no'. Then he will kill him and bring him back to life. The (man) will say after the *Dajjal* brings him back to life, 'by God I had never been more certain of you than I am now. The *Dajjal* tries to kill him (again) but would not be given the power over him to do so.[53]

أشهد أنك الدجَّال الذي حدثنا رسول الله... فيقول الدَّجال
أرأيتم إن قتلت هذا ثم أحييته أتشكُّون في الأمر؟ فيقولون
لا. فيقتله ثم يُحييه. فيقول (الرجل) حين يُحيي 'والله ما
كنت فيك قط أشدُّ بصيرة مني الآن...فيريد الدَّجال أن يقتله
فلا يسلَّط عليه

This same story was related on the authority of
Muhammad with variant details[54] in which he described the
way that man would be tormented and killed. But after the
Dajjal resurrects him and the believer continues defying all
his claims, the *Dajjal* becomes more determined to kill
him, but he fails because he is not given the authority over
him. The man will say to the people, 'O people, he will not
be able to treat anyone else in such a manner after me.'[55]

In his course of conquest, the *Dajjal* will fail to
enter two cities: Mecca and *Madina* (some other *hadiths*
add Jerusalem)[56] because they are guarded by angels with
unsheathed swords. He will camp at the edge of the
saltmarsh next to the Red *Dharib*. *Madina* will be shaken
by three tremors and every disbeliever and hypocrite will
desert it to the *Dajjal*. Most of those who will join him will
be women.[57] In that day, male believers will take every
precaution to keep away their close female relatives from
the spell of the *Dajjal*.[58] That day will be called the day of
salvation because the *Madina* will be purified from the
unfaithful[59]

As the *Dajjal* travels through Arabia, he will
endeavor to seduce the Bedouins by claiming that he can
bring back to life their parents. He would ask a Bedouin,
'(If I do so) will you bear witness that I am your lord? The
Bedouin will say, 'Yes'. So two demons will personify his
father and his mother and will say, 'O my son, follow him
for he is your lord.'"[60] Or he would come to a nomad
during the three years of extreme drought and tell him if I

59

bring your camels to life would you acknowledge that I am your lord? The nomad would answer, 'yes'. The demons accompanying the *Dajjal* will appear to him like his camels with full udders and fattest highest humps.[61]

It seems that the *Dajjal* and the host of demons who come to assist him in his devious plans will forge an alliance. The demons are his invisible helpers who would conspire with him to seduce even the believers if possible. The Qur'an calls the cursed devil the malice whisperer الوسواس الخنّاس who whispers evil things in the hearts of people. Subsequently Satan hastens to seize such an opportunity to enhance his wicked projects for the destruction of the human race. Thus, he would recruit his hosts of demons to woo people to the claim of the false christ towards that end.

The second area by which the Islamic Antichrist would attempt to bewitch the people is through controlling the weather and providing rain for those who would follow him. This strategy aims at drawing to him more partisans who would believe in his deity and miracles. He would pass among some people and invite them to believe in him. If they respond to his call he will command heaven to rain, the earth to bring forth its crops, and their livestock will return from grazing fatter, their flanks healthier, and their udders fuller. But for those who would reject him, the drought will destroy their lands and their flocks will die. He would pass by the ruins and would order them to reveal their treasures, which will follow him like swarm of bees.[62]

But what were the original sources that shaped the image of the Islamic Antichrist? How did these sources become available to Muhammad?

Two major sources created the legend of the Islamic Antichrist. One of them is the Beast of the Book of Revelation, and the other one is the story of the mythical Antichrist that was in vogue a few centuries before the time of Muhammad.

The New Testament points to two types of the Antichrist: the lesser Antichrists who precede the final Antichrist and the Antichrist of the end of time. The lesser Antichrists are the false prophets and the heretical teachers who pervade the church of Christ through the course of church history. Jesus Himself warned His disciples and the church against these false prophets who will come after Him.[63] These lesser Antichrists or 'like Antichrist of 1 John 4:3...are linked with false prophets who, speaking by the spirit of error (1 John 4:6), lead their hearers astray (Mark 13:22).'[64] The same concept is presented in the Islamic *Hadith* heritage in which Muhammad claims that about thirty false prophets will come after him, each one alleging that he is the apostle of Allah. Evidently, Muhammad was reiterating what Jesus had said. The difference between Muhammad's claim and Jesus' claim is that Muhammad emphasized that He was the last and the seal of the prophets and no other prophet will come after him. But Jesus warned against the false prophets who will come after Him, corrupting His teachings and preaching a different Christ, as the apostle Paul indicates in his Epistle to the Galatians.[65] Jesus did not negate the existence of true prophets in the church who will expound on His teaching, instruct the body of Christ in the faith and even prophesy.[66] These true prophets will not distort the biblical teaching about the deity of Christ, His crucifixion and resurrection. Moreover, it seems that the concept of prophethood in Islam has different connotation than the concept of prophethood in the New Testament. There were prophets in the church who possessed the gift of prophecy to reveal certain messages they received from God related to particular circumstances as in the incident of Paul. That did not mean that these prophets had claimed that they were sent to initiate a new faith. They only prophesied about certain events or matters that will take place in the near future; while prophethood in Islam implied the founding of a new religion and the revelation of a new scripture.

Evidently the lesser Antichrists 'were paving the way for the final Antichrist...(who) would lead a large scale departure from God.'[67] Muhammad, who believed that he was a true apostle of God, like Jesus, asserted also that the false prophets who would precede the *Dajjal* would prepare the way for him by creating a religious and political anarchism among the Islamic community. The hearts will be fertile to receive the false teaching of the *Dajjal*.

In his second epistle to the Thessalonians, 2:3-4, Paul talks about the man of lawlessness. He indicates that 'the day of the Lord' will not come unless the apostasy comes first. Apostasy is a revolt against the sovereignty of God, which will be a prelude for the emergence of the Antichrist. This same idea is reiterated in the *Hadith* as one of the signs of the end of time. A number of tribes will revert to polytheism and reject Islam. There will not be any power to restrain them from apostasy, as was the case in the first Islamic century during the caliphate of Abu Bakr.

The biblical Antichrist is also a man of destruction 'who opposes and exalts himself above every so-called god or object of worship, so that he takes his seat in the temple of God, displaying himself as being a God' (v. 4). Islam displays the portrait - as we discussed above - of a *Dajjal* who claims that he is God. The Islamic description of his allegations is almost an exact copy of the biblical remarks.

As we try to explore the apocalyptic Book of Revelation in search for the identity of the biblical Antichrist, striking resemblances seems to exist between the apocalyptic Antichrist and the *Dajjal*. But the Book of Revelation points to three different characters that are the epitome of wickedness. Their schemata are to oppose God and to wage war against the saints. They are the Dragon, or the Beast, that comes up from the abyss, the Beast that emerges from the sea, and the Beast that comes up out of the earth.[68] The Dragon, which is also called the old serpent, is Satan, who will head the forces of evil. The archangel Michael and his angles will defeat him and his hosts of demons. Soon, the other two beasts will join him. Satan will confer on the Beast that comes up from the sea his power, throne and great authority.[69] This beast, which is a symbol of the biblical Antichrist, will share the glory of the Dragon and receive the worship of the non-believers. He is also given the authority to blaspheme against God, apotheosize himself and   persecute the saints. He will reign over the earth and kill all those who defy him.

But it seems that the Islamic Antichrist is a distorted image of both the beast that comes up out of the sea and his deputy the Beast that emerges from the earth. They both speak like the Dragon, defy God, and blaspheme Him; and the second Beast 'performs great signs and makes fire come down out of heaven to the earth in the presence of men'.[70] He also deceives the people of the earth by the signs he is allowed to perform in the presence of the first Beast and allures them to make an image of the first Beast to worship him.[71] Even it is given to him the power to make the image of the Beast to speak. Satan, the Beast, and his deputy form an evil trinity. And as it is written on the forehead of the *Dajjal* the word "infidel", the second Beast has a number of a man, which is 666. The number of this Beast or his name is a mark that would be tattooed on the forehead or the right hand of every person to enable him or her to sell or to buy.[72] Though this number is difficult to decode, it will be a significant external symbol in the identification of the Antichrist and his deputy in the future apocalyptic events.

Most of these characteristics are manifested in the Islamic antichrist. It is obvious that the Islamic traditions have failed to comprehend the meaning and the symbolism of this evil triune, which is a devilish attempt to constitute a counterpart to the Holy Triune to entice people to worship Satan, the real power behind the Antichrist. It is true that Islamic traditions allude to a relationship between the *Dajjal* and the demons, but these demons are like 'the fifth column' that would cause enormous damage and dread behind the scene or the front lines. They are not part of a triune. After all, Muslims do not believe in a triune God.

The other sources that seem to mold the image of the *Dajjal* are the legends and views of some Christian theologians who lived before the inception of Islam.

In his book *the Antichrist Legend* (1895), Bousset indicates, as he reconstructs the Antichrist expectation, that his research into the ancient myth of the Antichrist, suggests that the Antichrist would

> appear among the Jews...He would be himself a Jew, born of the tribe of Dan...Elijah would appear and denounce him and would be put to death for his claims...True believers, refusing to give him worship which he demanded, would seek refuge in the wilderness and be pursued by him there, but when they are on the point of being wiped out, he is

destroyed by the intervention of God (who may use an agent such as Michael the archangel or the Messiah of David's line).[73]

Bousset concluded from a 'study of the relevant literature that the Christian expectation (of the Antichrist) was adapted from an existing Jewish conception.'[74] In this regard Jewish literature in the pre-Islamic time presents "a Roman Antichrist in the person of Armillus (probably a corruption of Romulus) who is to be slain by the Messiah (Tg, Isa 11:14, for example, says of the 'shoot from the stump of Jesse' that, with the breath of his lips he shall slay the wicked Armillus)."[75]

The Christian idea that the Antichrist will be of a Jewish descent "is first extant in Iranaeaus (C.A.D. 180)."[76] He, undoubtedly, relied on earlier Jewish and Christian sources and traditions. It seems that the belief that the Antichrist is of Jewish origin "and from the tribe of Dan" is based on Jeremiah 8:16, LXX. (It says): *'From Dan we shall hear the sound of the speed of his horses; at the sound of the neighing of his cavalry the whole earth shakes; he will come and devour the earth and its fullness, the city and those who dwell in it'*...The Antichrist is thus portrayed as an apostate Jew."[77]

Early Christians, along with the majority of today's theologians, adheres to the view that Antichrist, regardless of his origin, is "the false Messiah, the pseudo-Christ... first and foremost the great deceiver, the arch-hypocrite."[78]

Hippolytus (3rd. C.) who was a disciple of Iranaeus, listed six specific aspects in which Antichrist "will be a perverted imitation of Christ: (1) Jewish origin, (2) the sending out of the apostles, (3) bringing together people

65

scattered abroad, (4) sealing his followers, (5) appearance in the form of a man; and (6) the building of a temple (in Christ's case the temple of his body in the resurrection [see John 2:19]; in Antichrist's case the raising of a new stone temple in Jerusalem)."[79]

One of the most interesting legends that is related to this study is the myth that is recounted by a Latin Christian writer, whose name is Commodium (mid-third-to the mid-fifth centuries), who believed that the final antichrist will "proceed from Persia, will cross the Euphrates…and then will march to the land of Judea."[80]

But Commodium was not the only Christian writer that believed that the Antichrist is originating from the East. A Syriac legend dating to the fifth century, entitled *Testament of the Lord*, indicates that the Antichrist comes from the East (Chapter 10} and adds,

> And these are the signs of him: His head is as a fiery flame; his right eye shot with blood, his left eye blue-black and he has two pupils. His eyelashes are white; and his lower lip is large, but his right thigh slender; his feet broad, his great toe {or perhaps finger) is bruised and flat. This is the sickle of desolation.[81]

In another book entitled *The Apocalypse of the Holy Theologian John,* often dated to the fifth century (or could be several centuries earlier) a portrait of the Antichrist is briefly depicted in chapters 6 through 8. This account illustrates his queer appearance. Four features of his appearance are of great significance for this treatise. One speaks of his hair as 'the points of arrows'; the other one denotes that 'his right eye (is) like the morning star'; the third one indicates that 'his fingers are like the sickles'; and the fourth one reveals that 'on his forehead is the writing: The Antichrist'.[82]

This brief survey of the legends about the Antichrist that existed in the pre-Islamic period sheds light on the many features and characteristic of the Islamic *Dajjal*. Certainly the *Dajjal* does not manifest all the peculiarities mentioned in these legends, but the emphasis, it seems, is on these characteristics that fit well the imagination of the storytellers and appeal to the propensities of the audience within the context of their culture and social environment. Also the contradictions that permeate these stories are striking proof that the narrators may have had received their reports from different sources. Here is a repertoire of information available to the researcher to compare and contrast between the *Dajjal* and the legendary Antichrist. That will help to dispel the concoction that veiled the mythical characters of the *Dajjal*.

There are numerous similarities between the Islamic traditions and the pre-Islamic legends, or the Christian apocalyptic exegesis about the final Antichrist. Let us examine these divergent views based on the discussion above:

- Both the *Dajjal* and the Antichrist are going to emerge from the East.[83]
- Both the *Dajjal* and the Antichrist are of the Jewish origin.
- Both the *Dajjal* and the Antichrist will claim that they are gods.
- Both the *Dajjal* and the Antichrist will deceive the non-believers and create anarchism.
- Both the *Dajjal* and the Antichrist will instigate fear in the hearts of the believers. In the case of

Muslims, they will flee to the Smoke Mountain in Syria;[84] and in the case of the Jews, they will flee to the wilderness. But the gospel of Matthew informed us that Jesus had urged his followers who resided in Judea to flee to the mountains during the time of the tribulation.[85]

- Both the *Dajjal* and the Antichrist will have a mark written on their forehead. The word *'Kafir'* (infidel) will be written between the eyes of the *Dajjal* and the word 'Antichrist' will be written on the forehead of the Antichrist.
- Both the *Dajjal* and the Antichrist are formidable figures. Islamic sources claim that the former is very bulky فيلمان,[86] while the *Apocalypse of the Holy Theologian John* describes the latter *"His hair like the points of arrows,...his mouth is a cubit wide, his teeth a span in length, his fingers are like sickles. His footprints are two cubit long."* [87]

It is interesting that Islamic Hadith had described him with 'hen-toed' fingers that looked like sickles.

- Both the *Dajjal* and the Antichrist have hairs either like the twigs of a tree or the head of a snake[88] or like the points of arrows.[89]
- Both the *Dajjal* and the Antichrist will invade Jerusalem and will be killed at the hand of Christ. The former in Ludda and the latter in Jerusalem.
- Both the *Dajjal* and Antichrist will be a perverted imitation of the real Christ.

This comparison is not fully comprehensive. At least, it proves beyond any doubt that the concept of the Islamic Antichrist and the portrayal of his general behavior

68

are fashioned partially, by the perverted information that Muhammad or Muslim narrators were able to acquire from different extant sources of the time. Also, it shows that some biblical knowledge were available to them, though in distorted form. Muhammad was not acquainted with foreign languages; thus, if he was really the source of these *hadiths* they must have been related to him orally as the story of Tamim al-Dari suggests. Otherwise, they were the fabrication of later narrators who, either heard them from some unreliable Jewish or Christian sources, or read about them from written pseudo-Christian material that pre-existed the time of Islam. In the process of reshaping them, they re-created these materials to fit the environs of their society in order to be appealing to the imagination of the audience. There is no doubt that the narrators intended to entertain the audience, yet at the same time, they aimed at teaching the people a moral or ethical lesson. Many of the narrators were pious Muslims who cared about the deterio- rated ethical life in their societies. They wanted to warn the people of the consequences of their actions. Some of them were Muhammad's companions. In his interesting book, *Hadith Literature,* Muhammad Zuhair Siddiqi remarks,

> But the most dangerous type of *hadith* forgers came from the ranks of the devout traditionists themselves. Their sincerity and love for the traditions of Islam could not be doubted. But it has rightly been observed by an eminent English writer that 'everyone kills the object of his love'. Many pious traditionists attempted, unwittingly to kill the science of Tradition by forging *hadiths,* ascribing them to the Prophet, and spreading them abroad among Muslim community.[90]

Such spurious *hadiths* invented by some devout Muslims who were suppose to be a model for the Islamic community, paved the way for the fabricators to flood the market of the *hadith* literature with unreliable information. They also shrouded any scholarly research with uncertainty.

But what are the sources of the Islamic claim about the physical description of the Dajjal?

Islamic sources alleged that Muhammad is the source of the physical description of the Dajjal. Based on the sound *Hadith*, it is believed that Muhammad saw the person of the *Dajjal* on two occasions: once in a vision while he was sleeping in the Ka'ba, and the second time was during his alleged journey in the Night of Ascent. In *Sahih of al-Bukhari* it is recorded that Muhammad said,

> While I was sleeping, I saw myself in a dream performing circumambulation الطواف around the Ka'ba... Then I turned my face to see another man with huge body, red complexion, curly hair and blind in one eye. His eye looked as a protruding out grape. I asked, 'Who is this?' They said (to me), 'He is Ad-Dajjal.[91]

In the night of his Ascent, Muhammad claimed that among the many signs that Allah showed him, was the *Dajjal*.[92] Another source asserts that in the night of the Ascent Muhammad saw the *Dajjal* as a very bulky man with white skin and one of his eyes is protruding like a shining star.[93]

It is conspicuous that Islamic Traditions do not allude to the foreign sources from which they quote. And if

70

Muhammad was really the original source of these traditions, it is apparent that he did not refer to the sources from which he received his information. The Christian and the Jewish documents that were in vogue in the East had surely made this information available to any person who was interested in obtaining such knowledge. The caravans that traveled between Arabia, Syria, Yemen and Egypt were the major cultural and educational market in which Muslims found a great treasure of information. After the Islamic conquest, Arabs became more acquainted with the Hellenistic and Persian civilizations that expanded and opened to them a new horizon of knowledge they had never known before. In many instances, with great adaptation, later traditionalists acquired this abounding wealth of information from their stories.

The picture that Islamic Tradition depicted of the character of the *Dajjal*, instilled a profound fear in the hearts of Muslims. The picture is very bleak and the trial or tribulation of the *Dajjal* that will afflict the world nothing was or will be like it, since the creation of the world. Evidently, the Islamic *Hadith* cites the words of Jesus Christ, *"For those days will be a time of tribulation such as has not occurred since the beginning of the creation which God created until now, and never will."*[94] The *Dajjal* is a master of terror, accompanied by a formidable army of people and demons in an attempt to accomplish his mission. Thus, how can the believers protect themselves from his deception and atrocity?

Islamic Traditions furnish Muslims with the weapons by which they can shelter themselves from the spell and terror of the *Dajjal*. Muhammad urged the believers to memorize the first or the last ten verses of the chapter of the Cave. That would safeguard them from the *Dajjal*.[95] In another sound *hadith*, it is related that

71

whosoever memorizes the first three verses of the chapter of the Cave will be protected from the tribulation of the *Dajjal*.[96] Also, whosoever lives in the City of the Prophet or Mecca will be shielded from his horror.[97]

But after over one year and two months of the *Dajjal's* appearance, he will meet his fate at the hand of Christ Jesus, son of Mary.[98]

CHAPTER FOUR

Jesus Son of Mary
عيسى ابن مريم

Muslims do not concur with the biblical teaching of Jesus' crucifixion, death and His resurrection after three days, in His first coming. The Qur'an seems to be conclusive in proclaiming that God has spared His life and lifted Him up to heaven or paradise before His enemies were able to crucify Him,

> That they said (in boast), 'we killed Christ Jesus the son of Mary, the messenger of Allah', but they killed him not, nor crucified him, but it so appeared to them...Nay, Allah raised him up unto Himself [1]

وَقَوْلِهِمْ إِنَّا قَتَلْنَا الْمَسِيحَ عِيسَى ابْنَ مَرْيَمَ رَسُولَ اللهِ وَمَا
قَتَلُوهُ وَمَا صَلَبُوهُ بَلْ شُبّهَ لَهُمْ ... بَلْ رَفَعَهُ الله إِلَيْهِ

However, Muslims do believe that Jesus will return by the end of time. Actually, His return is one of the major signs of the end of time. He is coming to fulfill a great mission, which nobody else is entrusted to accomplish. It is worth noticing that the Qur'an does not explicitly point to Jesus' second coming. It is both the efforts of the exegetes as well as the corpus of the Islamic Tradition that manufactured the events that would take place during the period in which Jesus will achieve the task God has pre-ordained for Him to do.

There is only one verse in the entire Qur'an Muslims claim it alludes to the second coming of Christ.[2]

73

But this verse is subject to more than one interpretation. There are two reasons why it is difficult to unveil the actual meaning of this verse. First, the translation of this verse may be read, 'It is a sign for the Hour...إنه لَعِلمٌ للسَّاعَة'. It can also be translated as,' He is a sign for the Hour...'The Arabic language does not help so much in clarifying whether the pronoun is really 'it' or 'he'. Secondly, there is no connection between this verse and both the preceding and the succeeding verses. It is inserted between two unrelated verses, disrupting the meaning and putting it out of context. But Muslims insist that there is a tangible relationship between this verse and the other verses, and the word 'Innahu' (it, is really he) alludes to Jesus. Also based on the Islamic Tradition, expounders associated this verse with the eschatological Islamic episodes incorporated in the Hadith. But apart from the Islamic Tradition this particular verse would be ambiguous and subject to different interpretations.

There are two other verses in the Qur'an that Muslims relate to the future death of Christ in His second coming,

> And there is none of the people of the Book
> but must believe in him before his death;
> and on the Day of Judgment he will be a
> witness against them.[3]

وإنَّ من أهلِ الكِتابِ إلاَّ لَيُؤمِنَنَّ به قبلَ مَوتِهِ ويومَ القِيامَة
يَكونُ عَلَيْهِم شَهيداً

Muslim scholars believe that the possessive pronoun 'his' refers to Jesus. They say, "Jesus is still living in the body and that he will appear just before the Final Day, after the coming of the Mahdi,"[4] then he will die. In his commentary, ibn Jarir explains that the phrase 'before his death' implies 'the death of 'Isa Son of Mary' and that

74

none of the people of the Book but will believe in him.[5] Al-Hasan al-Basri comments that it means, "Before the death of 'Isa Son of Mary. By God he is now still alive with God, but when he descends, they will all (the people of the Book) believe in him."[6] The other verse is recorded in Sura 19:33,

> So peace is on me the day I was born, the day that I die, the day that I shall be raised from the dead.

والسَّلامُ عليَّ يومَ وُلِدْتُ ويومَ أموتُ ويومَ أُبْعَثُ حيًّا

Since most Muslims affirm that Jesus was not crucified and did not suffer from the agony of death in his first coming, they claim that this verse refers to His second coming. After forty years of His life on earth, he will die and be resurrected, in the Day of Judgment, like the rest of mankind. But the wording of the above cited verse was also said about John the Baptist, and John, as Muslims admit, died and no one claimed that this verse referred to His future death.

Then, how did Jesus become the focal point of the Islamic eschatology? Why was Jesus chosen, from among all the known prophets, to play such a prominent role in these future historical events? What prompted Muslims to find in Jesus the right figure who will complement the Islamic picture of the end of time? It was not difficult for Muslim scholars to provide an answer. They reasoned that Jesus must descend to earth at the end of time,

- To refute the Jewish allegation that they killed him. Thus, God will divulge their deception and will show that Jesus is the one who will eradicate them.

- To suffer death. Since Jesus is a human being, he must taste death. Thus, the time has come for him to die on earth. Being created from dust, he must be buried in dust, (The Qur'an does not claim that Jesus was created from dust but he was the word of God and of His spirit. Thus, he was called the Spirit of God), (Sura 4:171).

- To join the best nation created on earth. When Jesus recognized the sublime characteristics of Muhammad and His community, he pleaded with God to make Him one of them. God acceded to His request and kept Him alive, so Jesus will descend at the end of time to renew the vitality of the religion of Islam. His descent will also be simultaneous with the appearance of the *Dajjal*, who will be killed at the hand of Jesus.

- To proclaim the truth. Jesus' return would prove the falsehood of the Christians, disclose their spurious claims, and disprove their belief in His crucifixion.

- To corroborate Muhammad's assumption. He is allotted the above privileges as corroboration to Muhammad's saying: 'I am more entitled, to 'Isa Son of Mary than all the people (because) there was no prophet that emerged between him and me.'[7]

- To declare that Islam is the true religion of God. Muslims believe that Jesus predicted the advent of Muhammad and preached that the messenger of God will come after Him.[8] They also ascertain that He called all the people to believe and follow him.[9] Even Jesus himself will follow the teaching of Islam and will be a believer in Muhammad.

In Islamic eschatology, Jesus will return at the end of time to carry out God's plan, which He pre-ordained, against the *Dajjal* and his adherents, and the armies of Gog and Magog. It is an epic full of actions and intricate developments aimed at creating excitement.

In this chapter, we will examine the episode of Jesus and the *Dajjal* who is the inverse of Jesus. Furthermore, the *Dajjal* will become the symbol of the evil forces that bent to destroy what is good in God's creation and remove the faith from the hearts of the believers.

For some unknown reasons the armies of both Muslims and the Byzantines[10] sign a treaty of alliance against a third party. Islamic sources do not provide any information about the common enemy. The allied forces will vanquish their foes and win enormous bounty. Then they will camp in a plain with scattered hills in the suburb of Damascus.[11] But that alliance will not last for long. A fierce war will be waged between the two old allies in which innumerable soldiers from both sides will lose their lives. Though Muslims will win the war, grief will overwhelm them because of the large number of fatalities from which they will suffer. The victorious army will not rejoice in the spoils of the war it will capture from the conquest of Constantinople.[12] As they are being busy in sharing the spoils and their swords are hanging on the olive trees, Satan shouts: "The *Dajjal* has taken his place among your households." They will rush out but they will discover that it is just a rumor.[13] They, however, will decide to return to Syria in order to prepare themselve for the war. Subsequently the *Dajjal* and his forces will besiege them. At that moment Jesus Son of Mary will come to aid the Muslims against the *Dajjal.*

But this story, as numerous other stories of the *Hadith*, is shrouded with abstruse doubts and problems. Evidently, it is rather difficult to reconcile between the contrasting narratives, when the details are conflicting.

Originally, according to some *hadiths,* the cause for the war between the Muslims and the Byzantines is that a Byzantine man comes out of the ranks of the army raising a cross and saying, "Victory to the cross." One of the Muslims will come forward and kill him. The treaty is broken and the massacre takes its toll on both sides.[14] But some other Islamic sources recount different reason for the war and there is no mention of any alliance between the two armies. It seems that there will be prisoners of war from the Byzantine army in the Muslims' camp who were converted to Islam. The Byzantines wanted to fight the apostates but the Muslims refuse to concede. Thus, a vehement war will start between the two enemies in a place called *al-A'maq* or *Dabiq* in the surrounding area of Aleppo[15] and not Damascus as previously mentioned.

The significance of recounting this incident in this context is that it focuses on the conflicting information about the location in which the Muslims will take refuge after defeating their enemies. It is reported that the *Dajjal* will beleaguer them after the battle with the Byzantines and Jesus will descend amidst their military camp or nearby. That means there are also contradictory accounts about the location of Jesus' descent. One *hadith* indicates that they will gather their forces in the Smoke Mountain where the Dajjal will besiege them.[16] Another *hadith* remarks that they will be in Jerusalem in a mosque led in prayer by a righteous Imam when the *Dajjal* and his forces will surround them.[17] A third story points to a different location. It says "Muslims will retreat to *'Aqabat Afiq'* (beside the Jordan River)"[18] where the *Dajjal* will follow them. A fourth hadith attributed to Muhammad, asserts that Muslims will indeed fight the *Dajjal* at the Jordan River: "you will be at its eastern (bank) and he will be at its western (bank)."[19]

All these irreconcilable *hadiths* raise more questions than answers, especially as we try to examine the role of Jesus in these accelerating events. It is true that all these traditions emphasize that Jesus will come to rescue the Muslims from the atrocity of the *Dajjal,* regardless of the location of their camp. But these contradictions create doubts about the authenticity of these traditions and seemingly, point to the concoctions of the narrators or later storytellers.

Based on the information that could be extracted from the *Hadith,* Jesus will descend on the Muslims' camp while either they are preparing themselves for war against the *Dajjal,*[20] or he will come to them while they are fortified in the Smoke Mountain, besieged by the *Dajjal* and extremely suffering from famine.[21] Alternately, he will descend beside the white minaret, east of Damascus,[22] or at a mosque in Jerusalem during the time of the early prayer,[23] or in *'Aqabat Afiq* at the Jordan River.[24]

On the based of these unconfirmed but sole reports, Islamic Tradition furnishes, the researcher - any researcher - wonders how he could scrutinize or even accept any of these information as authentic and develop a sound Islamic eschatology. However, for the sake of comparison, we are here, again, obligated to accept them at their face value.

According to Islamic sources, when Jesus descends to accomplish His mission, His first task will be to kill the *Dajjal* and eradicate his forces. The *Dajjal,* who apotheosizes himself and bewitches the people, will be facing his crucial and last moment before he unexpectedly is killed at the hand of Jesus. Interestingly, it seems that the *Dajjal* is not aware that he is going to meet with Jesus Son of Mary, face to face. Though he is ostentatious, he is not omniscient. Islamic sources have attributed to him some

79

futuristic knowledge about the rise of Muhammad and Islam,[25] which in the best scenario, aimed at the glorification of the prophet of Islam and his faith. But the *Dajjal* in optimum conditions will fail to predict his encounter with Jesus.

Variant stories are recorded in Islamic Tradition about this encounter. These traditions agree that Jesus will kill the *Dajjal* at the eastern gate of the city of Ludda, in Palestine. There are different scenarios involved in this encounter. Mostly, a sort of dialogue will take place among Muslims themselves and later between them and Jesus. They have already suffered from the toil and famine so that they would burn their bows and eat them. While they are in such ordeal, they hear a voice at early dawn announcing the good news, "O, people the succor has arrived." This glad tiding will be repeated three times. The Muslims will argue among themselves saying that this is a voice of a sated man. Then *'Isa* Son of Mary will descend at the morning prayer. Their leader will call Jesus **Spirit of God**, and ask him to lead them in prayer, but Jesus declines and the leader will lead them. As soon as the prayer is over, Jesus will carry His spear and march towards the *Dajjal*. When the *Dajjal* sees him he will melt as the lead (or the salt) melts. Jesus will then stab him with His spear between his two breasts and kill him,[26] and He will show the Muslims the blood of the *Dajjal* staining the head of His spear.[27] This is a general portrait of the episode of the fate of the *Dajjal*.

But there are other details that are inserted in other *hadiths* that are of some interest. While the Muslims are fortified on the mountain, they will suddenly be covered with thick darkness that it becomes so hard for a man to see his palm. Then son of Mary will descend among them and dispel the darkness, and Muslims will see a man wearing a cuirass. As they ask him about himself, he will inform them

80

that he is the slave of God, His messenger, His word and His spirit, *'Isa*. Then he will ask them to choose one of three options against their enemies: "either God will afflict the *Dajjal* (and his forces) with a punishment from heaven, or the ground will swallow them, or He will let your arms overcome their arms and their arms will be powerless against yours. They will say, 'O, messenger of God this (last one) is more gratifying to our hearts.'"[28]

In other *hadiths* it is related that when Jesus descends at the minaret in east of Damascus the believers and true servants of Allah will assemble around him to support him. He will lead them against the *Dajjal* who will be on his way to Jerusalem. Jesus will overtake him at *'Aqabat Afiq*. The *Dajjal* will run away from Him, but Jesus will catch up with him at the gate of Ludda and kill him.[29]

In one of the *hadith* it is said that Jesus will descend among them in the early morning while they are camping in the Smoke Mountain in Syria. He will ask them why they are hesitant to attack this devious man. They will answer that he is a genie. But Jesus, after the time of prayer is over, will lead them in their war against the *Dajjal*, kill him, and his forces of Jews and polytheists will be completely annihilated.[30]

But the story of Jerusalem's battle has a different setting. Jesus will descend amidst the people assembled in the mosque at the time of the Morning Prayer, led by the *Mahdi*.[31] Meanwhile, the *Dajjal* and his troops will be surrounding the city and the mosque. As soon as the time of prayer is over, Jesus orders the Muslim worshippers to open the gate of the mosque. The *Dajjal*, accompanied by seventy thousand Jews who are carrying adorned swords and wearing crowns, will be standing behind the gate. When the Dajjal sees Jesus, he will melt like salt in water

81

and run away. Jesus will tell him, 'I have to deal you a blow from which you cannot escape.' Jesus will catch up with him at the eastern gate of Ludda and kill him.[32]

When the *Dajjal's* Jewish forces see that their leader has run away for his life, and his plans have been thwarted, they will be gripped with fear and try to hide from the swords of the Muslims. The tradition indicates that all the hiding places in which the Jews take refuge will speak, whether it is a rock or a tree, or a wall or an animal – except the boxthorn الغرقدة because it is one of the Jewish trees. All will say, "O, Muslim, slave of God, here is a Jew come and kill him.[33] It is also said that no infidel touched by Jesus' breath but dies; and His breath reaches wherever the range of His sight ends. Al-Qurtubi reiterates that God has invigorated the breath of Jesus so that as soon as the infidels see Him and are touched by His breath, will perish.[34] In his remark, Ali al-Qari, a Muslim scholar, expresses his amazement at how the breath of Jesus has the power to cause the death of some and the life of others.[35] But this phenomena, is a distorted quotation from Jewish literature. It is related that the Messiah shall slay the Antichrist in the person of the wicked Armillus, *with his breath,*[36] a statement that may have originated with Isaiah 11:4, that Christ *"will strike the earth with the rod of His mouth; and with the breath of His lips He will slay the wicked."* This same striking image is reiterated in 2 Thessalonians 2:8, *"Then that lawless... whom the Lord will slay with the breath of His mouth and bring to an end by the appearance of His coming."*

Obviously, Muhammad or the narrators altered the function of the breath of Jesus from being the cause of terminating the life of the Antichrist into the power that kills any infidel it touches.

This story of the eradication of the Jews has been repeated in several places in the collections of the *Hadith*.[37] After all, according to Islamic traditions, the Jews comprise the bulk of the *Dajjal's* troops. They will follow him and proclaim him as a god. They deserve the retribution that will afflict them because they have become infidels كفار . It is noticeable here that nothing is mentioned about the Christians. What happens to them? Muslims will claim they all have become Muslims after the descent of Jesus. Actually, Muslims believe that the second coming of Christ will entail the elimination of all religions except the Islamic faith.[38] But this does not agree with the existence of all the infidels who will continue to populate the earth after the death of Christ in His second coming.

Apparently, we have here a number of incompatible reports, even a credulous reader would be hesitant to accept. It is not easy to rectify the contradictions or to believe that these traditions are *bona fide*. A primordial question will be, is there a way for a researcher to seriously reconcile between these different stories? The enormity of the contradictions do not allow for any interpretive solution. Any critic who is *au courant* of the Islamic Tradition will recognize the trend of falsification despite the authentic names included in the chain of authorities, which, in the opinion of this writer, were fabricated by skillful narrators who mastered this art.

Killing of the *Dajjal* is not the only task entrusted to Jesus to accomplish in His second coming. One of his missions will be to prove to both the Jews and Christians that they had erred in their beliefs about Christ. The Jews will realize that He was really a prophet and the messenger of God, and that they did not crucify Him. Christians, who deified Jesus, will discover that He was a mere prophet, not the Son of God, and the Savior of the world. Thus, Jesus

83

will break down the cross, extirpate the pigs and fight all non-Muslims, either to force them to accept Islam or to exterminate them. All other religions, in His time, will be eliminated except Islam.[39]

As the *Hadith* provides a description of the *Dajjal*, it also furnishes a general physical description of the Messiah Jesus Son of Mary. This description is attributed to Muhammad. Muhammad alleged that he saw Jesus twice: once when he ascended to heaven in the Night Journey of the *Mi'raj,* and again, in a vision he saw. Any other information of Jesus' physical appearance is based on these two incidents. These two incidents were the same two occasions in which Muhammad encountered the *Dajjal* also. In his first encounter, he describes Jesus as a man *"of a medium height and of a red complexion, as if he had just come out of a bath,"*[40] or *"a curly-haired man of moderate height."*[41] In his vision while he was sleeping in the *Ka'ba,* he affirms, *"he* saw *a brown-skinned man with flowing hair, supported by two man, and water dripping from his head. I asked, 'Who is this?' They said, 'son of Mary.'"*[42]

This description continued to be quoted and repeated by Muhammad and the narrators of the *Hadith* with some additional slight variations. One episode reports that He will descend wearing two garments lightly dyed with saffron and placing His hands on the wings of two angels; whenever He lowers His head, His hair drips water like beads, and when He raises it up, beads like pearls fall from it.[43] In another place, Jesus was said to resemble *'Urwa Ibn Mas'ud,* one of Muhammad's companions.[44]

This same description was related in a more colorful picture: *'Abdullah ibn 'Umar* claimed that *"the Messenger of Allah... said, I dreamt at night that I was at the Ka'ba, and I saw a dark man like the most handsome of dark men you have ever seen. He had hair reaching to between his ears and his shoulders like the most excellent of such hair that you have seen. He had combed his hair, and water was dripping from it. He was leaning on two men or on the shoulders of two men doing the circumambulation around the Ka'ba. I asked: Who is this? It was said: al-Masih ibn Maryam* (Christ son of Mary).[45] He is also described as a *"reddish-white man with lank hair"*[46] or a *whitish-red lank-haired man."*[47] Some other *hadiths* imply that Muhammad encountered 'Isa in more than one occasion and shook hands with him.[48]

The Islamic version of Christ's mission does not conform to the biblical teachings. In Christianity, Jesus in His second coming will act neither as an agent to Muhammad nor as his deputy – as Muslims allege – to enforce Islam on people or even to practice Islam with its rituals.[49] The Bible made it clear that Jesus will come as the Lord of His creation to reward the righteous and condemn the wicked. Every knee shall bow to Him and He will judge the living and the dead. In his epistle to the Philippians, the Apostle Paul says,

> So that at the name of Jesus every knee will bow, of those who are in heaven and on earth and under earth, and that every tongue will confess that Jesus Christ is Lord, for the glory of God the Father.[50]

In another place Jesus says,

> The sign of the Son of Man will appear in the sky, and then all the tribes of the earth will mourn, and they will see the Son of Man coming on the cloud of the sky with power and great glory. In addition, He will send forth His angels with a great trumpet

85

and they will gather together His elect from the four winds, from one end of the sky to the other.[51]

Thus, Jesus will not come as a follower of any human being or of his traditions, because He is the Lord of the creation and *the redeemer of the world.* He is the *Way, the Truth, and the Life.* And all those who reject His redemptive act on the cross and deny His deity will sustain His judgment in that fearful day.

But what is the biblical view of the excruciating end of the Antichrist and his deputy the False Prophet? First, it is noted that the punishment of God's wrath will fall on the Antichrist and his deputy, and then on all those who worshiped the Antichrist, his image, and all those who received his mark on their forehead or their hands. The Beast, the False Prophet and the federation of ten kings with their armies that allied themselves with them have one purpose: to wage war against Christ who is called the Lamb, and His army.[52] However, the Lamb will defeat them because *"He is Lord of lords and King of kings and those who are with Him are the called and chosen and faithful."*[53] By the end of this war the Antichrist and his deputy, the False Prophet, are seized and thrown alive into the lake of fire, which burns with brimstone.[54] These two devious characters will be the first to be tormented in the lake of fire. All those who allied themselves with them will be eradicated by the *"sword which came from the mouth of Him who sat on the Horse, and all the birds were filled with their flesh."*[55] Evidently, all those who have received the mark of the Antichrist on their foreheads or arms and worshiped him and his image *"will drink of the wine of the wrath of God, which is mixed in full strength in the cup of His anger; (they) will be tormented with fire and brimstone in the presence of the holy angels and in the presence of the*

86

Lamb. And the smoke of their torment goes up forever and ever."[56]

But before this chapter is concluded, a point of profound importance should be denoted here. In the *Hadith* literature the descent of Jesus to carry out His mission, as it is depicted in Islam, is not surrounded by signs and the grandeur that befit the Savior and the Judge of the world. That is because Jesus, in the Islamic view, is a mere prophet and not the Son of God, as Christians believe. The image thus presented in the Islamic literature about the person of Jesus, fits well in the Islamic theology. Furthermore, in spite of the great veneration Muslims display for Jesus, Islam prohibits Muslims from elevating any prophet above Muhammad. Notwithstanding the role Jesus performs on the stage of the world history, He will descend quietly just in time to save the Muslims from the Dajjal's ordeal. He is like a mythical hero who appears unexpectedly to achieve some great feat. There are no guidelines, neither in the Qur'an nor in the *Hadith,* to prepare Muslims for his second coming. Actually, Jesus' second coming in Islam, is just one sign among many that ushers the end of time. He is one means to an end. Contrary to the Islamic perception of the second coming of Christ, the Christian scriptures assert that astral portents and paragons will appear in heaven signaling that the second coming of Christ is at hand. All the historical events and cataclysmic signs point to His coming. He is the focal point and they are the means, not the end. One Islamic *hadith* implies that Jesus will descend supported by two angels. Maybe this is a remnant image of the event that took place after the ascension of Jesus in His first coming. Two angels with white clothes came down to scold His followers who, amazingly, continued standing, watching the cloud that shrouded Him out of their sight.[57] Was that a real cloud or a cloud of angels that came to receive Him and accompany

Him to His glory? In Islamic context, the story of these two angels that descended with Jesus ends mysteriously as if their only task is to bring him down to earth safely and then disappear.

In the Christian account, there is a profound relation between the way Jesus ascended to heaven and His second coming. The two angels assured all the spectators who gathered together at the Mount of Olives that Jesus will come back '*in just the same way*'[58] as He ascended to heaven. His second coming will be visible, seen by the world. He will descend on the same Mount He had departed from.[59] Actually what these two angels told them was proclaimed by Jesus Himself. In Matthew 24:30 Jesus foretold His disciples that in His second coming "*all the tribes of the earth will mourn and they will see the Son of Man coming on the cloud of sky with power and glory.*" Jesus is not going to come down during a dusky morning or on a misty day. The entire world will witness His coming.

But there is a prelude of successive catastrophic events before the second coming of Christ. In predicting these events, He was careful to underscore what is imminent and what is futuristic. Some of the imminent signs are: wars and rumors of wars, nation will rise up against nation, kingdom against kingdom, earthquakes in various places, and famines; those '*things must take place; but that is not yet the end...these things are merely the beginning of birth pangs*'.[60]

Then after the tribulation and before the second coming of Christ, "*The sun will be darkened and the moon will not give its light, and the stars will be falling from heaven and the powers that are in the heavens will be shaken.*[61] Then the sign of the Son of Man will appear.[62] These signs are merely a few of many of the future 'guideposts' that will announce, loudly and clearly, the second coming of Christ.

The nature of this study does not allow this writer to examine all the details that precede the second coming of Christ, but any biblical component related to the topic under discussion necessitates a careful consideration and analysis.

CHAPTER FIVE

Jesus and Gog and Magog
عيسى ابن مريم ويأجوج ومأجوج

The episode of Gog and Magog is a mystery for Muslims and the expounders of the Qur'an. This is not an accusation but undeniable fact based primarily on what is presented in the corpus of Islamic commentaries. But before examining the story of Gog and Magog in the apocalyptic *Hadith,* we are obligated first to look into the Qur'an to discover what does the Holy Book of Islam says about these two mysterious nations that will perilously plague the world, especially the Middle East. In this case, it will be helpful to quote the entire segment of chapter 18:83-99 that is related to this event,

> They ask thee concerning *Dhu al-Qarnayn.* Say, "I will rehearse to you something of his story." Verily We established his power on earth, and We gave him the ways and the means to all ends. One (such) way he followed, until, when he reached the setting of the sun, he found it sets in a spring of murky water: near it he found a people; We said: *"O Dhu al-Qarnayn* (thou have authority), either to punish them or to treat them with kindness." He said, "Whoever doth wrong, him shall we punish; then shall he be sent back to his Lord; and He will punish him with a punishment unheard of (before). "But whoever believes, and works righteousness- he shall have a goodly

reward, and easy will be his task as we order it by our command. Then followed he (another) way. Until when he came to the rising of the sun, he found it rising on a people for whom We have provided no covering protection against the sun. (He left them as they were: We completely understood what was before him. Then followed he (another) way, until, when he reached (a tract) between two mountains, he found beneath them, a people who scarcely understood a word. They said: "O *Dhu al-Qarnayn*! The Gog and Magog (people) do great mischief on earth: Shall we render thee tribute in order that thou mightiest erect a barrier [1] between us and them?" He said: "(the power) in which my Lord had established me is better than (tribute): Help me therefore with strength (and labour): I will erect a strong barrier between you and them: "Bring me blocks of iron." At length, when he had filled up the space between the two steep mountainsides, he said: "Blow (with your bellows)." Then when he had made it (red) as fire, he said: "Bring me molten lead that I may pour over it."[2] Thus were they made powerless to scale it or to dig through it. He said: "This is a mercy from my Lord: but when the promise of my Lord comes to pass, He will make it into dust: and the promise of my Lord is true." On that day We shall leave them to surge like waves on one another...

ـ وَيَسْأَلُونَكَ عَن ذِي الْقَرْنَيْنِ قُلْ سَأَتْلُو عَلَيْكُم مِنْهُ ذِكْرًا

ـ إِنَّا مَكَّنَّا لَهُ فِي الْأَرْضِ وَآتَيْنَاهُ مِن كُلِّ شَيْءٍ سَبَبًا

- فَأَتْبَعَ سَبَبَاً
- حَتَّى إِذَا بَلَغَ مَغْرِبَ الشَّمْسِ وَجَدَهَا تَغْرُبُ فِي عَيْنٍ حَمِئَةٍ وَوَجَدَ عِندَهَا قَوْماً قُلْنَا يَا ذَا الْقَرْنَيْنِ إِمَّا أَنْ تُعَذِّبَ وَإِمَّا أَنْ تَتَّخِذَ فِيهِمْ حُسْناً
- قَالَ أَمَّا مَنْ ظَلَمَ فَسَوْفَ نُعَذِّبُهُ ثُمَّ يُرَدُّ إِلَى رَبِّهِ فَيُعَذِّبُهُ عَذَاباً نُكْرَاً
- وَأَمَّا مَنْ آمَنَ وَعَمِلَ صَالِحاً فَلَهُ جَزَاءً الْحُسْنَى وَسَنَقُولُ لَهُ مِنْ أَمْرِنَا يُسْراً ثُمَّ أَتْبَعَ سَبَباً
- حَتَّى إِذَا بَلَغَ مَطْلِعَ الشَّمْسِ وَجَدَهَا تَطْلُعُ عَلَى قَوْمٍ لَمْ نَجْعَلْ لَهُمْ مِنْ دُونِهَا سِتْراً
- كَذَلِكَ وَقَدْ أَحَطْنَا بِمَا لَدَيْهِ خُبْراً ـ ثُمَّ أَتْبَعَ سَبَباً
- حَتَّى إِذَا بَلَغَ بَيْنَ السَّدَّيْنِ وَجَدَ مِنْ دُونِهِمَا قَوْماً لا يَكَادُونَ يَفْقَهُونَ قَوْلاً
- قَالُوا يَا ذَا الْقَرْنَيْنِ إِنَّ يَأْجُوجَ وَمَأْجُوجَ مُفْسِدُونَ فِي الأَرْضِ فَهَلْ نَجْعَلُ لَكَ خَرْجاً عَلَى أَنْ تَجْعَلَ بَيْنَنَا وَبَيْنَهُمْ سَدَاً
- قَالَ مَا مَكَّنَي فِيهِ رَبِّي خَيْرٌ فَأَعِينُونِي بِقُوَّةٍ أَجْعَلْ بَيْنَكُمْ وَبَيْنَهُمْ رَدْماً
- إِيتُونِي زُبَرَ الْحَدِيدِ حَتَّى إِذَا سَاوَى بَيْنَ الصَّدَفَيْنِ قَالَ انْفُخُوا حَتَّى إِذَا جَعَلَهُ نَاراً قَالَ إِيتُونِي أُفْرِغْ عَلَيْهِ قِطْراً
- فَمَا اسْطَاعُوا أَنْ يَظْهَرُوهُ وَمَا اسْتَطَاعُوا لَهُ نَقْباً
- قَالَ هَذَا رَحْمَةٌ مِنْ رَبِّي فَإِذَا جَاءَ وَعْدُ رَبِّي جَعَلَهُ دَكَّا وَكَانَ وَعْدُ رَبِّي حَقَّا
- وَتَرَكْنَا بَعْضَهُمْ يَوْمَئِذٍ يَمُوجُ فِي بَعْضٍ...

Nevertheless, one more Qur'anic verse must be added to this lengthy citation from chapter 21:96,

Until the Dam of (the people) of Gog and Magog is opened, and they swiftly emerge from every hill.[3]

حَتَّى إِذَا فُتِحَتْ يَأْجُوجُ وَمَأْجُوجُ وَهُمْ مِنْ كُلِّ حَدَبٍ يَنْسِلُونَ

The first reference is associated with a controversial figure that was, according to the Qur'an, instrumental in

92

restraining the ferocious tribes of Gog and Magog. This powerful king is called in the Qur'an as *Dhu al-Qarnayn* (the man of the two horns). Muslim commentators have questioned the identity of this man and made a number of suggestions that were mere speculations. Some believed that he was Alexander the Great; others proposed that he was a "prehistoric king contemporary to Abraham,"[4] or he was an ancient king of Persia, or a prehistoric Himyarite king from Yemen.[5] But it seems, that most expounders are inclined to associate *Dhu al-Qarnayn* with Alexander. This is the popular identification among Muslim scholars. In his book *The Life of the Prophet,* Ibn Hisham says,

> *Dhu al-Qarnayn* is Alexander, the Greek, the king of Persia and Greece, or the king of the east and the west, for because of this he was called *Dhu al-Qarnayn,* or because he went about the two horns of the earth, east and west. Others claim that (he was thus called) because he had lived for two centuries or generations. Yet others hold that he had two horns, meaning two plaits, or that his crown had two horns. Perhaps he was thus called by reason of his courage, since he butts his enemies, Opinions are not unanimous about his being a prophet, but all opinions are agreed on his being righteous and a believer.[6]

In his commentary on chapter 18:83-86, Baydawi indicated that when the Jews asked Muhammad about *Dhu al-Quarnayn*, he said to them,

> That God established him in the land so that he could reach the place where the sun sets. He found that it sets in a muddy spring,

93

surrounded by idolatrous people! He also walked to the place where the sun rises and discovered that those who lived there went about naked, with no homes to shelter them from the sun. After that, he walked to a site that lies to the north between two mountains. He poured in the path between these two mountains a mixture of iron and molten brass erecting thus an impassable barrier, which only God can reach on the Day of Resurrection.[7]

A host of other scholars and commentators ascertained that *Dhu al-Qarnayn* is truly Alexander the Great. Among them are al-Fakhr al-Razi,[8] al-Tabari,[9] al-Qummi (whose book is published on the margins of Ibn Jarir's work), and al-Zamakh-shari.[10] All these scholars, apt to believe that *Dhu al-Qarnayn* is Alexander the Greek, forget that he was an idol worshipper, and claimed to be the son of Jupiter Amon, the sun god. He never acknowledged the sovereignty of the true God who was revealed in the biblical scriptures. Besides, Alexander, despite his military accomplishments, did not live long enough to achieve all the great feats attributed to him by Muslim commentators. He died when he was thirty-three years old in the city of Babylon in 323 B.C.

'A. Y. 'Ali remarks

> I have not the least doubt that *Dhu al-Qarnayn* is meant to be Alexander the Great, the historic Alexander, and not the legendary Alexander...[11]

He also tries very hard to justify the Qur'anic allusion to Alexander's righteousness by saying,

He was a man of lofty ideal. He died over three centuries before the time of Jesus, but that does not mean he was not a man of faith, for Allah revealed Himself to men of all nations in all ages. Alexander was a disciple of the philosopher Aristotle, noted for his pursuit of sound truth in all departments of thought. Alexander's reference to Jupiter Ammon may have been no more than a playful reference to the superstituous of his time. Socrates spoke of the Grecian gods and so did Aristotle and Plato; but it would be wrong to call them idolaters or men without Faith.[12]

It is obvious that 'A. Y. 'Ali and other like expositors of the Qur'an attempt, through speculation, to prove the validity of their Sacred Book. In this case historical facts become secondary or invalid if they contradict their Sacred Text. The reader does not have to go too far to discover that Alexander the Great was obsessed with his military career, and his own pleasure. Religious matters were not of his main concern unless they served his own political interest. History recounts that,

In the spring of 331, Alexander made a pilgrimage to the great temple and oracle of Amon-Ra, Egyptian God of the sun, whom the Greeks identify with Zeus. The earlier Egyptian pharaohs were believed to be the sons of Amon-Ra; and Alexander, the new ruler of Egypt, wanted the god to acknowledge him as his son. Apparently, the pilgrimage was successful, and might have confirmed in him a belief of his divine origin.[13]

This same Alexander, who endeavored to deify himself, after defeating Darius, the Persian king in the battle of Gaugamela, on October 1, 331 B.C., and then forcing his way to Persepolis, the Persian capital, and plundering the royal treasuries, burned the city "during a drunken binge".[14] Also, "shortly before he died, Alexander ordered the Greek cities to worship him as a god."[15] Thus, how can any serious researcher or historian claim that Alexander the Great was a man of faith in a true God?

Moreover, when the above Qur'anic verses are objectively studied, several interpretive problems demand honest answers. It is noted that this *Dhu al-Qarnayn* acted as a just and merciful ruler who followed the divine instructions and never boasted about his great military and political conquests. It is a prophetic image of a just ruler, who believed that Allah guided all his deeds. There is nothing mentioned about his cruelty, immorality, or drunkenness, and ungodliness - the facts that history verified. Thus, how can Muslim scholars reconcile between the historical Alexander and the Qur'anic *Dhu al-Qarnayn*? On what basis have Muslims considered *Dhu Al-Qarnayn* as Alexander the Great? The answer does not lie in the historical Alexander, but in the legendary Alexander of later times. This writer realizes that Muslim scholars may regard such a statement as an impulsive perpetrating accusation against what they believe as the impeccable Qur'an and its inspiration. From scholarly point of view this is not true. Thus, the following pages will introduce the readers, Muslims or non-Muslims, to historical evidence that will impugn the Islamic claim about *Dhu al-Qarnayn*, and virtually endorse the notational facts as they are recorded in the legendary documents. Eventually, intricate questions, problems and answers will be focusing on which of the two accounts is authentic.

96

A raison d'etre for focusing on Alexander the Great is that the Qur'anic Alexander is associated with the building of the dam or barrier to deter the people of Gog and Magog from infringing on other industrious peaceful people who inhabited the neighboring lands. This also has been the story of Alexander in the legends that mostly existed in the first six centuries prior to Islam. Thus, before the stupendous epic of Gog and Magog and Jesus is discussed, an analytical study of the Qur'anic *Dhu Al-Qarnayn* and the legendary Alexander has become an unalterable necessity.

Perhaps the best book that treated the story of Alexander's Gate behind which the people of Gog and Magog were enclosed is Andrew Runni Anderson's study entitled *Alexander's Gate, Gog and Magog, and the Inclosed Nations.*[16]

It seems several legends erupted around Alexander and his Gate. This study, however, is concerned only with the legend of Alexander and the people of Gog and Magog.

In his monograph, A. R. Anderson explains that "the union established between Greece and the Near East by Alexander's conquests brought into being a new conception, that of the civilized world of common interest."[17] He became the creator and the protector of the civilization of this New World "against the barbarians dwelling outside" its frontiers.[18] In the eyes of the mythical innovators he became the successor of Semiramis, Nebuchadnezar, Cyrus, and Sesonchosis. To the "Babylonians he became identified with Gilgamesh – the prototype of Heracles – and to the Greeks, a Dionysus and a new Heracles."[19] But the image of Alexander for which we are looking, is found in Jewish and Christian literature. The

97

Jews, who received a special treatment from Alexander after they showed him that he was mentioned in their Sacred Scriptures,[20] and had greatly benefited from his achievement, "came to conceive him as one of their own heroes, a champion and propagandist of the Most High."[21] Anderson then adds,

> Quite unconsciously, too, he prepared the ground in which Christianity was to grow, a forerunner of Jesus, earlier representation of whom portrayed him in Alexander's likeness, and the conception of Alexander Cosmocrator in time grew into Christus Pantocrator. In time also Alexander, as the champion of Jehovah to both Jews and Christians, became under the name and guise of Dulcarnain, the Lord of Two Horns, the hero of Mohammedanism in the Koran, xviii, 83f.[22]

But it seems that the earliest apocalyptic version of the legendary history of Alexander the Great is the Syrian *Christian Legend concerning Alexander.*[23] A thorough study of this legend led scholars to believe that the Qur'anic anecdote was echoing a legend that was in vogue in the East before the rise of Islam. In this legend, Alexander was made to predict the appointed time when the nations that were retained behind the Gate would be able to go forth "at the conclusion of eight hundred and twenty-six years."[24] Then, according to this legend, he also inscribes upon the Gate, "I have...prophesied that it shall come to pass, at the conclusion of nine hundred and forty years, ...another king, when the world shall come to an end by the command of God the ruler of creation."[25]

Since then, the *Syrian Legend* became susceptible to many changes in which the identity of Alexander the Great was transformed into a mature Christian leader who is guided by God to carry out His will, and " instead of building the gate as a pagan king, (he) builds it as a worshipper, a champion and instrument of God."[26] The Qur'an elicited this image from the legend. Any claim that the historical Alexander was a man of faith, or God revealed Himself to him, is a sheer calumny against history and the truth. Actually, if the story of *Dhu al-Qarnayn* is stripped from the Arabian fairy tales, we find that the title *Dhu al-Qarnayn* is borrowed from the Syrian Legend. It is believed that *"after the original in the Syrian Legend which arose in the vi century A.D. in which Alexander says to God, 'I know that thou hast caused horns grow upon my head so that I may crush the kingdoms of the world with them'. The Syriac Legend is, as Noldeke has shown, the source of the 'two horned' in the Koran."*[27]

A second historical source for this title is *"the widely current coinage of the conqueror and of the successor states generally depicted him in the guise of the horned god Jupitor-Ammon; hence the popular designation customarily used in the age of the Prophet."*[28] Another aspect of the legend is the building of the Gate to exclude the people of Gog and Magog in contrast to the non-Christian legends that asserted that the Gate was erected to restrain the Scythians, Alans, or other tribes called the Huns.[29]

The legend also exhibits that the Gate was built of iron and brass and some other material so that no fire could melt it, or steel could penetrate it[30] This Gate will permanently be closed, for about a thousand years as God decrees.

Obviously, historical studies proved that the historical Alexander did not build any gate to exclude any barbarian tribe, whether they were the Scythians, Alans or Gog and Magog. It is true that some Persian kings such as Khosro I Anushirwan (531-579 A.D.) finished the building of the iron gate of Derbend and the Caucasian Wall, a project begun by his father Kavath. But there is not any historical evidence that supports the claims of any of these legends, pagan or non-pagan. Encouraged by the Abbasid Caliph *al-Wathiq Bil-lah* and their curiosity to prove the authenticity of the Qur'anic story, Muslim explorers and historians had attempted to discover the location of the Gate.[31] Unfortunately, they pursued the legends' landmarks guided by the Qur'anic tradition "which itself continued the tradition of the *Christian Legend.*"[32]

In summary, this study ascertains that:

- The Qur'anic *Dhu al-Qarnayn* is identified with Alexander the Great.
- The Qur'anic Alexander is not the historical Alexander the Great.
- The Qur'anic Alexander should be identified with the legendary Alexander.
- The Qur'anic Alexander is a copy of the Christian legendary Alexander as depicted in the *Syrian Legend.*
- The historical Alexander was a pagan who deified himself and could not be a man of faith.
- The historical Alexander had never built a Gate to exclude the people of Gog and Magog.
- Middle ages Muslim explorers' who attempted to locate Alexander's Gate had failed because, historically, there was no gate built by Alexander the Great, and secondly, these explorers

were guided by legends and not by documented information.

Since the identity or personality of the Qur'anic *Dhu al-Qarnayn* is conclusively established, it remains to examine the story of Gog and Magog in its relationship to Jesus and the end of time.

The Qur'anic story is very brief. It acknowledges the existence of Gog and Magog who were excluded behind two mountains after the erection of Alexander's Gate. They will continue to be contained in their location, unable to escape until the appointed time that God Himself decreed. Then a breach will occur and these tribes will swarm out to destroy and ransack the world.[33] The Qur'an does not provide any information about the origin of these obscure people. In this case, we have to look for more detailed and reliable sources in order to acquire better understanding of the people of Gog and Magog. Actually, this study can only rely on one basic source. It is the Biblical account that became the source of most studies about the people of Gog and Magog. The Qur'anic references as well as the *Hadith* and all the legendary records about Gog and Magog are dependent on the Biblical account. Thus the question that needs to be asked is: Who are Gog and Magog?

The first reference mentioned in the Bible about Gog and Magog is found in the book of Genesis 10:2-4,

> The sons of Japheth were Gomer and Magog and Madai and Javan and Tubal and Meshech and Tiras. The sons of Gomer were Ashkenaz and Riphath and Togarmah. The sons of Javan were Elishah and Tarshish, Kittim and Dodanim.

101

The same list, with minor spelling variations, is repeated in 1 Chronicles 1:5-6. But the most important reference about Gog and Magog is recorded in Ezekiel 38 and 39. These two chapters are a detailed prophecy about Gog and Magog, and their allies who will invade the Middle East, and in particular the land of Israel. It is worth discussing these two chapters in some detail, and comparing them with the Islamic version as it is reiterated in the Qur'an and Islamic Hadith.

The name Gog is first mentioned in I Chronicles 5:4 as a son of Joel and descendent of the tribe of Reuben. But it does not seem that he is associated with the people of Magog. The Gog of Ezekiel is the chief prince of Rosh, Meshech and Tubal.[34] His territory was known as the land of Magog. He will lead his hordes of the northern tribes to wage a final war against the land of Israel, to plunder the country while enjoying the blessings of peace and security. Josephus identified the Magog as the land of Scythians, which is located in the north and northeast of the Black Sea and east of the Caspian Sea (now occupied by three members of the commonwealth of Independent States: Russia, the Ukraine, and Khazakhstan).[35] Rosh is believed to be modern Iran, while Meshech and Tubal "are always coupled together, in secular as well as biblical writings... (and) probably east of Asia Minor and are usually identified with Phrya and Cappadocia."[36] Ethiopia is Northern Sudan, Put is Libya, and Gomer is linked with Magog in Genesis 10:2.

> They were called Gimirrai by the Assyrians and Cimmerians by the Greeks. Originating north the Black Sea, by Ezekiel's time they settled in Asia Minor. Their name survives in Gamir, Armenian name for Cappadocia.

Beth-togarmah,[37] northeast of Asia Minor is Armenia.[38]

Ezekiel received a prophecy from the Lord that Gog, by the end of the time, will be recruiting armies from the land of Magog to invade the land of Israel. No certain date is mentioned about the timing of the invasion. Scholars of the Bible are somewhat baffled at the vagueness of this prophecy. They agree that it will take place in the future, but the mystery lies in predicting the time-period. Is it before the Messianic era or at a certain point of Jesus' reign? Is it in the middle of the tribulation or years before the apocalyptic time? In his commentary, Daniel I. Block says.

> Unlike Dan, 2:28 and 10:14 where it (later years) serves technically for the eschaton, here both expressions (in the course of time and in the future), refer simply to a later time, when the historical phase of the exiles is over and the new period of settlement in the land has arrived. [39]

All these speculations are full of enigmatic questions that have no answer. It is very difficult for a person to imagine that an uprising will occur during the Messianic era. By then, the Antichrist and his deputy will be thrown in the lake of fire, and Satan will be in chains in the Abyss until he is released to wage his final war against Jesus and the saints. Everything will be under the full control of the Messiah. In addition, this invasion could not happen during the tribulation first, because of the divine intervention against Gog, and, secondly, because the Antichrist will be dominating the world at this time, and the invasion of Gog will be an infringement on his sovereignty. The only speculation I entertain is that this invasion will occur sometime before the tribulation during a peace truce in the Middle East. Actually, these two chapters are unique among the Old Testament prophecies. They erupt suddenly without any warning and create emotional and intellectual shock.

In this prophecy, God reveals that Gog and his armies will be summoned, in the latter years, from the remote parts of the north to a land that is restored from the sword (6-8). This last phrase is significant because it clearly proves that this invasion cannot be during the tribulation. Gog with his troops will swiftly come like a forceful storm or a cloud covering the land (9). He will have an evil plan to attack a defenseless country to "capture spoil and to seize plunder" (11). Verse 16 explains that Gog is summoned from the remote parts of the north "in order that the nations may know Me when I shall be sanctified through you before their eyes, O, Gog." God's intervention will be manifested through the means of the natural elements such as earthquake,

> "The fish of the sea, the birds of the heaven,
> the beast of the field, all the creeping things
> that creep on the earth will shake at My
> presence; the mountains also will be thrown
> down, the steep pathways will collapse and
> every wall will fall against the ground (20).

God will also send pestilence, torrential rain, hailstones, fire and brimstone, and every man's sword will be against his bother (22), to destroy Gog and his armies. It will not be the people of the land, who will defend themselves, but God Himself will intervene, and His powerful hand will vanquish and annihilate Gog. It will be God's victory and deliverance. As God delivered the Israelites from Egypt by his own might, He will manifest

104

His power and greatness again in this unusual event, displaying His might over the forces of nature. But,

> Two conditions will antedate Gog's invasion. First, the land itself will have recovered from the sword, a metonymic expression for the destruction and slaughter of an invading army. The mountains of Israel are identified as Gog's target for the first time...The land that Nebuchadnezzar's forces had devastated, and which will have lain desolate for a long time. Second, the population will have been re-gathered from many peoples of the Diaspora and resettled securely within it[40]

One of the interesting verses in this chapter is verse 17. The reference to earlier prophets who may have alluded to this encounter "would be to such passages as Zephaniah 3:8; Joel 3:6; and perhaps seeing that the prophets spoke *in old times,* to prophecies known to Ezekiel but which have since perished."[41]

Chapter 39 predicts not only the attacking armies will be defeated and eradicated, but, for unstated reasons, their homeland will also be destroyed (1-8). The burning of the enemy's weapons will last for seven years, and the people of the land will collect the spoils of those who will come to despoil them (10). Some of the corpses of Gog's army will be buried in a valley, east of the Dead Sea (11-16), while predatory birds and wild animals will eat others (17-20). A group of inspectors and buriers will be assigned for cleansing the land from the dead bodies and the bare bones whose flesh were eaten by the ferocious animals and birds (15).

Before this part of this chapter is concluded, it is necessary to point to another reference in which the names Gog and Magog are mentioned. In the Book of Revelation 20:7, Satan, after being imprisoned for a thousand years in the abyss, is released and goes roaming the four corners of the earth, to gather the enemies of Christ for the final war. Gog and Magog here are symbols of the worldwide enemies of Christ. They are not the same Gog and Magog of Ezekiel 38. "The large number of rebels will come from the many people born during the millennium who, though giving outward obedience to the King, never accepted Him"[42] In Ezekiel, Gog and Magog are summoned by God for their destruction. "Gog's invasion of the land represents part of the calculated plan of God for His people,"[43] while in Revelation the nations are recruited by Satan to wage war against the Lamb. In both cases, their ruin by supernatural powers is decisive and conclusive. That is the account of the biblical story.

But what does the Islamic episode tell us about Gog and Magog? Undoubtedly the Islamic narrators have found abounding information in Ezekiel, chapters 38 and 39, concerning Gog and Magog. The Islamic Tradition also ascribes to Muhammad many *hadiths* about Gog and Magog. Whether these *hadiths* are sound or spurious is a matter of contention. Muslim narrators imply that Muhammad was the first among the Arabs to declare, "a gap has been made in the wall of Gog and Magog."[44] This is the indestructible wall or the barrier the legend claims that *Dhu al-Qarnayn* had erected around the people of Gog and Magog. This *hadith* is related on the authority of *Zainab bint Jahsh*, one of Muhammad's wives. She alleged that Muhammad saw the gap in a vision. She said, "the Prophet got up from his sleep with a flushed red face and said, 'None has the right to be worshipped but Allah. Woe

106

to the Arabs, from the great evil that is nigh. Today a gap has been made in the wall of Gog and Magog..."[45]

The Islamic Tradition presents more than one version of the invasion of Gog and Magog. But all the versions agree that Gog and Magog will attack the East after the demise of the Antichrist at the hand of Jesus. One version indicates that Allah will reveal to Jesus that He will be bringing forth "from among My servants such people against whom none will be able to fight."[46] As God revealed to Ezekiel His plan to bring forth Gog and his coalition to the Land of Israel, God here reveals to His prophet Jesus that *He is the one who is bringing forth, in His own time, the people of Gog and Magog, after incurring a gap in the barrier, to the Holy Land.* God even commands Jesus to take the faithful to the mountain of Tur before the people of Gog and Magog 'swarm down from every slope' after the gap is opened in the barrier.[47] The invading crowd will be so formidable that "the first of them will pass the Lake of Tiberius and drink out of it. And when the last of them passes, he will say: there was once water here.[48] Jesus and His companions will be besieged on the mountain and hard pressed, but as Jesus and the faithful supplicate Allah, He will send harmful insects that will attack the necks of Gog and Magog. Thus all of them, without exception, will perish.[49] When Jesus and His companions descend from the mountain, the whole area will be filled with putrefaction and stench.[50] Then Jesus and His companions will beseech Allah,

> Who will send birds whose neck would be like those of Bacterian camels and they will carry them away and throw them where Allah wills. Then Allah will send rain which no house of mud-brick or (tent of) camel-

107

hair will keep out and will wash the earth
until it resembles a mirror.[51]

But this is not the only report we have about Gog
and Magog. These barbaric forces will devastate the land,
creating horror, and claiming that they have defeated and
terrified the people of the earth, and none can confront
them anymore. Then they will turn their faces toward
heaven and one of them will wave his lancet, and hurl it
against the sky and it will come back stained with blood.[52]
When they miraculously meet their terrible fate, Muslims
will come out of their fortresses and fortified cities in
which they will take refuge, and send their flocks and cattle
to the fields where they will feed on the flesh of the people
of Gog and Magog.[53] Other traditions include some details
that do not conform to previous information obtained from
other sources. It is related on the authority of ibn Mas'ud
that Muhammad said that Jesus shared with him and other
prophets in the Night of the Ascent that after the death of
the Antichrist, people would go back to their homes and
countries. Then Gog and Magog will invade the land and
destroy it. Then the people

> Will come back to me complaining against
> (Gog and Magog), I supplicate God (to
> punish them), and God will annihilate them
> and the earth stinks from the putrefaction of
> their bodies. He (Jesus) said: Then God
> ...sends heavy rain that will sweep away
> their bodies and throw them in the sea.[54]

In this *hadith* there is nothing mentioned about the
birds that carry the bodies to where God wills, or any
intimation to the flocks and cattle feeding on the flesh of
their enemies.

One other *hadith* reports that this event will not take place at the Tur Mountain, but inside Ludda in Palestine. And when they perish God will send a strong wind to throw them into the sea.[55]

As we examine the Islamic story of Gog and Magog and compare it with chapters 38 and 39 of the Book of Ezekiel, the similarities become apparent, despite the distortions that afflict them. Some of the similarities are:

- God revealed His plans to bring forth Gog and Magog to the East: to Ezekiel in the Old Testament and to Jesus in Islam.
- In both cases, God is the One Who will bring Gog and Magog from the North to Palestine.
- They are defeated by supernatural power. They are not really engaged in any war; God destroys them.
- The deadly insects that attack them and cause their death are symbols to the woes that afflict Gog and Magog in Ezekiel.
- According to Ezekiel, their flesh becomes a banquet to the wild animals and the ferocious birds, while in the *Hadith* they become food for the cattle and flocks.
- In both cases, the war is not between the inhabitants of the land and Gog and Magog, but rather between God and Gog and Magog. They become arrogant and challenge God.

In both events Gog, with his allies, are brought forth from the North to the East by the omnipotent God to punish them for their wickedness. Their motive for the assault on the peaceful lands is to plunder and to destroy. But there is a very interesting contrast between the Islamic account and the Biblical account. While in the *Hadith* they will come to wage war against the Muslims, in the biblical account they will set out to invade and fight against the Jews. Also, the *Hadith* ascertains that Gog and Magog will appear on the world stage as a perpetrating power after the death of the Antichrist, while the biblical story does not set a certain time for their military expedient.

The post-Gog era depicts a stupendous time for the faithful Muslims. After the eradication of Gog and Magog, the world will experience an Elysian time during the Messianic age. Jesus will be the sole ruler on earth, and the custodian of the Islamic faith and the Law. According to the *Hadith*, Jesus will be a just ruler,

> He will break the cross, and kill the pigs. Peace will prevail and people will use the sword as sickles. Every harmful beast will be domesticated; the sky will send down rain in abundance, and the earth will bring forth its blessings. A child will play with a fox and not get harmed; a wolf will graze with sheep and a lion with cattle, without harming them.[56]

On authority of *Abu Hurayra* who reported that the Messenger of Allah said, "During his (Jesus) time, Allah will end every religion and sect other than Islam...Then peace and security will prevail on earth, so that lions will graze with camels, tigers with cattle, and wolves with sheep; children will be able to play with snakes without being harmed."[57] It is obvious that these *hadiths* are quoted from the book of Isaiah, 11:4-5 and 6-8, with slight adaptation appropriate to the cultural life of Arabia during the time of Muhammad. Isaiah prophesied,

110

But with righteousness He (Christ) will judge the poor, and decide with fairness for the afflicted of the earth; …and the wolf will dwell with the lamb, and the leopard will lie down with the young goat, and the calf and the young lion and the fatling together; and a little boy will lead them. Also the cow and the bear will graze, their young will lie together, and the lion will eat straw like the ox. The nursing child will play by the hole of the cobra, and the weaned child will put his hand in the viper's den.

In addition to that, all instruments of war will be converted into instruments of peace, since wars will be obliterated from earth. This image is also cited in Isaiah 2:4, *He (the Messiah) will judge between the nations, and will render decisions for many peoples; and they will hammer theirs swords into plowshares and their spears into pruning hooks. Nation will not lift up sword against nation, and never again will they learn war.* This Elysian world becomes feasible, not because Christ will be a just and fair ruler only as Muslims claim, but because He is King of kings and Lord of lords, as the Bible asserts. The prophet Isaiah declares that Christ *"will strike the earth with the rod of His mouth; and with the breath of His lips He will slay the wicked* (11: 4). Both phrases, *the rod of His mouth* and *the breath of His lips,* are mere figures of speech symbolizing the power of the Word of God. Christ, thus, will govern the world by His own laws and ordinances, and all nations will implement His will and be subjugated to His divine constitution.

According to Islamic sources, Jesus will live on earth for forty years after his second coming.[58] He will be the coercive force that impedes the powers of evil. After 21 years of His life, He will get married to a woman from the tribe of *Judham*, from whom, as Muslims claim, Moses had married, and will beget children.[59] After 19 years of his marriage He will die. For forty years while Jesus is still alive, no one will get sick or die.[60] An interesting observation is found in the pseudepigrapha of 4 Ezra that echoes the view of Muslims about the second coming of Christ. We read that the Messiah will emerge and bring "rejoicing for four hundred years, then die, after which comes the resurrection and the judgment."[61] This manuscript was in existence in the year 100 A.D., and must have been well in vogue among the Jewish and Christian communities in the seventh century.

During His lifetime on earth in His second coming, Muslims believe that Jesus will go to Mecca to perform the rituals of pilgrimage[62]. Based on some *hadiths*, He will also visit the tomb of Muhammad and salute him. Muhammad will respond to his greetings from beyond the grave. When Jesus dies, Muslims will conduct His funeral and He will be buried beside Muhammad in His tomb in Madina.[63] This story is incongruent with other traditions. 'Abd-ul-lah ibn 'Amru said,

> After (the termination of) Gog and Magog God sends sweet wind that causes the death of 'Isa, his companions, and all the faithful that (live) on the face of the earth. Those who stay (alive) are the remnant of the infidels. They are the wicked of the earth.[64]

This *hadith* contradicts several other traditions quoted in the context of this study. It is related that when Jesus dies Muslims will conduct His funeral. In this case, *the hadith* indicates that Jesus and all the faithful will die simultaneously by the fragrant wind. Thus, who is going to

112

preside over His funeral? Besides, another hadith asserts that Jesus will appoint a man from the tribe of Tamim by the name of al-Muq'ad to be His successor.[65] Three years after the death of al-Muq'ad, the Qur'anic text and teachings will be obliterated from the hearts of men, and the copies of the Qur'an will not be available[66]. Moreover, the traditions made it clear that during the lifetime of Jesus the entire world will embrace Islam and there will be only one religious sect, the people of Islam. From where, then, will the wicked of the earth come?

So Jesus will die and he will be buried beside Muhammad, awaiting the Day of Resurrection like any other human being. He has already accomplished his mission, and saved the world from the Antichrist and his devilish forces. Through his supplication, God will annihilate the army of Gog and Magog and the world will live in unprecedented peace. He will be a fair judge, and a just ruler and the land will be fruitful and naturally fertile as it was during the time of Adam and eve before the fall. The world will be restored to its pristine purity. In the opinion of this author, *such an end is extremely anti-biblical and detrimental to the person of Jesus Christ the Son of God. Christ the Lord of lords will come, in His second coming to judge the living and the dead, and not to be judged. He is the way, the truth and the life. He is the RESURRECTION.*

CHAPTER SIX

The Shi'ite Mahdi and Christn

ألمسيح والمهدي عند الشِّيعة

T he concept of the second coming of Christ, the return of the Shi'ite *Mahdi* (linguistically means the rightly guided one), and the end of time, take a different dimension and new direction in the Shi'ite eschatology. Apparently, Christianity and Judaism have made their deep marks on the historical and theological Shi'ism, especially at an early age,

> Judeo-Christian messianism had at an early stage, deeply influenced Muslim communities who gave it the synonymous nomenclature in Arabic, namely *Mahdiyya*.[1]

The messianic *Mahdi* is the embodiment of the earnest longing and hope of the Shi'ites who have been oppressed and persecuted through the course of history, especially during the Umayyad and 'Abbasid monarchies. In his revolutionary book *Mihnat al-'Aql fi al-Islam* (The Ordeal of Reason in Islam) Mustafa Jiha says that the belief in the awaited *Mahdi* is the result of the political and social circumstances to which the Islamic society was subjugated, especially the Islamic schools of thought and the religious sects that did not conform to the opinions of the caliphs, the rulers and princes who did not care for the welfare of the subjects.[2] In her remarkable study, Riffat Hassan points to seven characteristics of Shi'a messianism:

- Shi'a Islam and the theory of the Imamate[3] rest upon the idea that blood kinship to the prophet confer superiority and merit in this world as well as the next.

- Shi'a Islam came to regard the Imam as being more than human.

- Shi'a Islam holds that the Imams are infallible and protected from error and sin.

- Shi'a Islam regards the Imam as extending the prophet's function, as inheriting not only the temporal authority but also his religious and "prophetic" role and attributes, and holds that the world cannot be without an Imam.

- Shi'a Islam regards the Imam as an intermediary between human beings and God. His intercession is sought by his followers for peace and prosperity in this world and the next.

- Shi'a Islam focuses heavily upon the *Mahdi*; however, there is no reference to this concept in the Qur'an.[4]

- Shi'a Islam has developed a network of intense messianic expectation around the idea of the *Mahdi*'s return.[5]

The Shi'ite Twelvers (the largest Shi'ite sect) believe that the Imamate is a divine office like prophethood consecrated by God Who elects whom He wills, to execute the duties of the prophet in his absence.[6] The only difference between a prophet and any of the twelve Imams is that the Imam does not receive a revelation like a prophet. The prophet relates God's message, while the Imam proclaims the ordinances he receives from the prophet. Each of the Imams appoints his successor, who must be from the line of "Ali and Fatima, the daughter of Muhammad.[7] The Imam, in view of perfection, is less than a prophet and above the rest of the people.[8]

115

Contrary to the Sunni's claim, the Shi'ites interpret verse 61 of Sura 43, 'and he shall be the sign for the Hour,' to mean that 'he' refers to the *Mahdi*[9] and not to Jesus. They also emphatically "argue that (Islamic) messianism is an essential part of Islam,"[10] a concept that is alien to orthodox Islam.[11] But the Shi'ite messianism carries in its perception

> The expectation for the end of tyranny and wickedness through the establishment of ju- tice by a descendant of the prophet means, not merely a hope for a better future, but also a re-evaluation of present social and historic life.[12]

Thus, the *Mahdi* is called the Savior Imam and is regarded as an eschatological figure.[13] But the term 'savior' does not imply the concept of redemption or spiritual generation or rebirth,[14] but it holds the concept of an utopian society as it will be manifested in the establishment of the 'ideal religio-political community, the *Umma,* with a worldwide membership of all those who believe in God and His revelation through Muhammad.'[15] The role of the *Mahdi,* therefore, will be to fill the earth with goodness, justice, and equity; to eradicate corruption and to purify the religion from the depravity that permeates it. In this respect the Shi'ite sect believes that the *Mahdi* is the person who is destined from eternity, to save the world from the forces of wickedness. In other words, he aims at establishing the ideal society or the kingdom of God on earth. Moreover, one of the *Mahdi's* missions is to direct man's spiritual life and orient

> the inner aspect of human action toward God. Clearly his physical presence or

absence has no effect in this matter. The Imam watches over men inwardly and in common with the soul and spirit of men even if he be hidden from their physical eyes. His existence is always necessary if the time has not as yet arrived for his outward appearance and the universal reconstruction that he is to bring about.[16]

The Imams in general and the *Mahdi* in particular are regarded as sinless and infallible,

> The question of the human sinlessness and infallibility (*'isma*) عصمة is one of the principal doctrinal issues distinguishing Shiism from Sunnism... Unlike the Sunni caliph, the Shiite Imam is (at least in theory) not only a worldly ruler but the highest spiritual authority. He is characterized by *'isma* – sinlessness and infallibility- a claim never put forward by the Sunni *'ulama* (Muslim religious scholars) for the caliph; hence the Imam is catapulted in rank above the caliph. The Imam's appointment takes place not through any process of collective election, but through *nass* نص (designation) by his spiritual predecessor alone.[17]

But why is he called the *Mahdi*?

Based on the *hadiths* ascribed to Muhammad, it is related that he is (traditionally) called the *Mahdi* because he will be guided to a mountain in Syria from which he will recover the original Torah;[18] and from Antioch he will restore the Arc of the Covenant.[19] Thus, he is called the

117

Mahdi because his commission is to reveal the truth and refute the Jewish and Christian claims.

The Shi'ites claim that the *Mahdi* is mentioned in the Torah and the Gospel, and his character and person are described in the revealed scriptures.[20] This claim, if proven, will obligate the People of the Book to acknowledge him as the awaited rightful Imam. His name, also, will be exactly similar to the name of the Prophet: Muhammad ibn 'Abdullah, and his father's name will also match the Prophet's father's name.

The Shi'ites bestow on the *Mahdi* numerous titles no other Islamic figure, even Muhammad, has enjoyed. Among his titles are: God's Evidence, the Seal of the Imams, the Deliverer of the Nation, the Awaited One, the Heir, the Righteous Successor, the Revealer of Faith, the Spreader of Justice, the Remnant of God on Earth, the Master of Time, the Lord of the Sword, and the Awaited One for the State of Faith.[21] These are not the only titles that the Shi'ites confer on him,[22] he is also empowered by God to perform miracles. In his countenance, character and dignity he resembles 'Isa (Jesus). God will favor him with what He favored the prophets before him and even more. He endears him more than He endears others.[23] In another source, he is depicted as a person who is endowed with the perfection of Moses, the glory of Jesus and the patience of Job.[24] The moment he was born he fell down on his knees, lifted up his index finger and sneezed; then he said,

> "Praise be to God the Lord of the worlds, and peace be upon Muhammad and his family; (I am) a servant who remembers God, without detest or haughtiness. The oppressors allege that the Evidence of God

is untenable; if we are permitted to speak, the doubt will be dispelled."[25]

The Shi'ites believe that when the *Mahdi* reappears from his great occultation, he will recover the original book of Psalms from the Lake of Tiberias,[26] the Torah and the Gospel, the Arc of the Covenant, the Tablets of Moses and his Staff, and the Ring of Solomon, from a cave in Antioch.[27] The variant accounts of this claim reveal the chaotic information that permeates the Shi'ite Tradition about the era of the *Mahdi* and his accomplishments. The *Mahdi* will conquer the world and destroy all the infidels. He would take over every city, even Jerusalem, that Alexander the Great vanquished and reform them. That will gratify the hearts of the people of Islam.[28] Upon the return of the *Mahdi* God will support him with a host of angels: Gabriel will be his fore guard, Michael will be his rear guard, Israfil at his left hand, and terror will walk in front of him, after him and at his right and left hands, and the angels who are nearest to God, are his servants.[29] With the support of the angelic hosts, and the miraculous powers that emanate from the sacred relics of the previous prophets, he will be able to subdue all the unbelievers all over the world. Either a heavenly fire or the fire of his wars will burn all the idols and symbols of ungodliness.[30] As he embarks on his religious reformation, the 'people of heaven, people of earth, the birds of the air, and the whales in the sea will rejoice in him.'[31] He will be sent as the sword of God to avenge the blood of al-Husayn and to restore the pristine essence of Islam. All those who fail to embrace Islam will be killed. He will employ the original Torah and the Gospel of Jesus that he recovers from the cave of Antioch in Syria to argue with and prove to the Jews and Christians that Islam is the true and final revelation of God.[32]

The conquest of Constantinople will be at the hand of the *Mahdi,* assisted by an angel and the *Khadir,* and seventy thousand faithful Muslims. They will vanquish the city by *al-Takbir* (God is greater) and Muslims will witness the great massacre in the plain of Accra.[33] Obviously, the detail of this event contradicts the account of the Sunnis' Tradition. There is no mention of the *Mahdi* in the Sunni story and the seventy thousand soldiers who conquer that city with *Takbir* are the Jews, not the Muslims.

Apparently, the Shi'ites have mythologized the concept of the *Mahdi.* He became the symbol of their hope as their future savior, and a salient feature of their ideology. The universal Islamic community he establishes is not based on peace or love. It is an earthly militant kingdom under the banner of Islam in which people either will accept the Shi'ite type of Islam, or will be killed, including the Sunni sect who may defy the Shi'ite's claim. The attributes ascribed to the figure of the *Mahdi* and his celestial characters do not conform to the teaching of the Qur'an. Though Shi'ites admit that the *Mahdi* is not a prophet, the way they venerate him elevates him to a higher plateau than any prophet. He is the heir of the sacred relics of the former prophets, as well as the Arc of the Covenant and the Ten Commandments Tablets. He possesses the blessings and the miraculous power that have been endowed to them. From his seat he will fill the earth with righteousness, justice and equity. He knows the secrets of men's hearts and no intention can be hidden from him. The Shi'ites acknowledge that these attributes are bestowed on the *Mahdi* by God because God favors him more than any other human being. After his reappearance, the *Mahdi* will go to *Kufa,* sitting on the throne of King Solomon with the staff of Moses in his right hand. The Faithful Spirit and 'Isa Son of Mary will be his companions. He will be wearing the cloak of the Prophet, and girded with Dhi al-Faqqar (the

120

prophet's sword). His face will be like the ring in the night of the full moon. From his mouth emanates a light like a radiant lightning, and on his head there is a crown of light.[34] After eight months of war, he will reign over the East and the West, and peace will prevail over the world. On the authority of 'Ali, Muhammad's son-in-law, it is related that during the reign of the *Mahdi* the Shi'ite's millennium era will take place. Here again the Shi'ites borrow the images of Isaiah 11.[35] It is obvious that this image of the *Mahdi*, in his grandeur and glory, is the creation of a vivid imagination that garbed him with a supernatural power that surpasses the glory and the greatness of all the previous prophets. He will become omniscient since he will be able to watch the deeds of all the peoples of the world through a pole of light that is erected for him from earth to heaven.[36] In some respects, it seems that the Shi'ite writers, inspired by the image of Christ in his second coming, created a celestial character of the *Mahdi*.

Ahmad Kasravi (1890-1946), an Iranian reformer and social thinker, examined the issue of the Imamate with a critical mind and said:

> The Shi'ites, with their beliefs concerning
> their imams, place their imams on the same
> level as prophets, and even consider them as
> more exalted at times, because, to the
> Shi'ites, an imam was chosen by God, knew
> all things, understood all languages, and had
> knowledge of the unknown. Every one had
> to obey him. Heaven and earth could be at
> peace because of his being. And no one but
> the imam knew the meaning of the Koran
> and religion. With such praise for the

imams, the Shi'ites place them above the prophets.[37]

But for how long will the *Mahdi* reign? The Shi'ite accounts do not help too much. According to their various *hadiths,* the scope of his reign ranges from 17 years to 309 years.[38] Yet different Shi'ite sources indicated that he would reign for 19 years and a few months.[39] The life of the *Mahdi* will be tragically terminated. A woman by the name of *Sa'ida,* from the tribe of *Tammim* (she has a beard and moustache like men), will kill him by hurling at him a trough from the roof of her house while he is passing by.[40] This tragic ending of the life of the *Mahdi* resembles the unfortunate episode of Abimelech mentioned in the book of Judges 11:53, *"But a certain women threw an upper millstone on Abimelech's head, crushing his skull."* Was the author who reported this incident familiar with the biblical story and, thus, weaved it into his futuristic prediction? Moreover, if the *Mahdi* will be so omniscient as the Shi'ites claim, how did he fail to perceive the tragedy that will befall him and end his life?

Jesus and the Mahdi

Whereas the *Mahdi* is the focal point in the Shi'ite eschatology, Jesus Christ plays a minor role in the end of time. Sachedina indicates that,

> In the development of the eschatological role of the *Mahdi* in the Shi'ite traditions, much emphasis was laid on the function of the *Mahdi* as the descendant of Muhammad and the Imam, who will be followed in the prayer by Jesus. The latter point is repeatedly emphasized in the Shi'ite eschatological

traditions. This distinguished the roles of the *Mahdi* and Jesus, which at times became confusingly alike.[41]

The information about Jesus in the Shi'ite episode, are mostly cited from Shi'ite sources. Sunni sources are listed and quoted as long as they corroborate the Shi'ite point of view. While the mission of the *Mahdi* in the Shi'ite religious literature is universal, Jesus' mission is limited to propagating Islam among Christians and Jews and aiding the *Mahdi* in killing the Antichrist. It is true that the Shi'ites believe in the second coming of Christ, but his mission is clouded with obscurity when it is compared to the mission and the heroic deeds of the *Mahdi*.

The Shi'ite sources contend that Muhammad referred to the *Mahdi* as "one of us who 'Isa Son of Mary will pray behind him,"[42] When Jesus descends in Jerusalem among the Muslims while they are performing their early morning prayer, the *Mahdi* will ask Jesus to lead them in prayer. Jesus will decline and insist on the *Mahdi* to lead in prayer and Jesus will pray behind him, according to the law of Muhammad, saying, "You belong to a house that has the right of preeminence."[43] In another place, Jesus pledges his allegiance to the *Mahdi* after praying behind him, saying, "I have been sent as a vizier and not as a commander."[44] This bit of information is repeated several times in different Shi'ite and Sunni sources.[45] When Jesus descends, seventy thousand angels will accompany him. He will be wearing a green turban, girded with a sword, and riding a mare. As he settles down on earth, a voice will call, "O, Muslim people, the truth has arrived and the falsehood has passed away."[46] He is also called the Spirit of God. Yet in spite of that, the Shi'ite eschatology focuses on the *Mahdi* as the major player in the events of the end of time. The *Mahdi* is the one who will establish the kingdom of God on earth. He will be the force that will fill the earth with goodness and justice. He is the one who will be the world ruler. He will eradicate the power of evil and exalt the religion of Islam.

Numerous Shi'ite Muslims quote biblical verses, claiming that they attest to the authenticity of their traditions uttered by Muhammad and their different Imams.[47] But these Shi'ite writers who make this claim may not be aware that they fall short in three areas of their thesis.

First, they quote these verses out of context. For instance, Roman 15:12 is quoted as proof that the Bible predicts the coming of the *Mahdi*. The verse says, "There shall come the root of Jesse and He Who arises to rule over the gentiles, in Him the gentiles hope." The author of *Yawm al-Khalas* ("The Day of Salvation") claims that the Bible mentions the title of the *Mahdi al-Qa'im* ("the rising," or "the one who arises"), not by insinuation, but explicitly.[48] He does not realize that *the Mahdi* is not from 'the root of Jesse', and the emphasis is on 'He who' and not on the verb 'arises'. The one who is from the root of Jesse is Jesus Christ who is also called son of David. He is the only hope of the gentiles. In their book *Hagarism: The Making of the Islamic world*, Patricia Crone and Michael Cook indicate, "It is worth adding that the Shi'ite usage of the term *qa'im* has a precedent in Samaritan heresy."[49] Another example is partially cited from Acts 17:31,

> Because He (God) has fixed a day in which He will judge the world in righteousness through a Man He has appointed, having furnished proof to all men by raising Him from the dead.

The above same author does not quote the entire verse, but stops short at 'through a man He has appointed' without including the rest of the verse, especially the phrase 'by raising Him from the dead'. Then the author comments, "Who is this man but the Awaited Imam who will implement justice and fill the earth with equity; the one that is mentioned in Roman 15:12?"[50] This lack of integrity in citing the biblical references in order to prove his point of view disqualifies the author and perverts the truth.

In his commentary on Haggai 2:7, the author alleges that the phrase 'the desire of all the nations' (as it is translated in the Arabic version of the Bible) alludes to the *Mahdi*.[51] In reality, according to the context and the best commentaries, it refers to Christ. The author also refers to Matthew 24:29-31, implying that verse 31 points to the followers (elects) of the al-*Qa'im* (*al-Mahdi*) who will heed the trumpet of the archangel Gabriel and be gathered together from the four winds, from one end of the sky to the other end, and raptured to the high.[52] One of the passages that the author cites is the First Epistle of Paul to the Thessalonians 3:15. He insists that this passage is similar to what the Shi'ite Imams predicted. He intimates that the image of people being raptured and walking in the air, are of those of the adherents of the *Mahdi*.[53] He does not consider the phrase 'the dead in Christ will rise first', and that this passage talks about the Christians. The Shi'ites are not dead in Christ and will not rise in the first resurrection. What interesting and puzzling is that the concept of the 'rapture' does not exist in any Islamic context. There are many other references the author of *Yawm al-Khalas* (The Day of salvation) has quoted from the Bible, claiming they refer to the *Mahdi* and his faithful partisans.[54] He asserts that the kingdom, over which the *Mahdi* will rule, will be the kingdom of God on earth because the suffering humanity will not be saved from its long excruciating agony except at the hand of its savior the *Mahdi*.[55]

In his book *'Aqidat al-Masih al-Dajjal fi al-Adyan* (The Doctrine of the Antichrist in Religions), Sa'id Ayyub, an Egyptian author, relies heavily on Jane Dickson and other secondary biblical commentaries, in addition to his Islamic sources. He quotes what fits his eschatological perspectives without any regard to the original text or context. Besides, his political views as well as his religious ideology dictate on him to follow an illogical line of subjective thought conducive to radical interpretations. He believes that behind the problems of the world are the Jews who seek to corrupt the world society, control the international economy, pervert the revealed faiths, and mold the political trends to serve their own interests. He asserts that they deceitfully interpret the prophecies of their Torah to mislead the political and religious leaders of the world, including the Pope. Christians have blindly embraced their claims and, wittingly or unwittingly, become an essential part of their political scheme. Even many Muslims have fallen into their trap, especially those who are deceived by western culture, values, political and philosophical thoughts, and their corrupted societies. Their long-range objectives are well planned and calculated. He emphatically claims that the West, motivated by the Jewish strategies to rule the world, attempts to exploit the Islamic world, psychologically, culturally, politically, economically and religiously. He alleges that the 'prince of peace' the Jews are expecting to appear on the world stage is not but the Antichrist. Like most Muslims, Sa'id Ayyub associates Christianity with the West.

But he also utilizes the dangerous ploy of citing number of biblical verses out of context, interpreting them coercively to fit his obscure pre-conceived ideas about

Judaism, Christianity and the *Mahdi*.[56] In his opinion, the *Dajjal* or the Jewish prince of peace is the creation of their devious minds, and he will come at the end of time as a fulfillment of their wishes. He will be the epitome of evil, and the Jews and all of those who will be enmeshed by their deception will follow him for their own destruction.[57] He believes that Christianity was corrupted at the hand of the apostle Paul, who invented a Christology that was foreign to Christ himself. In his own way, Paul was executing the devilish plan of the Jews to eliminate the danger of Christianity or orient it toward the gentiles by recruiting them to serve the interest and the welfare of the Jews.[58] Therefore, all those who are in the camp of the Jews will be subject to the deceptive leadership of the *Dajjal*. But who is going to confront the *Dajjal*?

> The camp that will confront the *Dajjal*, his followers, and the apostate church leaders, is Islam, headed by the awaited *Mahdi*, the leader of this camp.[59]

One of the titles of the *Mahdi* in the Shi'ite belief is the 'Faithful and True'. Ayyub claims that the *Mahdi's* name is mentioned in the book of Revelation 19:11. But as it is his habit, he quotes this phrase out of context and perverts the meaning. The passage clearly indicates that these titles are Jesus' (vv. 13 and 16), because He is called the Word of God and King of Kings and Lord of Lords. Actually, these titles have been used previously in Revelation 1:5 and 3:7 to allude to Christ. Ayyub and those who fall in the same category will make every attempt, without any discretion, to discredit the Bible or pervert its meaning in order to subject it to their ideology.

The author also quotes the second part of Revelation 19:11, '...in righteousness He judges and wages war'

127

and compares it with the actions of the *Mahdi* who will fill the earth with justice and equity as it was filled with oppression and tyranny.[60] He implies that the two statements talk about the same person, the *Mahdi*. He also cites some portions of Revelation 12:1-5, '...A women clothed with the sun, and the moon under her feet, and on her head a crown of twelve stars...and she gave a birth to a son, a male child, who is to rule all the nations with a rod of iron...' Here again he boldly presents his own erroneous interpretation indicating that the women is Fatima, and the sun representing her father Muhammad, and the moon is a symbol of her husband 'Ali, and the twelve crowns are the twelve Imams.[61] But as usual he does not link his quotation to the rest of the text, especially verse 6, in which the woman fled into the wilderness where she had a place prepared by God for her protection. One wonders whether *Fatima* had to flee to the wilderness from persecution or her descendent the *Mahdi* 'was caught up to God and to His throne' (v. 5). The images of those passages, point to Israel (or the church), and the person of Christ. However, Ayyub has endeavored to hijack the symbols and their Christian interpretation in order to engulf them with a Shi'ite Islamic garment.

Ayyub, who has mastered the art of misquoting and misinterpreting the biblical verses, cites Revelation 3:12 and 14,

> He overcomes, I will make him a pillar in the temple of My God; and he will not go out from it anymore; and I will write on him the name of My God, and the name of the city of My God, the new Jerusalem, which comes down out of heaven from My God, and My new name...To the angel of the church in Laodicea writes: The Amen, the

Faithful and true Witness, The beginning of
the creation of God, says this...

Then he also quotes Revelation 21:1 and 22 about
the new heaven and the new earth, as well as the New
Jerusalem in verse 10. In his view, Mecca and the Ka'ba
are the New Jerusalem, without any regard to the rest of
verse 22, 'for the Lord God the Almighty and the Lamb are
its temple.' He claims too that the water of life (22:17) is
the well of Zamzam. He does not realize that this chapter
describes the future heaven that God has prepared for his
faithful, and not an earthly place that already existed, and
that Jesus is the water of life. He also ascertains that the
'Amen, the Faithful and true Witness' is Muhammad or the
Mahdi and not Jesus as the text indicates. Actually the
entire chapter (91-138) is filled with such fairy tales and
incredible interpretations, since all his citations are taken
out of context, and are based on his erroneous pre-
conceived ideas. At one point he claims that Daniel 7: 22,
*'Until the Ancient of Days came and Judgment was passed
in favor of the saints of the Highest One, and the time
arrived when the saints took possession of the kingdom,'*
alludes to the *Mahdi* and the Muslims.[62] Accordingly, the
Ancient of Days is the *Mahdi* who will lead the faithful
saints of the Highest (the Muslims) to possess the kingdom
of God on earth. He does not realize that the Ancient of
Days is the eternal God Who is going to sit on His throne to
Judge the world, the boasting beast, and the kingdoms that
surrendered their powers to the beast. It seems also that
Ayyub, as usual, had cited his quotation out of context and
failed to show the relationship of this verse to verses 13-14
that clearly elucidate the meaning of 'the Ancient of Days
and the Son of Man'. The tragedy in this case is that
Muslims who have little or no knowledge of the biblical
prophecies or the apocalyptic terminology, will be misled
and embrace such misguiding interpretation.

Secondly, the Shi'ites rely heavily on the *hadiths* attributed to their twelve Imams. Again, we encounter here the same problems that we encounter when we attempt to cite the Sunnite *Hadiths*. It is so difficult to discern the false *hadiths* from the authentic. Even Shi'ite scholars like Ayatollah Ibrahim Amini, the General Secretary of Majlis-i Khubragan in the Islamic Republic of Iran, admits that not "all the traditions on the subject of the *Mahdi* are highly reliable and that all its narrators are trustworthy."[63] Besides, the Sunni scholars, though they do not deny that the notion of the *Mahdi* is not foreign to them, either claim that these hadiths are weak or fabricated, and only few of them are really authentic. The Shi'ites reject this claim and assert that there are enough of the authentic hadiths about the Mahdi, and the existence of the falsified *hadiths* does not nullify the veracity of other *hadiths*.[64] The validity of this argument depends mainly on the depth of the Shi'ites' faith in their Imams and their infallibility. In their views, their Imams are the heirs of the prophet and the knowledge that God reveals to him. He, in turn, entrusted his household with the secrets of the future. Thus, apart from the prophets, God has singled them out with his blessings and bestowed on them the light of His divine knowledge. Is this really what their Imams claimed about themselves, or do their partisans attribute these claims to them? The spectrum of these traditions does not suggest that they originated with the Imams. The Shi'ites decisively deny that the texts that are handed down to us prove that the Imams are superior even to the prophets, especially in the later Shi'ite heritage, but their biographies tell different stories. One of their significant claims is that, in the absence of prophets, God does not leave the world without an Imam to guide humanity in the right path. But what about the revealed books; aren't they the source of guidance to the straight path? Is this not what Muslims believe? What about the

130

non-Muslims and other ethnic groups? Amini believes that some of the Qur'anic verses seem to suggest that the People of the Book will be judged according to their original Holy Books, but that does not answer the question: Who are their Imams? Are they doomed and left without any guidance? It seems that the Shi'ites have, in reality, substituted the Qur'an with the Imams. If we have to accept the Shi'ite heritage, or what their followers have falsely ascribed to them, there is no palpable proof to substantiate their claim except the arrogations of their Imams But for the Shi'ites, without such faith the reliability of their proclamation becomes invalid. All that is available to the researcher are the traditions attributed to them. In most cases, these traditions are orally related to the later Shi'ite generations. Modern Shi'ites tend to interpret many of the Imams proclamations in the light of current events.[65] This is a Shi'ite attempt to prove that the Imams' knowledge is a God-given knowledge by which God has distinguished them from the rest of the human race. What is the difference between this type of knowledge and revelation? If the future is really revealed to them, even in a symbolic way, doesn't that mean revelation? According to some Shi'ite authors, they interpret many of the Imams traditions as predictions referring to futuristic inventions such as military tanks, artilleries, warplanes, satellites, televisions, nuclear weapons, etc., either by intimation or symbols. We hardly encounter such information prophesied by Muhammad or revealed in the Qur'an. The *ahl-al-bayt* (the household of the Prophet) are endowed, as it seems, with more merits than the prophets. Based on this view, the role of the *Mahdi* will be more significant in the events of world history than Jesus'. It is true that the Shi'ites are anticipating the second coming of Christ and they agree with some of the Sunnis traditions about this historical event, but the *Mahdi*, not Jesus, is the deliverer of the world. He is the one who will make Islam the dominant religion and eradicate the non-monotheistic faiths.[66] Among non-Muslims, only the People of the Book "will be around until the Day of Judgment occurs."[67] They will be treated as the people of the covenant, and they will pay the poll tax "while accepting their inferior position."[68] There are other traditions that claim that, during the reign of the *Mahdi*, only the community of Islam will be in existence. The *Mahdi* will give the People of the Book the option to accept Islam or to die.[69] This does not conform to reliable Sunni traditions or other Shi'ite *hadiths* that indicate that Jesus is the one who will present Islam as the true religion of God to the People of the Book. Those who defy his invitation will perish. However, the Shi'ites will be inclined to accept those traditions that "agree with the Qur'an...over those that do not."[70]

Thirdly, the Shi'ites have failed to acknowledge that a corpus of their "authentic hadiths" have been either borrowed from the holy books of the People of the Book, or other apocryphal materials that influenced their interpretation of the futuristic events.

> The circulation of non-Islamic materials for use as the basis for Qur'an commentary was present during Muhammad's lifetime and saw a considerable increase in the two generations after his death. The companion Abu Hurayra, although illiterate, had extensive knowledge of the Torah as did Ali, Salman al-Farisi, and, of course the 'Ocean of *Tafsir*' Ibn 'Abbas, who is often called *'hibr al-'umma'*, or the Rabbi of the (Muslim) commentary because of his intensive knowledge of Judeo-Christian as well Muslim scripture and commentary.[71]

Moreover, Muhammad, Abu Bakr and 'Umar, were accustomed to visiting Beit Midrash in Madina to dialogue with the Jews. Muhammad's amanuensis also, is reported to have studied Judaism in Beit Midrash "at Muhammad's behest in order to read Jewish material."[72] 'Abdullah ibn al-'As, who acquired broad knowledge of the Talmud and learned Syriac, had engaged in theological discussion with Jewish converts.[73] 'Abdullah ibn Sallam admitted to Muhammad that he was accustomed to read the Torah and the Qur'an.[74] Converted Jews, like Ubayy Ibn Ka'b and Ka'b al-Ahbar, transmitted information originally cited from the Talmud as well as the Midrash, though "some of it is preserved in Islamic versions"[75] only. Ka'b, occasionally, used to narrate to the Caliph 'Umar some of the stories from his old books.[76] It was also said about 'Abdullah ibn Suryyah that there was no one in the entire Hijaz who was more knowledgeable in the Torah than he was.[77] Some of the generation of the followers of the companions followed their paradigm and sought knowledge from the People of the Book; among them, Abu Jald of Basra who was accustomed to reading both the Torah and the Qur'an, believing that reading eheither or both books will bestow on him God's mercy.[78] Other scholars also introduced more Judeo-Christian materials to Islamic sources and circles, among them Wahb Ibn Munabbih, who transmitted a corpus of Talmudic and Midrashic informa-tion.[79] Such material found its way into the Islamic commentaries, whether they were Sunni's or Shi'ite's. Others who transmitted interpretive traditions from the books of the People of the Book were non-Arabs, converted to Islam (*mawali*), "whose family background and place of origin could have given them special knowledge of Jewish-Christian and Zoroastrian sources"[80] such as Al-Hasan al-Basri and Qatada Ibn Di'ama. Both were regarded in their era as reliable interpreters of the Qur'an.. "From the point of view of modern investigation, they show a remarkable reliability in faithfully transmitting traditions from Judaism and Christianity when commenting on figures in the Qur'an that also appear in the Bible and other texts."[81] Later, a group of storytellers whose main vocation was commenting on the Qur'an, resorted to what they learned from the Jews and the Christians, to explain the obscure passages of the Qur'an.[82] They, also, employed their colorful imagination to complete the final touch of what they learned or read in the literature of the People of the Book. In order to bestow on these innovations a sense of reliability, they ascribed them to authentic chain of authority.[83] History has proven that most of these stories were cited from the folkloric literature that was in vogue among the common people[84] and lack veracity. The spectrum of this information would, indeed include stories about the awaiting Jewish Messiah or the Christian second coming of Christ. One of the accusations with which the Sunnis charge the Shi'ites is that the Shi'ites made the same claims of those of the Jews concerning the appearance of the expected *Mahdi*: "The Jews said, no strife in the cause of God until the awaited Messiah comes, and a call heralds from heaven. The *Rafida* (the Rejectors of the Shi'ite sect) said, no strife in the cause of Allah until the return of the *Mahdi* and by an order from heaven.[85] Elsewhere, the Jewish Tradition indicates that Elijah who was taken to heaven, will sometime return to restore the religion and the Mosaic laws, the same mission allocated to the *Mahdi*.[86] It is obvious, despite the doctrinal differences between Shi'ism and Judaism "it is clear enough that the *Mahdi* had inherited the role of the political redeemer which lies at the heart of Judaic messianism."[87]

Thus, the concept of the *Mahdi* did not originate from the Shi'ites. Zoroastrianism[88] ascribing all evil to Ahiram, believed that Saoshyant,[89] from the race of Zoroaster, will emerge at the end of the time and kill Ahiram, and cleanse all the world from all wickedness.[90]

134

Both Christians and Jews, within the context of their theology, anticipate the coming of the Messiah. Though each of the two faiths embraced such an ideology, they expect the establishment of the Messianic age sometime in the course of history. Both Jews and Christians sustained severe persecution and atrocities, and they looked forward for a deliverer. Such a hope continued to dominate the Jewish history as a nation, as well as the church. The Shiʻites, who experienced similar oppressions and paid a heavy price at the hand of their enemies, found in the concept of the return of the Messiah, which was transformed in the Shiʻite ideology, into the return of the *Mahdi,* the hope that would inflame their quest for an equitable society. The Master of Time will fulfill and gratify their expectation of a pristine Islamic society in which they will rule the world under the banner of the *Mahdi.* The concept, thus, was not, at all new. Psychologically as well as emotionally, the Shiʻites were ready to adopt the Islamic Messianic concept, without precluding any of the characteristics of the Judaic Christ, or as in the case of biblical Christian Messianism, as they are precisely delineated in the scripture, except Christ divinity and His role as the judge of the world.

Jesus, the Mahdi, and the Antichrist

How do the Shiʻites view the Antichrist?

The majority of the Shiʻites endorse the concept of the Antichrist. They believe that he will appear on the world stage for a short period of time during the reign of the *Mahdi.* Shiʻite literature does provide enough details about the Antichrist. But they mainly rely on the Sunni Hadith that incorporated into their corpus of Tradition.[91] Actually, original account of the Antichrist in the Shiʻite sources is rare, and follows the same views of the Sunnis that are attributed to his role in the world events. But at one point, contrary to the Sunni's prophetic literature, some Shi'ite reports claim that the *Mahdi* is the one who will kill the Antichrist. Also, a minority among the Shi'ites believe the Antichrist is an imaginary figure, created by the vivid delusions of the Muslim narrators.[92] He could be, according to the author of *Yawm al-Khalas* (The Day of Salvation), a high-ranking Jewish general who believes that acquiring modern weaponry will secure for his nation victory over their enemies;[93] or he could be the *Sufyani*, the archenemy of the *Mahdi*.[94] But unlike the Sunnis, the Shi'ites do not regard the Antichrist as a major player in the world events. His vicious tribulation is, undoubtedly, matchless in world history, but his massive forces will not be able to confront the superpowers of Jesus and the Mahdi. His destruction is inevitable.

The Imamate doctrine of the *Mahdi,* however, "merges with the return of Christ...The doctrine of the return of Jesus, as described in the Sunnite sources and cited by the Shi'ite traditionists is explained in a more or less uniform manner."[95] It is assumed that the return of Jesus is pending the appearance of the blessed *Mahdi*. This assumption implies that the second coming of Christ will not take place if the Shi'ite *Mahdi* does not emerge from his occultation. At the same time, the appearance of the Antichrist coincides with the presence of these two super beings: the Prophet and the Imam. The destruction of the *Dajjal* is reserved for the *Mahdi* whose return will be preceded by a time of severe trial.[96] The role of the *Dajjal* at the end of time is regarded as "almost identical with that of Satan, as explained in the traditional sources, because he will tempt people by bringing food and water, which will be scarce at the time."[97] The synchronization of the emergence of the *Dajjal,* the *Mahdi,* and Jesus, is aimed as a "test for sifting the true believers of God from the false ones."[98] Those who respond to the call of the *Mahdi* are the faithful and the partisans of *ahl al-bayt*, and those who heed the temptation of the Antichrist are the misguided and non-believers. In this case, the Jews, the apostate church, and all those who fail to believe in the *Mahdi,* including the Sunni Muslim community, who reject the eschatological concept of the *Mahdi* are the enemy of the true Islam and must be eradicated. Besides, the Shi'ites believe that the appearance of the Antichrist ushers the end of the grace period in which the door of repentance was still open.[99] All those who do not heed the call of the *Mahdi* and accept his invitation to relinquish their corrupted religions are, indeed, doomed. This is the moment of reckoning in which the two camps will distinctively be separated and the universal battle between the powers of good and the forces of evil will take place.[100]

In conclusion, before the reappearance of the *Mahdi*, the world will be flooded with the blood of the victims of wars.[101] But the black banner of Islam will continue to fly high,[102] blemished with dark blood until the awaited Imam reappears. This Imam will wage vehement wars against the enemies of *ahl al-bayt*. His motto will be 'revenge', to avenge the blood of all the persecuted Shi'ites who have been oppressed, suffered, and ostracized after the establishment of the first Islamic state, and to the present time.

CHAPTER SEVEN

The Beast, the Smoke, and the Three Land-slidings
الدَّابة والدُّخان والخسوفات الثلاثة

The Beast ألدَّابة

The story of the Islamic Beast finds its origin in the Qur'an.[1] Because of their impudence, a segment of the society who is blind and disobedient, will disbelieve in God's signs.[2] These people are the remnant of the evildoers who will continue to defy God and indulge in their wickedness. That does not preclude the existence of the believers. Thus, God will send the Beast to speak to them:

> Nor canst thou be a guide to the Blind, (to prevent them) from straying: only those wilt thou get to listen who believe in Our Signs, and they are Muslims.
> And the Word is fulfilled against them (*the unjust*), we shall produce from the earth a Beast to (face) them: She* will speak to them (*the unjust*) for people did not believe with assurance in Our Signs. (Italic is mine)

وَمَا أَنتَ بِهَادِي العُمْي عَنْ ضَلَالِتِهِم إِنْ تُسمِعُ إِلاَّ مَنْ يُؤْمِنُ بِآيَاتِنا فَهُم مُسْلِمُونَ.
وَإِذَا وَقَعَ القَوْلُ عَلَيْهِمْ أَخْرَجْنَا لَهُمْ دَابَة مِنَ الأرْض تُكَلِّمُهُمْ أنَّ النَّاسَ كَانُوا بِآيَاتِنا لا يُوقِنُون .

It is conspicuous that the Qur'an in verse 81 addresses Muhammad during the Meccan period while he was struggling to preach monotheism to the polytheists of the city. It is also obvious that Muhammad was frustrated because the people failed to heed his message. God, in this verse, was informing Muhammad that his commission was to preach and to call people to worship the One Allah. He was not responsible for their rejection and rebellious attitude towards Allah. This verse does not relate to the subsequent verse 82 that erupts suddenly, to usher into the picture the indefinable identity of the Beast. This is the first and the only time that this particular Beast is mentioned in the Qur'an, as one of the signs that herald the end of the times. This unexplainable disruption in the text creates an unbridgeable gap in the mind of the reader. In verse 81, Allah was comforting His messenger Muhammad, who was disappointed with the hostile reaction of his contemporaries, the people of Mecca. While in verse 82, the theatrical stage changes, leaving an uncovered historical time that is only known to Allah. It is a move from the present to the uncertain future without any prefatory remark to set up the stage for the new event.

But the story of the Beast is very ambiguous. Muslim scholars and expounders do not agree on its identity and function. Is there any relationship between the *Jassasah* that is mentioned in the epic of Tamim al-Dari and this Beast? Or, is the gist of this episode based on the Beast of Revelation 12? A. Y. 'Ali believes that the Beast is one of the portents of the Last Day to come "before the present world passes away and the new world is brought into being"[3] is a symbol of materialism which will appeal to the degenerated world and will close the door of repentance.[4] Even he makes a suggestion that the word *tukallimuhum* (to speak to them) could be read as

139

taklimuhum which means to 'wound them'[5] which would lead to their destruction. According to the Islamic Tradition, this Beast will emerge after the death of 'Isa', the widespread of wickedness, the decline of Islam, and the indulgence of people in iniquity. At this point, Allah will bring forth the Beast to discern between the believer and the non-believer, so that they may ponder their sinful life and reconsider their futile spiritual situation.[6]

But former Muslim scholars and commentators attempted to formulate a different anecdote from the fragmental information that was available to them. Their deformed composition delineated a mythical portrait that most modern scholars reprobate as a collection of superstitions foisted into the Islamic Tradition, aiming at explaining an ambiguous verse.[7] Apparently, the fore-cited Qur'anic verse, replete with vagueness, created an unexplainable problem for the commentators. There is nothing in this verse that would, implicitly or explicitly, reveal the description of the Beast, or tell us about the content of its speech. Furthermore, the Qur'an does not indicate whether it is a real beast or a symbolic person characterized with good or bad dispositions. The word Beast (capitalized) suggests that his innate characters manifest beastly manners. This notion did not fit well with the opinion of most of the former Muslim expositors and narrators who sought after exciting and thrilling episodes. The lack of information about this Beast opened the door wide for speculations and innovations. In his commentary, Ibn Kathir said,

> This Beast will appear by the end of time, when people become corrupted, deviating from the commandments of God and replacing the religion of God (with ungodly-

140

ness). Then God will bring forth a Beast from the earth that will talk to the people about that.[8]

Another expounder by the name of Al-Alussy remarked,

It will tell the people that they do not believe with assurance, in the Signs of the exalted Allah, that allude to the coming of the Hour and its phenomenon, or in all His signs, including these Signs. In short, the utmost thing I shall say about this Beast is: it is a formidable Beast that has legs, essentially unlike humankind; the exalted God will bring it forth from the earth by the end of time, at a time when there will be among the people, the believer and the infidel.[9]

Other Muslim compilers of the *Hadith* like Abu Dawud al-Tayalisi,[10] Ahmad,[11] al-Tirmidhi[12] and ibn Maja,[13] narrated on the authority of the prophet by way of Abu Hurayra, the following *hadith,*

A Beast will come forth (carrying) with it the ring of Solomon son of David, the staff of Moses son of 'Imran, peace be upon them. It will clear up the face of the believer - that is, enlightening and whitening it - with the staff, and snout the nose of the infidel - that is, branding and leaving a mark on him - with the ring, so that the inhabitants of the quarter, when they meet together to draw water from a well, one will call the other: O, you the believer or, O, you the infidel

141

(according to the obvious brands that mark their faces).[14]

There are other numerous reports about the Beast in which the creative power of the narrators painted them with colorful shades. But most of these stories are succumbed to the imagination of the narrators and even preachers. Fabricated chains of authorities that ascribed these hadiths to Muhammad stigmatized these reports. In his book *al-Fitan wa al-Malahim*, ibn Kathir records some of these *hadiths* without questioning their validity.[15] One of the foisted tradition describes the Beast as "its head is like an ox head, its eye is as the eye of a pig, its ear is as the ear of an elephant, its horn is as a horn of a deer, its chest is as a chest of a lion, its color is as a color of a tiger, its waist is as a waist of a cat, its tail is as a tail of a ram, its legs are as the legs of a camel, and between every two joints there are twelve cubic."[16] Another *hadith* ascribed to Muhammad implies that he said that the Beast will come forth three times: one at the utmost edge of the desert and the people of Mecca will not hear about it. Then, after a long period of latent, it will come forth for the second time inside the desert and the nomads as well as the sedentary of Mecca will hear about it. Then, while, the people of Mecca are worshipping in the Sacred Mosque it will appear to them between the *Rukn and the Maqam*.[17] But there are other traditions ascribed also to Muhammad or his companions that allude to different contradictory locations from which the Beast will come forth.[18] All these accounts, as they seem, have stintless power over the mind of the ordinary people. The narrators retained repositions of information from which they drew their stories to thrill their audience, to compete with the preachers, and to enhance their fame.

142

It seems that the identity of the Beast in Islam can be interpreted, based on three theories:

1. That the beast is just a symbol of a political system or ideological order.
2. That the Beast is a human being endowed with a special power.
3. That the Beast is an animal, unlike any other animal, created by God to reward the believers and penalize the infidels.

All these theories are implied in the various *hadiths* that are ascribed to Muhammad or his companions; though most Muslim scholars consider them as spurious and fabricated. The difficult task, in this case, is to discern the authentic from the fake.

But is there any relation between this Beast and the beasts of Revelation 13? Were the storytellers and the compilers of the Islamic Tradition aware of the episode of these two beasts of the book of Revelation? If so, how well acquainted was the ordinary Muslim with this story?

Chapter 13 of the book of Revelation provides a brief description of the two beasts: the one who comes out of the sea and the one who emerges from the earth. The beast who comes out of the sea "was like a leopard, and his feet were like those of a bear, and his mouth like the mouth of a lion" (v. 2). The second beast that emerges from the earth "had two horns like a lamb but he speaks as a dragon" (v.11). Christian scholars assert that these descriptions are only figures of speech, portraying the inner characteristics of these two extraordinary characters who are not but the agents of the great dragon (Satan). They are not 'beasts' but are subversive human beings, and indomitable leaders who

143

will recruit their forces against the saints of the mighty God. But what is interesting about both the biblical and the Islamic folkloric depiction of the beasts is that the lists of animals mentioned in both descriptions are almost similar. Both accounts include the lion, the ram or lamb and the leopard (the Islamic *hadith* used the word cat). It is true that other animals are mentioned in both descriptions such as the bear (Revelation), the elephant, the pig, the tiger, the ox, and the camel. But it is obvious that these additional animals in the folkloric *hadith* are intended to make the *hadith* more thrilling and exciting. It is also noticeable that Muslim narrators have combined the two beasts of Revelation in one, producing that deformed picture of such a mythical Beast.

The description of the first beast of Revelation 13 corresponds thoroughly with the four beasts of Daniel 7, only they are now combined in one huge human monster who, with his deputy, will force people to worship him. In his commentary on the book of Revelation, Leon Morris remarks,

> The beast is now likened to a leopard. ...The feet are like those of a bear and the mouth like that of a lion. Since the animal had seven heads the singular *mouth,* is curious. ...He (John) is making use of a variety of the features of the animals mentioned in Dan.lvii. His composite beast thus becomes indescribably horrible.He combines in one the terrible features hitherto associated with different beasts. The Beast of Daniel vii are to be understood of the various world empires and it may well be that this is in mind with John's beast. In this case he

stands for a final empire in which will be concentrated the fruitfulness of all its predecessors.[19]

The intention of the second beast that comes out of the earth is to force the world to worship the first beast and to stress the futility of resisting him;[20] subsequently, they will give homage to the Dragon (Satan) and worship him.

Contrary to that purpose the Islamic Beast is limited in its role and its mission to either separate and distinguish the believers from the infidels, or to create, as A.Y. 'Ali speculates, a repressive or tyrannical society ruled by stringent laws to punish those who failed to believe in Allah's signs. Besides, the description of the Islamic Beast adapts well to the superstitious life and the vibrant imagination of the storytellers since the Qur'an itself does not provide a specific image of the Beast. That allowed the narrators to resort to their fantasy and stretch it as far as they could go. Although the Islamic folkloric description of the Beast does not imply any figure of speech or symbolism, it does functionally relate to the second biblical beast. Each one of them leaves its mark or brand on the forehead of the people. The Islamic Beast, however, will carry with him the ring of Solomon and the cane of Moses to snout the nose of the non-believers, write on their forehead the word 'infidel' and to adorn the faces of the godly men and write on their forehead the word 'believer'. The biblical beast also will leave his mark on the forehead or the right hand of the non-believers only, but fails to brand any of the believers with his mark. It is difficult to assess the identity of the Islamic Beast whether he was righteous or wicked. The claim that he will appear carrying with him the cane of Moses and Solomon's ring, suggests that he is a good Beast.

The Smoke ألدُّخان

Smoke is also one of the ten major signs that will usher the end of time. This event is based on another obscure Qur'anic verse which Muslim expositors found difficult to interpret. Sura 44:10-16 says,

> Then watch for a Day that the sky will bring forth a plainly visible smoke, which will engulf the people. This is an excruciating anguish. Our Lord! Dispel this (cause of) agony away from us for we are really believers. How would they remember when, after a messenger came to them with a lucid (message), they turned away from him, saying: (he) is a possessed teacher. We (Allah) shall indeed dispel away the (cause of) anguish for a while, (but) surely, you will revert (to your old ways). (But) a day (will come) when We will exact Our greater onslaught; We, indeed, will take revenge [my translation].

فارْتَقِبْ يَومَ تأتي السَّماءُ بِدُخانٍ مُبينٍ
يَغْشى النَّاسَ عَذابٌ أليمٌ
ربَّنا اكْشِفْ عنَّا العَذابَ إنَّا مؤمنونَ
أنَّى لهُمُ الذَّكرى وقد جاءَهُم رَسولٌ مُبينٌ
ثُمَّ تَوَلَّوا عَنهُ وقالوا مُعلَّمٌ مَجنونٌ
إنَّا كاشِفُو العَذابَ قليلاً إنَّكُمْ عَائدونَ
يومَ نَبْطِشُ البَطْشَةَ الكُبْرَى إنَّا مُنْتَقِمونَ

The people of Mecca were froward men who rejected Muhammad's message and contested God's signs. Thus Allah condemned them and resolved to penalize

146

them. A visible dense smoke will cover them, causing the people to suffer severely from indefinable calamity. At this point, Muslim scholars disagree on the nature of this calamity and question whether it was a current event or a futuristic plague. Some interpret the 'smoke' as a famine that afflicted the Meccans "in which men were pinched with hunger that they saw 'mist' before their eyes when they looked at the sky."[21] Some Islamic sources talk about two famines that befell the people of Mecca, one in the 8th year of Muhammad's mission, and the second one in the 8th year after his immigration from Mecca to Medina.[22] The above interpretation was rejected and refuted by Ibn Kathir on three bases: (a) only ibn Mas'ud from among the companions is assumed to have related this interpretation, and thus, it may not be reliable; (b) that the 'smoke' is one of the ten signs of the end of time; and (c) it is a real smoke and not a delusion that so appeared to the people of Quraysh as they suffered from severe starvation.[23] In other words, the 'smoke' is one of the signs of the end of time that will take place prior to the day of resurrection. 'Abdullah ibn 'Umar, one of Muhammad's companions, speculates that the 'smoke' will attack the believer as a common cold, while it will penetrate the ears of the infidel and the hypocrite until his head looks like a roasted head on a charcoal.[24] It is obvious that all these interpretations are mere speculations. Furthermore, the text suggests that two catastrophes are going to inflict the infidels at different times. One is during Muhammad's era, and the other one is prior to the Day of Judgment. The first one was a warning to catch the attention of the people of Mecca who were susceptible to the curse of Muhammad and later prompted him to plead with his Lord to dispel away that curse of famine. According to Islamic Tradition, Allah accepted Muhammad's plea and repealed the retribution for a while. Verse 16, however, points to a different time, to the day of

147

the wrath of Allah on all those who defy Islam and reject the Signs of the Hour. That will be the great day of onslaught when Allah will punish the ungodliness. The sign of the 'smoke', thus, becomes a signal that the day of reckoning is nigh. Therefore, between verse 10 and verse 16 there is a long period of grace for the people to repent and to accept Islam before it is too late. Otherwise, it will be difficult to reconcile between this text and the tradition of the sign of the 'smoke' as one of the signs of the end of time.

Is it possible that the basis of the sign of 'smoke' is derived from Revelation 9:2-3? Undoubtedly, the concept of the Day of Judgment and Resurrection was familiar to Muslims even during the time of Muhammad. He relentlessly preached this basic doctrine against the reprobating attitude of the Qurayshites. However, there were other poets and preachers from among the Christians community and the monotheistic *Hanifs,* who were prior to Muhammad or his contemporaries, who emphasized almost the same message. It is believed that,

> Much biblical material was known on the Arabian Peninsula in the pre-Islamic period and incorporated by poets into their work. Christian elements in pre-Islamic composition have long been a subject of study. ...A prominent poet who made use of biblical material was *Umayya ibn Abi al-Salt...* was related to the Meccan patricate of Kuraysh, was a contemporary of Muhammad and is believed to have died in 630...he was a *Hanif.* He professed faith in a single God, whom he imagined as the "Lord of the Servants." He used apocalyptic images to

148

describe the residence of God, the household of the angels, the Last Judgment, Paradise, and Hell. Based on a biblical model, he told of the creation of the world and described important episodes of the history of salvation: the Flood, Abraham, Lot, Moses, and the Pharaoh; He also included non-biblical judgments such as the destruction of 'Ad and Thamud, who are also mentioned in the Koran.[25]

Such information proposes that some accurate or inaccurate images of the apocalyptic time have found their way, possibly orally, to the religious circles in the pre-Islamic era or during the life of Muhammad, and at a later incorporated into Islamic Tradition and among the exegetes time. Thus, Revelation 9 could be one of the sources that some of these preachers or poets verbally quoted to delineate effective and impressive images of the end of time to convince people to relinquish their idols.

The notion of the 'smoke' is; in particular, mentioned in chapter 9, verse 2. As the fifth angel sounded the trumpet, a star from heaven

> ...opened the bottomless pit and smoke went up out of the pit, like the smoke of a great furnace; and the sun and the air were darkened by the smoke of the pit.

With the smoke will come locusts (interpreted as demons) that will be given the power to agonize the godless inhabitants of the earth (v. 3). They will cause such unbearable pain that people will desire death, but death will elude them. These locusts are subjugated to the sovereignty

149

of God. However, in reality they are the vehement enemies of the saints of the Highest, "those who belong to God are not included in the commission given to the locusts."[26] This plague does not differ from the Islamic plague except that the book of Revelation reveals that the source of the smoke is the pit that will be opened at the assigned time that God designated to punish the godless of the earth. Whereas, the story of the Islamic smoke in the Qur'an does not give any indication to its source, apparently, it is sent by Allah. Both plagues are posed to penalize the ungodliness, regardless of their historical epochs. Therefore, in the opinion of this author, the sign of the smoke in Islam is an unfinished replica of the story of Revelation 9:2 and 3.

The Three Land-slidings الخسوفات الثلاثة

The three land-slidings are regarded as three of the ten signs of the end of time. The compendium of Islamic Traditions does not furnish enough information about these land-slidings. It is related that each of these land-slidings will occur in three different places: one in the East, one in the West, and one in Arabia.[27] The Sunnite *hadith* does not indicate the significance of these land-slidings nor why they are considered as signs. The lack of sufficient information is problematic. It is difficult to associate these land-slidings with any particular event that may explain the purpose for their occurrence. They could be part of the total picture that portrays the physical changes that impact the natural world, such as floods, earthquakes, wars, seditions and famines. But what makes this interpretation unfeasible is that the land-slidings is the only natural phenomena associated with the ten major signs.

The *hadith* predicts that the land-slidings will occur in the East, the West and Arabia. What does the *hadith* mean by the East and the West? Is it the West of the Arabian borders and the East of its boundaries? Or it is alluding to both the Eastern and Western hemispheres? Are these land-slidings three disastrous earthquakes that will swallow up some portions of the earth in three parts of the world? Assuming that these land-slidings are the result of earthquakes, what is the difference between these earthquakes and any other earthquake of a great magnitude? In other word, what makes them special signs that will precede the Hour? Sunnite Muslim expounders failed to provide a reasonable answer to show the link between these land-slidings and the other seven major signs.

There is nothing mentioned in the Qur'an that underscores the land-slidings as one of the signs of the end of time. In addition, there is not any indication to explain the cause for these land-slidings. At the same time, it is difficult to assume in this vein that these signs of the landslidings are borrowed from Christianity as a prelude to the end of time. If there is any connection between these signs and any similar event recorded in the Bible, it should be the plights of the earthquakes that are mentioned in Matthew 24. Seism usually creates landsliding that will cause destruction and swallowing up of people, homes and even mountains. But Sunnite sources do not provide satisfactory comment, if any.

So what is the traditional source of this sign? The explanation is found in the *Shi'ite* heritage. The *Shi'ites* refer to a futuristic event that they believe will be fulfilled at the end of time, when the *Mahdi* emerges from his occultation. As the *Mahdi* resorts to Mecca before he begins his military campaigns, a rancorous brutal man from Syria, known as the *Sufyani*,[28] will appear on the stage of world history, overcome his foes, and seize the power. His rapacity is embodied in his wars against his enemies, especially in his attack on the *Medina* and *Kufa*. He will recruit a formidable army from the tribe of *Kalb* and send it against the *Mahdi*. While the Syrian army is camping between Mecca and Medina, the desert will split open and swallow them up.[29] That will weaken the forces of the *Sufyani*, who will be later captured and killed at the hands of the *Mahdi's* army. The *Sufyani* is the archetypical persona of the old relentless enmity between the Umayyad dynasty and the Alides family - an enmity that never ceased to victimize the two religio-political sects through the course of the Islamic history. This apocalyptical event in the *Shi'ite* eschatology has far-reaching implication. The death of the *Sufyani*, however, will subjugate the Middle East to the authority of the *Mahdi* and will pave the way for him to conquer the rest of the world.

It seems, however, that there is another interpretation for the story of the landsliding; a dichotomy that is derived from the historical legacy of the conflict between the Umayyads and *'Abd Allah B. Al-Zubayr*. After the death of the Umayyad caliph Mu'awiya, *Ibn al-Zubayr* "refused to pledge allegiance to his son and successor *Yazid*. He fled from Madina to seek asylum in the sanctuary of Mecca."[30] Soon, after the death of *Yazid*, *Ibn al-Zubayr* claimed the caliphate and began to receive the allegiance of the people of Mecca, Madina and Iraq. In order to solidify the position of *Ibn al-Zubayr*, his supporters publicized a spurious *hadith*, predicting that the Syrian army that will be sent against *Ibn al-Zubayr*, and is mainly constituted of the tribe of *Kalb*, will be swallowed up by the desert. That prediction was confirmed with one exception. The forces that were sent during the caliphate of *Yazid* to subvert Mecca and Madina disintegrated when the news of *Yazid's* death was enunciated.[31] Historically, *Ibn al-Zubayr* was

152

defeated and killed at the hand of the Umayyad troops during the reign of the caliph *Marwan,* a descendent of *Yazid.* The *hadith* proved to be feigned and lost its credibility.[32] Nevertheless, one generation later, this *hadith,* enwrapped with a Shi'ite gown, "came to be associated with the *Mahdi,* and *Ibn al-Zubayr's* revolt against the Umayyad caliphate as pictured in it became the prototype for the events at the time of the appearance of the Expected Restorer of the Family of the Prophet."[33] Thus, a historical event that took place during the life of the second Umayyad caliph had been transformed into an apocalyptic episode in the *Shi'ite* legacy and viewed as a proof of a divine providence in support of the *Mahdi.* If this reading of this segment of the Islamic history proved to be true, then the entire *hadith* and its implication were the artisanship of the traditionalists who falsely ascribed it to Muhammad. In this case, this putative historical fact cannot be regarded as one of the signs of the end of time, and by all means, to the dismay of all those who believe in its authenticity, they will suffer from the anguish of disappointment. Moreover, this fraudulent claim will cast more doubt on other Islamic eschatological signs that Muslims attribute to Muhammad. Virtually, there may be a need for *de novo* interpretation, or a second look at the signs of the end of time to purify the Tradition from the extraneous information that lack credibility. The contradictory *hadiths,* in regard of any of these signs, attest to the propensity of the narrators to authenticate their stories on the account of the Prophet or one of his respectable companions by the way of the chain of transmission. Besides, when such signs or contrasting traditions become, truly or falsely, part of the prophetic legacy, they will lack their logical acumen. In this case, Islamic insistence on the soundness of these *hadiths* will subject them to the diatribe of the critics, create

153

unmitigated hostility towards the religious heritage and elicit unfavorable impression on the prophet himself.

CHAPTER EIGHT

The Rising of the Sun from the West,
The Fire that Erupts from South of Eden
شروق الشمس من الغرب والنار المتفجِّرة من قعر عدن

On the authority of the companion Abu Hurayrah, it is reported that the Prophet said:

> The Hour does not come until the sun rises from its sunset. When the people see it, whoever is living on it (earth) will believe (in the sign), but that will be the time in which no soul who did not believe before, will benefit from believing then.[1]

> لا تقوم الساعة حتى تطلع الشمس من مغربها، فإذا رآها الناس آمن من عليها، فذاك حين لا ينفع نفساً إيمانها لم تكن آمنت من قبل.

This *hadith* and few others alike, are ascribed to Muhammad on the authority of Abu Hurayra. It seems that these *hadiths* are derived from the Qur'anic verse:

155

Are they waiting to see if the angels come to them, or thy Lord (Himself), or some of the Signs of thy Lord? The day that some of the signs of thy Lord do come, no good will it do to a soul to believe in them then, if it believed not before nor earned righteousness through its faith. Say: 'Wait ye: we too are waiting'. " 6:158

هَلْ يَنظُرُونَ إِلاَّ أَن تَأْتِيَهُمُ الْمَلائِكَةُ أَو يَأْتِي رَبُّكَ أَو يَأْتِي بَعْضُ آيَاتِ رَبِّكَ يَومَ يَأْتِي بَعْضُ آيَاتِ رَبِّكَ لا يَنفَعُ نَفْساً إِيمَانُها لم تَكُن آمَنَتْ مِن قَبْلُ أَو كَسَبَتْ في إِيمانِها خَيْراً قُل انْتَظِرُوا إِنَّا مُنْتَظِرُونَ.

It is related on the authority of Abu Sa'id al-Khudri, that Muhammad explained this verse saying that in the day in which certain of God's signs do come, any unbelieving soul will not sustain any good if it did not believe in these signs before they happen, "referring to the rising of the sun from the place of its sunset (the West)."[2]

Moreover, Abu Hurayra indicated that the Prophet said,

There are three things, which, if they appear, no soul will sustain any good if they happened and it had not believed in them from before, nor earned righteousness by its faith. They are: the rising of the sun from the West, the *Dajjal*, and the Beast of the earth.[3]

But it appears that the narrators of the Islamic tradition attempted to add some colors to the *hadith* to make it more thrilling and interesting to their audiences. An exciting explanation to this supernatural phenomenon was

156

needed to gratify the curiosity of the people who, presumably, wondered why and how the sun will rise from the West. At the same time, the answer must retain some prophetic authority in order to be practiced, acceptable and convincing.

Abu Dharr, one of Muhammad's companions, claimed that the Prophet asked him:

> Do you know where the sun goes when it sets? I said: 'I do not know.' He said: 'It travels until it prostrates itself beneath the Throne, and asks for permission to rise again. But it will be almost told, 'Go back whence you came.' That will be the time when "No good will it do to a soul to believe in them (the signs) then, if it believed not before nor earned righteousness through its faith.'[4]

قال لي رسول الله : "أتدري أين تذهبُ هذه الشَّمسُ إذا غرُبتْ؟" قلتُ: "لا أدري." قال: "إنَّها تنْتَهي فتَسْجدُ تحت العرش، ثمَّ تَسْتأذنُ فيُوشكُ أن يُقالَ لها ارجعي من حيثُ جئتِ؛ وذلك حين لا يَنفَعُ نفساً ايمانُها لم تكُن آمنتْ من قبلُ أو كَسبَتْ في إيمانِها خيراً.

This interpretation, it seems, was widely circulated among the traditionalists and narrators, with some additional variations. Abdullah bin 'Amr, the famous transmitter of the *hadith*, who was widely read, repeated this explanation to those who inquired about this episode. He claimed that the sun

> "Whenever it sets, it goes beneath the Throne, prostrates itself and seeks permission to return to its rising place; and

157

permission is granted. But when God intends to it to rise from where it sets, it will do as it usually does and place itself beneath the Throne, then prostrate itself asking for a permission to return to its rising place. But it will not receive a reply. Then it would seek a second permission to return but with no avail. Again it will ask for a permission (for the third time), and no consent is received. But when a part of the night will pass as God wishes and the sun realizes that even if it is given the permission to return, it will not be able to reach the rising point on time, it will say, 'O my Lord, the rising point is too far for me, What will happen to the people? Then when the horizon looks like a ring, it will ask for a permission to return. It will be told 'rise from where you are'; thus it will rise from the West.[5]

It is clear that this exposition was invented to explain the meaning of the Qur'anic verse 6:158, because the rest of the *hadith* concludes with this statement: Then 'Abdullah recited the Ayah (verse).' Although, originally the essence of this exegesis is ascribed to Muhammad, there is no reason to accept it as authentic. Ibn Kathir alludes to many other extraneous *hadiths* attributed to 'Abdullah ibn 'Amr which he reprobates their credibility and alleges that 'Abdullah related them from the two sacks of books he captured from the People of the Book in the battle of Yarmuk.[6] 'Abdullah ibn 'Amr was not the only one who was indicted by the critics for falsifying some of the *hadihs*. Ibn Mas'ud, one of Muhammad companions, is reported to have said that the Beast will kill the Devil.[7] Another companion by the name of 'Abdullah ibn Awfa, reiterates the same story with some variation after

158

attributing it to Muhammad.[8] But any inquisitive mind with critical objective sensibility, must consider another probability that may vindicate these traditionalists from false accusations. For there is also every reason to believe that some storytellers have fabricated both the *hadith* and the chain of transmitters and attributed them to these respected companions to lend them the veracity they lacked. Ibn Khathir, as well as al-Bukhari and others, as they investigated the characters of some of the transmitters, confirmed that they were of infamous reputation and liars.[9] Unfortunately, Muslim scholars have failed to identify many of the fabricators and thus, a large volume of concocted Islamic traditions went unnoticed and became part of the traditional legacy. Among the few Muslim scholars who recognized this fact is Taha Husayn who said,

> The Muslim storytellers were accustomed to narrate to people (stories) in the territorial mosques. They related to them the ancient legends of the Arabs and the Persians and that is associated with prophecies. They also pursued with them in the interpretation of the Qur'an, the *Hadith*, (Muhammad's) biography, the wars and the conquests, to wherever the imagination can take them...[10]

It is also worth mentioning here that every *hadith* about the rise of the sun from the West has concluded with the statement that the original relater, either recited verse 6:158, or hinted at it.[11] That entails that these interpretation are devised to explain the obscurity of the Qur'anic verse, though there is no authorized basis to attest to their validity except the word of the narrator. On the other hand, there are those who interpret the "rise of the sun from the West metaphorically. They claim that Islam will erupt in the West with forceful impetus as it was at its inception, and the people of the Occident will carry the banner of Islam to the uttermost parts of the world.[12] But all these *hadiths* and their interpretations are blatant contradiction to the Sura 18:86, *"When he (Alexander the Great) reaches the setting of the sun he found it set in a spring of murky water."*[13] There is no mention in the Qur'an about the prostration of the sun beneath the throne of God. Modern Muslim scholars attempt to solve this non-scientific interpretation of the setting of the sun by reiterating that 'reaching the setting of the sun' "does not mean the extreme West, for there is no such thing. West and East are relative terms. It means a western expedition terminated by a 'spring of murky water'."[14]

But how can a spring of murky water terminate such a military expedition? How it is possible that such a great brilliant conqueror who surmounted incredible natural and strategic obstacles fail to cross with his formidable army a spring of murky water?

The rise of the sun from the West also ushers the end of the grace era. The gate of repentance that was wide open until that fateful moment would be closed forever. A man may repent and profess his belief in the signs of God, but at this point his faith will be inevitably rejected.[15]

But what is the origin of this sign?

The expositors do not refer this sign to any known origin. They cite it as one of Muhammad's predictions. To them, that is sufficient to accept it at its face value. There is no need to prove the validity of this sign or whether it is authentic uttered by Muhammad or not. Muslim scholars, in this case, did not poise between fact and fantasy. It is true that some of them were cautious to accept precarious conclusions or doubtful interpretations. But that would stop short when the *hadith* is believed to be related by Muhammad. What is interesting in this regard is that the Qur'anic verse does not mention this sign. It says, 'some of the signs of thy Lord.' Actually, the Qur'an lists only three signs out of the ten major signs[16] and the rise of the sun from the West is not one of them. Thus, to trace the origin of this sign, we have to look for that outside the Islamic sources. Since Christianity and Christians possess an elaborated eschatological revelation, it is expedient to consult the Christian religious literature to discover, if possible, the resurgence of this sign as a real coherent part of the Islamic eschatology. At the same time, it is an effete attempt to claim that the biblical account has an exact parallel to what the custodians of the Islamic Tradition have developed in their comment on verse 6:158.

It is my conjecture, then, that traditionalists or narrators intended to point to some exceptional prodigious which they considered to be the first heavenly sign among the ten major signs of the end of time.[17] On this basis, the biblical description of the various astral phenomena as a prelude to the appearance of the sign of the Son of Man[18] may be the origin from which the Islamic 'sign' is developed. This portrait is a leitmotif of different verses in the Bible. In the book of Isaiah 34:4, it is stated, *"And all the host of heaven will wear away, and the sky will be rolled up like a scroll; all their host will also wither away as a leaf withers from the vine, or as one withers from the fig tree,"* Or, as 13:13 of the same book indicates, *"For the stars of heaven and their constellations will not flash forth light; the sun will be dark when it rises and the moon will not shed its light."* Since most of the *hadiths* have been compiled and recorded during the eighth and the early part of the ninth centuries, after the Muslims became acquainted with the Christian religious literature and scripture, it is not improbable that Muslim scholars found sufficient informa-

161

tion to interpolate into their eschatological views. This rich reservoir of scriptural images, it seems, has fascinated the storytellers who, additionally, may have also incorporated what they discovered in the apocryphal material, into their corpus of episodes.

But it seems also that the story of the sun's journey to the west and its prostration in front of God's throne could be traced to the Christian legend of Alexander who became a mythological hero redressed with a garment of Christian piety. It is said,

> And when the sun enters the window of heaven, he straightway bows down and makes obeisance before God the Creator; and he travels and descends the whole night through the heavens, until at length he finds himself where he rises[19]

The similarities between the Islamic interpretation and the Christian legend are very striking. Within the context or the scope of such comparative study, these similarities cannot be ignored or disregarded by any means.

The Fire that Erupts from the South of Eden * النار المتفجرة من قعر عدن

Islamic sources demonstrate that the fire that will burst forth from the Southern of Eden will be the last sign before the Hour or the Day of resurrection.[20] It is not clear whether this sign will appear before the first blast of the trumpet or not. This fire is designed, as unbeatable force, to drive the people to the place of their final assembly before resurrection.[21] It is a sign from God to force those who lag behind, to move forward to the designated place of

162

gathering. But another *hadith* hints that this fire will drive people from the 'East and the West.'[22] This implies that this fire will not be local but rather a global force that will circle the earth and drive people to their assembly place.

Nevertheless, as an attempt to make sense of the contrasting traditions, a thorough reading into *hadith* may reveal that they are two different stages involved in this event. The first stage propounds that there are three ways of transportation by which people will conventionally and involuntarily, travel to the place of Assembly: Some of them will be well equipped and owning their own rides; others will alternate between walking and riding, sharing one camel.[23] A third group will be crawling on their faces, "And the One who made them walk on their feet is able to make them walk (crawl) on their faces."[24] On the authority of Muhammad, Abu Hurayra relates another *hadith* in which he alludes to three types of ways of traveling by which the people will go to the designated place. They travel either walking, or riding, or crawling on their faces.[25] This *hadith* does not talk about taking turns. Moreover this *hadith* begins with "People will be driven to the place of assembly in the Day of Resurrection..."[26] Thus it runs counter to the general consensus of Muslim scholars who believe that the day of the first assembly supercedes the blast of the first trumpet. It also denotes that these *hadiths* have been subject to alteration.

The second stage of this fateful trip involves those who lag behind and do not respond to the call (whether it is the blast of the trumpet or a supernatural power). A fire will burst forth from the direction of Eden.[27] This strange fire will drive them, in spite of themselves, to move to the gathering place. It will alight with them when they alight, and sleep with them when they sleep. It will get up with them in the morning when they wake up, and will halt with

163

them wherever they halt in the evening.[28] But it will devour those who will lag behind. There is no way that these people can obviate their sinister journey. Their destiny is pre-ordained by God and it is unthinkable that they can change their fate.

This anecdote of this fierce fire is reminiscent of the Old Testament account of the pillar of fire that accompanied the children of Israel whenever they traveled or alighted in the desert whether during nighttime or daytime.[29] Surely, the function of the Old Testament pillar of fire differs than the function of the Islamic end of time fire. The Pillar of fire in the Old Testament was a physical manifestation of God's presence in the desert camp of the ancient Israelites and as a guide to lead them in the vast wasteland, whereas the Islamic fire will be a signal ushering the approach of the Hour.

But who are these people who will be forced to go to the final place of assembly? And where is this place of assembly? As mentioned before, all the righteous as well as anyone who has an iota of faith will die before the coming of the fearful Hour. On the authority of Muhammad, 'Abdullah ibn 'Amr reported that "the Hour will not arrive until Allah causes the death of the best people on earth; only the wicked will be left: they will not know any good or prohibit any evil."[30] Ibn Mas'ud indicated that he heard the prophet saying, "The worst of the people are those who will be still alive when the Hour comes upon them, as well as those who will convert their graves into mosques."[31] In his book *al-Fitan wa al-Malahim,* Ibn Khathir cites a number of *ahadith* in which a bleak spiritual environment will prevail over the Islamic society so that the name of the exalted God will be obliterated from the mouth of the people.[32]

It is conspicuous from these traditions, whether they are authentic or fabricated, that the Hour will come upon the worst segment of the society that has not been taken away or died after the demise of Christ and the reign of al-Muq'ad.[33] Those people are kept alive in order to sustain the anguish of life. They are the non-believers who lost their final opportunity to repent and to believe in God's Signs. Their skepticism and ferocious deeds will witness against them in the Day of Judgment. The images these traditions portray imply that their forced journey into the place of assembly manifests the hopelessness from which they will suffer. It will be a moment of 'pre-reckoning' as they gather for the Day of Resurrection. The real puzzling question is what will happen to the believers who will be set apart from the infidels during the time of the Islamic Beast?

The tragic journey of the people who are left on earth will end up in the land of *al-Sham* (Syria).[34] They will travel, wave after wave, from all over the world to Syria. This is the first place of assembly. It is somewhat difficult to explain why Syria was designated to be the place of assembly. Islamic traditions do not point to a certain place in Syria. It is such a general term that Islamic expounders have to speculate without being specific. It may come to mind, in this case, that Syria has already become the designated place in which the wicked of the earth will gather because Syria will be the historical stage of the greatest events of the end of time. Jesus Son of Mary will descend in Syria to accomplish his mission, the Antichrist will be killed in Ludda, the people of Gog and Magog will perish around Jerusalem and the golden era of Jesus' reign will take place in that part of the world. It is true that these justifications are mere speculations, but the ambit of these speculations covers broad apocalyptic events that lend sense to these views. These are not *impromptu* oversight,

165

but a mixed collage of observations implied in the Islamic traditions. Some of these speculations may evoke sound objections, yet it is reasonable that these suggestions may turn out to be the true reasons that explain why Syria is designated to be the final destiny of the evildoers and infidels. Those wicked people are those whose lands will spit them out, the spirit (soul) of the Merciful will vomit them, and the fire will drive them with the apes and swine,[35] and will face the consternation of the end of time. They have lost the divine pathos and become the subject of God's wrath.

In conclusion, could those who rendered these traditions (whether it was the prophet or the narrators) also envisaged in their mind the image of the fire of hell, as it is described in the Qur'an or in the scriptures of the People of the Book, and applied it to the last major sign of the end of time? Could the traditionalists harbor the notion that these iniquitous people should have a foretaste of the agony of hell before the judgment day? Such possibilities do not seem to be illogic or inapprehensible.

CHAPTER NINE
The Resurrection
ألقيامة أو البعث

The concept of resurrection is one of the fundamentals of the three monotheistic religions: Judaism Christianity and Islam.[1] But in Judaism this most significant event lacks the details and the descriptive language that both Christian and Islamic eschatology have provided. This descriptive language, despite its evocative symbolism in Christianity and aesthetic figurative simile in Islam, aims at emphasizing the reality of its realization against the attitude of the Arab polytheists and the Jewish Sadducees.

The Islamic view indicates that after the death of Jesus and the Muq'ad, all the righteous people will die; only the wicked will survive to populate the planet earth for a while. This is to spare the virtuous from the anguish the evildoers will suffer in their first gathering in the land of al-Sham.[2] The ordeals and the trials are part of the chastisement the ungodly people will undergo before the blast of the Sa'qat (the blast of the trumpet that causes the death of all the living creatures in the universe). It seems that there is some significant attenuation in the legend of the Islamic Beast and the story of the fire. The hadith remarks that one of the tasks of the Beast is to discern between the virtuous and the infidels. This implies that after the death of Jesus and the Muq'ad, believers will continue to constitute a segment of the society that will not pass away before the Day of the assembly. Does that mean that these virtuous will be propelled to the land of al-Sham like the non-believers? Or, does it mean that the believers will die after the Beast accomplishes its mission and before the burst out of the fire? If so, then this allusion contradicts the claim that all the believers will also taste the death after the demise of Jesus and the Muq'ad. However, the different accounts of the eschatological events mentioned in Islamic Tradition vary in their chronological order. This variation makes it difficult to draw an accurate chart for the end of time drama without creating disruption or flaws. Moreover, it is beyond the spectrum of this study to discuss 'the behind the scene' scenario, that will take place in the grave prior to the resurrection, of those who died before the first *hashr* (assembly). Yet where appropriate, we will try to examine some of these perplexed issues within the context of this chapter.

Islam, like Christianity and Judaism, teaches that death does not terminate the process of life. Al-Ghazali (d. 501/1111) indicates, "it is man's soul and spirit that constitute his real nature, which is immoral."[3] The earthly life is only one phase of the continuous stream of existence that will find its last abode either in paradise or in hell. The waiting period in the grave, in which the soul and flesh have been separated, comprise a segment of life; though different from the biological presence before death, the soul continues, within the Islamic eschatology, recognizes itself as it faces the trial of the grave. Al-Ghazali explains that upon man's death his state becomes subject to two types of changes: he will be deprived of his biological features, power of senses, family, property, and "there is no distinction to be drawn between his being taken from these things and these things being taken from him, for it is separation itself which causes pain."[4] Secondly, upon death there are certain things that will be revealed to him such as his good deeds and evil works on which his final destiny will be determined in the day of reckoning.[5] Such belief stresses that death does not cause the extinction of the spirit and its consciousness, which "is proved by a number of

Verses and Traditions."[6] In *Sahih of Muslim,* it is related that Muhammad, as he was passing by some graves with his companions, informed them that

> When the dead body is placed in the grave,
> he listens to the sound of their (his friends)
> shoes as they depart (from the cemetery).[7]

Another tradition remarks that Muhammad went to where the casualties of the *Battle of Badr* had been thrown into a well one after another. He started to call each one of them by his name, asking them if they found that the message God entrusted to him was true. 'Umar Ibn al-Khattab inquired if they could hear him though their bodies were lifeless. Muhammad told 'Umar that they can hear him distinctly more than he can hear him (Muhammad) but they cannot answer.[8]

Other similar *hadiths* indicate that the dead will continue to be aware of their entities as they were before they passed away. Their deeds, good or bad, will determine their status in the hereafter. The two mysterious angels *Munkar and Nakir*, who will question the dead and prepare the preliminary report, will allow the dead to see some glimpses of their ultimate destiny. On the authority of Ibn 'Umar, he said,

> The prophet said: When a person dies his
> seat is displayed to him morning and
> evening. If he was one of the people of
> paradise, he would (belong) to paradise. If
> he was one of the people of hell, he would
> (belong) to hell. Then he will be told: This is
> your seat until God raises you in the Day of
> Resurrection.[9]

It is evident from the *Hadith* that no one is exempted from the trial of the grave[10]. It was said that Muhammad himself used to plead with God asking for refuge from this gruesome temptation.[11] This is rather surprising since the two obscure angels who will descend to interrogate the dead are supposed to interrogate Muhammad too. Among the questions they usually ask is, whether the dead person believes that Muhammad is the true messenger of God. One wonders what type of questions these two angels had asked Muhammad in the grave. Moreover, why, in the first place, was Muhammad afraid of the trial of the grave? Apparently, when the basis of reward and punishment is ethical, the consequences are always unpredictable. Such unpredictability creates terrible fear of the unknown. Men's eternal fate is at stake here. No one knows if his good deeds will be acceptable to God.

The Islamic Tradition provides us with an incongruent list of questions by which the two designated angels investigate the creeds, beliefs and deeds of the dead person. In his book *Life between Death and Resurrection in Islam,* Ragnar Eklaund surveys "several problems connected with this matter."[12]

After the two angels *Munkar* and *Nakir,* complete the interrogation of the believer and he answers all the questions correctly, at this very point

> There approaches one who is beautiful of countenance, sweet-smelling and decked in finery, who declares, 'Rejoice at the mercy which is come to you from your Lord, and at Gardens *in which there is bliss everlasting'.* 'May God give you good tidings!' he replies. 'Who are you?' 'I am your righteous deeds,' he says.[13]

170

But for the unbeliever who

Travels into afterlife and severed from this world, there descend to him *Angels strong and severe* bearing *garments of fire* and *mail-coats of tar,* who beset him on every side until, when his soul emerges, he is cursed by every angel between heaven and earth, and every angel that dwells in heaven. The gates of heaven are locked and shut, for there is not a single one of them that would not loath his entry by it. And when his spirit ascends it is cast back, as it is declared, 'O Lord Your bondsman so-and-so, who, neither heaven nor earth will accept!' And He says, 'Return him, and show him the horror I have prepared for him, even as I promised: *From it did We create you; to it shall We return you.*'[14]

Then when the unbeliever fails to answer the questions of the two interrogating angels, he will be then approached by "one of vile countenance, corrupt-smelling and meanly attired" who will inform the unbeliever that he is his foul deeds.[15]

Islamic eschatology hints at a human state between death and the time of resurrection, which is called the intermediate state. It is "that time/space often referred to as the Barzakh"[16] or "the place that the souls are to be stored after departure from their flesh"[17] until the day of resurrecttion when the soul will join its newly born body. The trial of the grave, the preliminary interrogation and the prospect of his eternal fate will take place in this period. Among the three monotheistic religions, Islam is replete with details

171

about the invisible activities during this span of time. It seems, as Smith and Haddad indicate that

> ...Islam in actuality espouses a belief in two judgments, the first to take place through and after the questioning of the grave, and the second and the ultimate judgment to be passed on the day of resurrection.[18]

The Islamic Tradition also reports that after the death of the believer the attending angels ascend with his spirit up through the "seven layers of the heavens, passing by previous community... until they reach the majestic pavilions and the *Sidrat al-Muntaha.*"[19]

Some Islamic sources state that the spirit of the dead may have permission from God to view its former body. It will return to the grave, and from a distance it will look at the corpse and even converse with it. These visits may recur in short sequences before the final departure.[20]

As we try to trace the sources of the above Islamic perspectives, we can easily recognize the influence of the Eastern ancient religions, in particular Zoroastrianism. Undoubtedly, Muhammad found in Salman al-Farisi his main source about Zoroastrianism. This remarkable person was originally a follower of Zoroaster and, according to Islamic sources, was converted to Christianity before he embraced Islam.[21] Moreover, he was accustomed to share with Muhammad his knowledge about the tenets of his ancient faith. Even 'A'isha, Muhammad's favorite wife, complained against Salman because these late private night meetings he used to hold with Muhammad, had already deprived her from the company of her husband.[22]

In his study *Zoroastrianism and Judaism,* George Carter explains that "When death takes place the soul remains in the vicinity of the body for three days and three nights which indicates a kind of transitional stage, in which the soul of the good man has a foretaste of Paradise and that of the evil man the torments of hell."[23] Both the pious and the impious souls will be lingering about the body for three days and three nights and in the dawn of the fourth day the souls will pass over the Chinvat Bridge.[24] These three days and three nights "are filled with happiness and confidence for the righteous soul, and anguish and fear for wicked souls."[25] Evidently, the Islamic concept of permitting the soul to view its deteriorating body is an adaptation of a Zoroastrian perspective. As the soul in Zoroastrianism enjoys a foretaste of delight or hell before the last Day of Judgment, likewise both Muslim believers and unbelievers will go through similar experience before the preliminary judgment. At the same time, in Zoroastrian eschatology, as the pious soul crosses the bridge, "it will meet a balmy and sweet scented wind."[26] Then the *doena* (conscience) of the deceased "appears to the soul in the shape of a beautiful maiden, if righteous, or a hideous hag, if wicked."[27] The later Avestian Texts, *Hadhokht nask* reveals more details about this maiden: "She is beautiful, radiant, white-armed, robust, fair-faced, erect, high-breasted, of stately form, noble born, of glorious lineage, fifteen years old in appearance, as beautiful in form as the most beautiful of creatures."[28] When the righteous inquires about the identity of the maiden, she informs him that she is "the personification of his beautiful conscience, the fruit of his own good words, deeds and thoughts. The soul of the righteous will then begin to rejoice and will enter a beautiful and fragrant region."[29] Conversely, the wicked soul will suffer from the frost and inhaling stenches, and from the north a wind foul smelling blows towards him – more foul smelling than all others do. Then, "the conscience

173

of the wicked soul appears to him in the form of an ugly hag. When the terrified soul asks the hag who she is, she responds that she is the personification of his conscience, the fruit of his own evil words, deeds and thoughts."[30]

Obviously, the Islamic account, as Ghazali recounts on the authority of Muhammad, strikingly resembles the image of the Zoroastrian episode. For the "one who is beautiful in countenance, sweet-smelling and decked in finery' is a reflection of the fair maiden of Zoroastrianism, and the "one of the vile countenance, corrupt-smelling and meanly attired" is a picture of the ugly hag. The former claims that she was the personification of the righteous deeds of the righteous soul, while the later indicates that she is the embodiment of the foul deeds of the wicked soul.

The impact of Zoroastrianism on Islam does not end at this point. The images of the Day of Judgment, the paradise, hell, and the story of the *Sirat* (the bridge) include significant elements borrowed from Zoroastrian eschatology. But Zoroastrian apocalypse is not the only source that influenced the Islamic eschatological events. Christianity has indeed furnished Islamic eschatology with numerous details of the end of time.[31]

For those evildoers who will be gathered in *al-Sham,* propelled by the super natural fire, the time has come for them to pay their due. The resurrection will come upon them unexpectedly. As they are waiting at their place of assembly, suddenly they hear the sound of the trumpet blown by the mighty angel Israphiel. According to ibn Kathir there are three trumpet blasts that will sound before the resurrection. The first one is the trumpet of terror,

> And in the Day when the trumpet will be sounded - those who are in the heavens and

174

on earth, will be smitten with terror save those whom Allah wills (to spare), and all will come to Him with humility. And you will see the mountains that you think that they are firmly established while (in reality) they pass away (hastily) as the passing cloud. This is the handiwork of God Who has masterly (created) every things: He is cognizant of all that you do   (Sura 27: 87-88, my translation).

ويَومَ يُنفَخُ في الصُّورِ فَفَزِعَ مَن في السَّماوَاتِ ومَن في الأرْضِ إلاَّ مَن شَاء اللهِ وكُلٌّ أتَوهُ داخِرينَ. وتَرى الجِبالَ تَحسَبُها جامِدَةً وهِيَ تَمُرُّ مَرَّ السَّحابِ صُنْعُ اللهِ الَّذي أتْقَنَ كُلَّ شَيْءٍ إنَّهُ خَبيرٌ بِمَا تَفعَلونَ.

Anyone who will hear the trumpet will be terrified. People will be distracted from their daily normal work due to the occurrence of this incredible matter.[32] Even Muhammad, as the Tradition indicated, was concerned about the approach of this moment. When he was asked about Sura 74:8, 'When the trumpet is sounded, he said, "How can I be delighted and the One with the trumpet has placed it in his mouth and bowed his forehead waiting (for the moment) when he will be ordered to blast it!"[33] This trumpet of terror is aimed at preparing the inhabitants of heaven and earth to expect the approach of the Hour with fear and uncertainty. This will be the prelude for the end of the present perishable world and commencement of the new everlasting world.

Most Islamic eschatological studies do not elaborate on the trumpet of terror. But there are some obscure *hadiths* attributed to Muhammad, accepted by a number of Muslim scholars, portrays a terrifying picture. Israphiel[34] is commanded to blow his trumpet with a long stretched blast so

175

that the earth will tremble as a lamp that is hit by the wind or a ship attacked by the waves. People will stagger on its surface, wet nurses become startled, pregnant women will prematurely give birth, lads will grow white hair, the earth will split asunder from one end to the other, stars will scatter in heaven and the sun and the moon will eclipse.[35] The narrator of this hadith based his description on a number of Qur'anic verses such as,

> These (today) only wait for a single mighty blast which (when it comes) will brook no delay (38:15,).

وَمَا يَنْظُرُ هَؤُلاَءِ إِلاَّ صَيْحَةً وَاحِدَةً مَا لَهَا مِن فَوَاقٍ

Another Qur'anic reference cited in this vein is Sura 79:6-10,

> When the trepidation violently convulses, followed by another tremor; in that day the hearts will be throbbing, their eyes will be cast down and they will say: Are we indeed reverting to our original state? (My translation).

يَوْمَ تَرْجِفُ الرَّاجِفَةُ، تَتْبَعُهَا الرَّادِفَةُ، قُلُوبٌ يَوْمَئِذٍ وَاجِفَةٌ، أَبَصَارُهَا خَاشِعَةٌ، يَقُولُونَ أَئِنَّا لَمَرْدُودُونَ فِي الْحَافِرَةِ.

When all the inhabitants of the universe are smitten by horror, the people of the earth will be the most to suffer from God's retribution. Another Qur'anic quotation is cited here to describe the terror that will befall the wicked,

> O mankind! Fear your Lord! For the convulsion of the Hour will be a thing terrible. When you see it, every mother shall

forget the baby she is nursing and every pregnant woman will prematurely give birth. Humankind will seem intoxicated though they are indeed not, but God's punishment is truly awful (Sura 22:1-2, my translation).

يَا أَيُّهَا النَّاسُ اتَّقُوا رَبَّكُمْ إِنَّ زَلْزَلَةَ السَّاعَةِ شَيْءٌ عَظِيمٌ. يَوْمَ تَرَوْنَهَا تَذْهَلُ كُلُّ مُرْضِعَةٍ عَمَّا أَرْضَعَتْ وَتَضَعُ كُلُّ ذَاتِ حَمْلٍ حَمْلَهَا وَتَرَى النَّاسَ سُكْرَى وَمَا هُمْ بِسُكْرَى وَلَكِنَّ عَذَابَ اللهِ شَدِيدٌ.

But Muslims are more concerned about the impact of the second trumpet. There is a period of respite between the first trumpet and the second. No one knows the exact length of this respite. Abu Hurayra reiterates on the authority of Muhammad that the span of this interval is unfixed. It could be forty days, months, years or more. Obviously during this period God's creations will be in a state of expectation and fear. People will wonder what will happen next. The first trumpet is indeed a wake up call. The people will be afflicted with all types of agony and uncertainty. Then at the right moment God will order Israphiel[36] to blow his trumpet for the second time,

The trumpet will be sounded, thus, all that are in the heavens and on earth will swoon, save those whom Allah wills (to exempt them from that), Sura 39: 68.[37]

وَنُفِخَ فِي الصُّورِ فَصَعِقَ مَن فِي السَّمَاوَاتِ وَمَن فِي الأَرْضِ إِلاَّ مَن شَاءَ اللهُ.

The trumpet of the *sa'qa* that will cause the swoon, leads to the cessation of the normal order of life and impedes the progress of the usual daily activities. Actually, this blast will cause every living being in heaven and on earth to die save those whom God wills to spare, i.e. the martyrs who are alive in paradise.[38] This view contradicts another *hadith* that denotes that, in the final analyses, only the eternal living God on His throne will defy death. Everything else shall become extinct; even the angel of death who is commanded by God to seize his own spirit, will taste death[39]. "He comes to a place between the Garden and the Fire and casts his gaze up to heaven. Then he withdraws his spirit and utters a loud cry, which, were all the creatures still alive, they would die from hearing it."[40] And "with the extinction of all save the divine we have the final and perfect cosmic setting for God's proclamation of His absolute and omnipotent oneness."[41] As the universe becomes void of every living being, the exalted God will announce with an authoritative voice His sovereignty, omnipotence and eternity. He will repeat three times: "'I am the mighty'; then He will shout three times: 'To whom does the kingdom belong today?' When no one answers Him, He will soliloquize: 'It belongs to the only One God, the Conqueror.'"[42] Apparently, this Islamic tradition intends to restore the universe to its former state before the creation when nothing was in existence save the eternal God. The monologue echoes the creation version of the first two chapters of Genesis when God, through the course of the process of creation, was in constant monologue with Himself.

When the second trumpet sounds every activity on earth ceases to exist. This trumpet heralds the beginning of the end of time. According to the Islamic Tradition, Muhammad had foreseen the suddenness of the coming of the Hour. Abu Hurayra narrates:

> Allah's Apostle said, "The hour will be established (so sudden) that two persons spreading a garment between them will not

be able to finish their bargain, nor will they be able to fold it up. The Hour will be established while a man is carrying the milk of his she-camel, but cannot drink it; and the Hour will be established when someone is not able to prepare the tank to water his livestock from it; and the Hour will be established when some of you has raised his food to his mouth but cannot eat it."[43]

Evidently, this hadith reflects the same picture delineated by Christ about the end of times as he was responding to the inquiry of his disciples.[44] The only difference between the two images is that Muhammad mirrors the life and the culture of his time and environ to which the Arabs can relate. There is no shade of doubt in the mind of this author that these images are inspired by the words of Jesus. Also, Jesus was alluding to the moment of the rapture while Muhammad was denoting the event of the sa'qa. As the result of the blast of the sa'qa, death will strike everyone so that no one will have time to dispose of his affair or to return to his people (Sura 36: 47).

The events of the second trumpet create some serious problems that are difficult to explain or reconcile. Chronologically, the second trumpet blasts after the evildoers are propelled to the land of al-Sham by the fire that bursts from Yemen and subsequent trumpet of terror. That means that people have already been driven away from their own lands, jobs, houses and businesses. They have been gathered together to face the coming judgment. Actually, we have here an interval that precedes the interval between the trumpet of terror and the trumpet of the sa'qa. But it seems that the above hadith reveals an irreconcilable contradiction because it suggests that the wicked people have continued to inhabit their land and living their normal

179

daily life. It also suggests that neither the fire nor the trumpet of terror has impacted their lives. The terrifying turmoil that is depicted, especially after the trumpet of terror, has failed to incur any change in the order of the people's lives. Thus, these reports point to a chaotic collage of information invented by the narrators to explain the cryptic Qur'anic verses. It is true that the Qur'an lucidly mentions the trumpet, Israphiel and other relevant events; but the Qur'an lacks the logical process by which a coherent chronological order may be formulated. Unfortunately, the commentators as well as the storytellers and the traditionalists seized the opportunity to incorporate the data they collected from different sources without any regard to their chronological order or their authenticity.

After the trumpet of the *sa'qa* which causes the demise of all the living beings save God, there will be a third interval that lasts as long as the Creator wills. But when the time comes, God will create first, new heavens and a new earth[45]. He will stretch them out, flattened them and spread them like the *'Ukazyan* hide without any crookedness and curves.[46] Ibn 'Abbas comments on this text: "It will be raised up and lowered: its trees, mountains, valleys, and all else that it contains shall disappear, as it stretched out like the leather of 'Ukaz to form a land as white as silver, upon which no blood shall have been shed nor any sin committed. And in the heavens, the sun, the moon and stars shall have vanished away."[47] This is a cosmic disintegration. Then the trumpet will blast for the third time.[48] This is the blast of the resurrection. Several verses in the Qur'an denote the means by which the resurrection will take place:

> The trumpet will be sounded...Then will a
> second one be sounded, when, behold, they
> will be standing and looking on (39:68).

وَنُفِخَ فِي الصُّورِ... ثُمَّ نُفِخَ فِيهِ اُخْرَى فَإِذَا هُمْ قِيَامٌ يَنْظُرُونَ.

Also in Sura 36: 51-52 we read,

> The trumpet shall be sounded, when behold!
> From the sepulchers (men) will rush forth to
> their Lord! They will say: "Ah! Woe unto
> us! Who had raised us up from our beds of
> repose?"...(A voice will say:) "This is what
> Allah, Most gracious had promised, and true
> was the word of the messengers.

وَنُفِخَ فِي الصُّورِ فَإِذَا هُمْ مِنَ الأَجْدَاثِ إِلَى رَبِّهِمْ يَنْسِلُونَ ...
قَالُوا يَا وَيْلَنَا مَنْ بَعَثَنَا مِنْ مَرْقَدِنَا (؟) هَذَا مَا وَعَدَ الرَّحْمَانُ
وَصَدَقَ الْمُرْسَلُونَ.

The Qur'an makes it clear that the act of
resurrection strikingly manifests the power of God and his
sovereignty. As the omnipotent Creator, He is able to join
together every soul to its original body, regardless of what
may have happened to that body or the decay that may have
corrupted it[49]. This notion is implied in the Qur'an as it
reiterates,

> Does man think that we cannot assemble his
> bones? Nay, We are able to put together in
> perfect order the very tips of his fingers
> (Sura 75: 3-4).

أَيَحْسَبُ الإِنْسَانُ أَنَّا لَنْ نَجْمَعَ عِظَامَهُ ؟ بَلَى قَادِرِينَ أَن
نُسَوِّيَ بَنَانَهُ.

That means that there "will not be any confusion at all as to
the identity of each person."[50] This basic concept, implicit
in the Qur'an, does not provide the reader with enough

181

information and details explaining how God is going to execute the resurrection. In this case, Islamic Traditions become again our major source. We have to probe cautiously these traditions, before we can project a coherent and reasonably acceptable picture, to comprehend the process the Creator employs in the story of resurrection.

The resurrection of the body is an essential belief in Islam. God will recreate the bodies and prepare them to receive their spirits. Though human bodies are not the first to be restored to life, they will be prepared to receive their spirits. God will make the water to flow from underneath the throne to the new earth, which contains the decayed bodies of people. He will also order the sky to rain for forty days so that the water will be as high as twelve cubits.[51] The barren land will "quiver with life."[52] Then God will command the individual bodies to begin to re-grow, starting with the coccyx,[53] like the medicinal plants or the herbage plants. Medically speaking, "this *hadith* is not correct. All major bones deteriorate at the same rate."[54] Then the bodies attain their completed form as it used to be before death.

The resurrected bodies will be preceded by the full resurrection of the inhabitants of heavens. The first to be restored to life by a direct command from God are the carriers of the Throne. It seems that the Throne will not be susceptible to annihilation. Among those who are restored is Seraphiel. Seraphiel will resume his role as the blower of the trumpet. At the command of the sovereign God, he places the trumpet in his mouth and says, "Let both Gabriel and Michael be restored to life"; they become vibrant with life. Then God will summon all the spirits.[55] When they are brought to His presence, Muslim spirits will be glowing with light, whereas other spirits will be blackened with darkness. God, then, will cause them all to die and store them in the trumpet[56] including the spirits of the martyrs. Does this mean that the spirits of the martyrs or even the spirits of the righteous and the wicked will taste death when God empties the universe from all the living creatures? Maybe the question that should be asked: Do spirits experience death? The Arabic word that is used in the above text, *yaqbiduha,* has two meanings in this context: a) to seize, or b) to cause to die. The text does not shed enough light on the meaning. The objection to the first meaning is that it suggests that the spirits did not perish when God made the universe to cease to exist, though the text indicates that only God remains beyond the dominion of death. The argument against the second meaning revolves around the nature of the spirit. It is believed that the spirit does not perish. In this case, it cannot mean that the spirits will die. It is hard to reconcile between the notion of the destruction of the cosmos except God and the notion of preservation of the spirits or terminating them.[57]

Now the stage is set for the crucial moment of resurrection. Here, the concept of time is not a significant factor. Neither the Qur'an nor the Islamic Tradition provides us with a timetable. For instance, how long will the universe remain in its primordial state after it becomes void of life, save God? How long will it take to restore the angels to life? Lastly, how much time will pass before the process of the growth and resurrection of the bodies begins? It seems that Muslim scholars did not concern themselves with either the order of events or the time span between these events.

When Seraphiel blasts the trumpet of the resurrection, all spirits, good or bad, will burst forth like bees filling in the space between heaven and earth. Then, by the command of God, the spirits will penetrate the ground and enter into the bodies through their nostrils first, then, they will stream into the rest of the bodies. The ground will split and all the quickened bodies will hastily burst forth.[58] As they gathered together, the beginning of the perilous Day of Assembly is heralded as a prelude for the Day of reckoning. This is the second Day of Assembly but on a larger scale. This time all the human race since the creation of Adam until the death of the last man will meet in the designated location, including all the prophets. The only exception, as it seems, are the martyrs.

It is appropriate at this point to examine the apocalyptic sources that left their mark on the Islamic eschatology. Zoroastriaism, Judaism and Christianity have all believed in the Day of Awakening and the Day of Reckoning. Thus, these two concepts were not the invention of Islam and "it is not surprising, therefore, to find a number of Qur'anic concepts coinciding with Zoroastrian theories, in particular ideas derived from the *Avesta,* one of the great works of ancient Zoroastrian legend and lore."[59] We have just alluded above to these mysterious personas, who will become the embodiment of the good or bad deeds of the deceased people. In both, Islam and Zoroastrianism, they play the same role in revealing, during the intermediate state, what is awaiting the dead on the Day of Judgment. This view does not conform to the general Qur'anic teaching that stresses that the destiny of each person depends totally on God's mercy and will, and only He has the final word. However, the role of these maidens does not end nor is limited to the intermediate state. They will continue to resume their relational interactions, whether they are good or bad, after the Day of Reckoning.[60]

Though Judaism shares with Islam the tenets of the Day of Judgment and eternal life, it did not impact the Islamic eschatology as Christianity did. Conceptually, both

184

religions believe in the ideology of the resurrection, the Day of Judgment and the bliss of Paradise. They also assert that God is the Judge who will judge the people on the basis of their deeds[61]. But Christianity furnished Islam with apocalyptic elements that were not available to Judaism. This study will analyze four issues within the context of the concept of resurrection.

a) The concept of the Hour. It seems that the term 'hour' has at least five different meanings in the Qur'an. One of these meaning is *al-ajal*[62] (instant of death). The second meaning of the 'hour' denotes time or moment as in Sura 9: 117, *"Who followed Him in time (hour) of distress."* The third meaning indicates a period of time of this earthly life that will seem like an hour.[63] The fourth meaning alludes to the time of the Day of Assembly as in Sura 10: 45, *"One day He will gather them together: (it will be) as if they had tarried but an hour of a day."* But the fifth meaning and the most significant one is the Hour of Resurrection, followed by the Day of Reckoning. Within this context, this term is repeated at least thirty-nine times in the Qur'anic text.[64] This fifth meaning has apparently, been borrowed from Christianity, especially as it is recorded in the gospels of Matthew, Luke, and John.[65] The only difference between the biblical meaning and the Qur'anic meaning is that the biblical meaning points to the second coming of Christ. Thus, that Hour that will be preceded by a number of supernatural portents will usher the second coming of Christ in His glory. But as the Qur'anic Hour is going to be sudden and will take people by surprise, likewise the second coming of Christ will be sudden and unexpected. Jesus made it clear that *"of that day and hour no one knows, not even the angels of heaven nor the Son but the father alone* (Matthew 24: 36). This 'suddenness' is repeated several times in the gospels, yet with the second coming of Christ the resurrection of the

185

righteous and the rapture of the living believers will also take place. In this case, there is a correlation between the biblical teaching and the Qur'anic views. The connotation of the Biblical Hour, therefore, lent itself to the Qur'anic apocalyptic apprehension with some adaptation appropriate to the Islamic ideology. It should also be noted here that the term 'day' in Luke 21: 34 carries the same connotation of the Hour. After Jesus delineated to his audience the terrifying picture of the horrors that will afflict the world, He urged them, and through them, the future church, to be always alert, lest that *"day will come on you suddenly like a trap."*

b) The intermediate state. It is a state of life that continues to exist between death and resurrection. There is only one Qur'anic verse where the *Barzakh* or the partition is mentioned as a stage in which the soul becomes subject to the interrogation of the angels *Munkar* and *Nakir*[66]. In Islamic theology this intermediate state begins as soon as the deceased person is buried. We have shown above that the soul in this stage is aware and self-conscious of its environment. When death comes upon the unbeliever, *"He says: 'O my Lord! Send me back (to life) that I may do righteous in what I neglect'. No, it is only (an empty) word he utters - Behind them is a barzakh till the day they are resurrected,"* (sura 23:99-100; my translation). Evidently, the soul recognizes its spiritual condition and realizes that the time has come to be accountable for its deeds. Such state of self-realization removes the veil that conceals what is invisible to the soul. Thus, this encounter will be a cause of delight to the believers and a source of terror to the unbelievers.

The intermediate state is hardly an Islamic ideology. In his book *The End of Times,*[67] Herman A. Hoyt discusses the concept of *Sheol-Hades.*[68] He intimates that there are other terms that refer to the same place that hint to the existence of two major compartments within *Sheol-Hades* "separated from each other by a gulf (Luke16:22)."[69] The upper compartment is "referred to as 'Abraham's bossom' (Luke 16:26) or paradise (Luke 23:43. The lower part of *Sheol-Hades* is referred to as 'the lowest Sheol 'in the Old Testament' (Deut 32:22; Ps. 86:13, ASV)."[70] Among other terms that refer to the same place is Abyss, translated (twice) as deep (Luke 8:31; Rom. 10:7) and as bottomless pit, (seven) times (Rev. 9:1, 2, 11; 11:7; 17:8; 20:1, 3.)[71] It is apparent that the upper level (paradise) is a temporary place of delight in which the righteous find rest and happiness until the Day of Resurrection. That was Jesus' promise to the repented thief on the cross when he told him, *"Truly I say to you, today you shall be with Me in Paradise"* (Luke 23: 43, NAS), whereas the lower compartment is a temporary place of torment and anguish[72] where God's anger *'burns to the lowest part of Sheol'* (Deut.32:22, NAS). This is the temporary abode of the rich man in the story of the poor Lazarus: *In Hades he lifted up his eyes, being in torment, and saw Abraham far away...he cried out and said, 'Father Abraham...I am in agony in this flame'*(Luke 16: 23-24, NAS). In this same place God reserved the rebellious angels for Judgment (2 Peter 2:4; Jude 6-7), but suffering the retribution of the eternal hell. The abyss is also described as a place of torment of which the demons were terrified and tried to evade (Luke 8:28-31).[73]

The concept of intermediate state, thus, is not an Islamic trait but is an integral part of the orthodox Christian theology, well expounded in the Bible. The righteous deceased will be rewarded by foretasting the happiness of paradise before the final Judgment, and the evildoers will partially suffer the torment of hell as they wait for the fearful day of the eternal condemnation. In both cases, the soul is aware of itself, condition and environment. Moreover, Sheol-Hades is not death, the grave, or the final hell. It is a realm where God is present and has absolute control over their dominions.[74]

From a biblical point of view, Sheol-Hades are not mythical places. They are actual places though it is impossible to pinpoint the exact location.[75]

c) The destruction of the universe: at the beginning of this chapter, we alluded to the transformation and destruction of the natural world and celestial planets. In both the Biblical and Islamic eschatology, these phenomena are part of the tragic events that will afflict the universe. But there is a difference in the timetable. In Islamic apocalyptic time, this destruction will take place after the Second Coming of Christ and upon the blast of the first trumpet. This is the blast of terror.[76] The universe becomes ruins and people will be struck with horror.

As we examine the Biblical apocalyptic timetable, the destruction of the world will occur just before the Second Coming of Christ and the rapture. It is a partial destruction[77], since the complete destruction and the creation of New Heaven and New Earth will be realized after the Day of Judgment.[78] These remarkable events will be supernatural portents by which Christ announces His glorious Second Coming.

d) The trumpets: In the Qur'anic eschatology, the term 'sur' الصّور (a ram horn) is used for trumpet. The Jews most often used this type of trumpet during their religious festivals as well as to announce the times of prayers. Undoubtedly, the Jews of *al-Madina* followed the tradition of their ancestors as they called their people to come to pray in the synagogue on Saturdays. The context in which the trumpet is utilized in the Qur'an suggests that Muhammad had received some knowledge about the Christian apocalyptic events, since the New Testament frequently mentions the trumpet in several eschatological occasions. The book of Revelation points *to seven trumpets* that will cause a formidable destruction to the world (8:7-9:21). Also, Jesus declared that *"He will send forth His angels with a great trumpet and they will gather together His elect from the four winds, from one end of the sky to another* (Matthew 24: 31). In 1Thessalonians 4:16, the Apostle Paul says, *"For the Lord Himself will descend from heaven with a shout, with the voice of the archangel and with the trumpet of God, and the dead in Christ will rise first."* Evidently, the apocalyptic concept of the trumpet in Islam is, shaped after the Christian model. The major differences between both accounts are related to the number of the trumpets and their functions.

It remains here to underscore two significant contrasting analogies in the episode of resurrection between Islam and Christianity. The first one involves the concept of resurrection. We have remarked briefly, in chapter two, that there are two types of resurrection in the Christian eschatology. In general terms all the dead, righteous and wicked, will be resurrected.[79] But this is an overview summary of the resurrection. The emphasis here is on the reality of the event. The resurrection is true: the justified 'to the resurrection of life' and the unjustified 'to the resurrection of judgment'. But as we look further into the biblical concept of resurrection we realize that there is a record of two resurrections: one preceding the other. The literal interpretation of the biblical intervals, as it is stated in Revelation, indicates that the righteous will rise from the grave before the evildoers. This is the first resurrection. But that does not exclude the living righteous from being raptured to meet their Lord in the air.[80] Here we have a complete picture of the first resurrection. And those who are included in the first resurrection are the ones who will not be under the condemnation of God. Revelation 20: 6 says, *'Blessed and holy is the one who has a part in the first resurrection; over these the second death has no power, but they will be priests of God and of Christ and will reign with Him for a thousand year.'*

The second and final resurrection will take place after the Millennium. This is the resurrection of the wicked. The wicked, both living and dead, will face the Day of Judgment with fear and terror. Every soul that did not have part in the first resurrection will stand before the White Throne of God to give an account of its life; even death and Hades will give up the dead which are in them so that every one will be judged according to their deeds; This is 'the second death, the lake of fire'.[81]

Islamic eschatology refers to one resurrection only. It is the resurrection of the entire humankind. Both the righteous and the wicked will rise from the dead to be judged by God. The universe will be laid in ruins. No living soul will be alive. All should die first, then, they will be resurrected to face their eternal destiny.[82] The process is gradual and is not instant as it is in Christianity. The Day of Judgment does not follow immediately but there is an uncertain interval filled with terrible anguish.

The second difference appertains to the idea of the Millennium. Muslims believe that the golden age of peace, justice, fertility and wealth will be after the Second Coming of Christ, and before his demise and the Day of Resurrection. Since Jesus is just a prophet, he has to taste death like any other human being. Yet, before his death, the Islamic Millennium will prevail for a short period during his lifetime. The nature of this Millennium is similar to the

Millennium as delineated in the book of Isaiah, chapter 11. But The Christian Millennium starts with the Second Coming of Christ and with the first resurrection of the believers. It will last for one thousand years[83] (Revelation 20: 6). During this period Jesus will be the absolute ruler surrounded by the believers who will reign with Him.

It is worth noticing here that both Millenniums will occur after the second coming of Christ, the destruction of the Antichrist and the eradication of Gog and Magog. Jesus will be the sole ruler, overseeing that justice, equity and goodness will characterize His reign. Islam emphasizes that Jesus' rule will be according to Muhammad's Shari'a, whereas in Christianity Christ will rule as the Lord of the creation and according to His own will and laws.

CHAPTER TEN

The Day of Judgment
يوم الدينونة

In both Islam and Christianity the Day of Judgment falls after the resurrection. Islamic Tradition as well as the Qur'an indicates that there is an interval between the Day of Resurrection and the Day of Reckoning. There is no consensus among Muslims about the length of this interval.[1] Some traditions state that people will stand for a period of three hundred years; others imply that it will be for fifty thousand years.[2] This difference in opinions and views creates interpretive problems and weakens the reliability of the tradition. At this point, the veracity of the content is not the concern of this chapter as much as the verity of the tradition.

But who will be the first to be resurrected? Islamic sources are quick to assert that Muhammad will be the first to be resurrected from among humanity.[3] This is a privilege bestowed on him by God. But other traditions denote that Jesus and Muhammad will be resurrected together.[4] In another place, a *hadith* ascribed to Muhammad reiterates that when he is resurrected he will find Moses has already outraced him, clinging to the Throne of God. Muhammad continues, "I do not know whether he would be awakened before me or he had already paid his due when he swooned in the Day of the Tur* or he will be resurrected before me."[5] In *Sunan of al-Tirmidhi*, an obscure *hadith* is recorded that Muhammad went to the mosque leaning on Abu Bakr at his right and 'Umar at his left, and he said, "As such we shall be arising in the Day of Resurrection."[6]

These contradictory *hadiths* make these reports unverifiable and, thus, create more questions than answers.

In effect, the Day of Resurrection serves two purposes: "It is to judge the deeds of man for the purpose of rewarding the faithful and punishing the guilty. Not only mankind but also the *Jinn* and irrational animals will be judged";[7] and, secondly, for God to exert His justice and sovereignty as the judge of the universe.

But what will take place in the interval between the Day of Resurrection and the Day of Judgment? First of all, it seems, that all those who will be resurrected will be naked, barefooted and uncircumcised. It is reported that 'A'isha said, "The Messenger of God said, 'people will be raised in the Day of Resurrection barefooted, naked and uncircumcised', 'A'isha said, 'What about the private parts?' The Messenger of God said, 'In that day everyone will have his own worry that would make him indifferent to the others.'"[8] A similar statement is related by Ibn 'Abbas[9] (Muhammad's cousin), but he added that Muhammad recited also the following Qur'anic verse:

> As we made the first creation, likewise we
> will re-create him. This is a binding promise
> we undertook that truly we will keep (Sura
> 21:104; my translation).

كما بدأنا أوَّل خَلْقٍ نُعيدُهُ وَعْداً عَلَيْنا إنَّا كُنَّا فاعِلِينَ.

The same tradition indicates that Abraham would be the first person to be clothed in the Day of Resurrection. There is no rational reason given for why Abraham, not Adam, Noah, Moses or any other prophet will be the first to be clothed.[10] In the view of this author, most probably Abraham will be the first to be clothed because Muslims regard him as the father of the prophets as well as the friend of God. In a *hadith* ascribed to Muhammad, 'Abdullah ibn Mas'ud, one of Muhammad's companions, said, "The Messenger of God said, 'the first to be clothed is Abraham; God, may He be exalted, will say: cloth my friend. Two white pieces of clothes will be brought to him. When he (Abraham) wears them, he will sit facing the Throne.'"[11] The idea of clothing the righteous with white robes is also mentioned in Revelation 6:11, *"And there was given to each of them (the martyrs) a white robe..."* This could be the source of the Islamic reference.

As we try to draw a timetable or a chronological order for the events that will take place during the interval between the Day of Resurrection and the Day of Judgment, we will encounter a serious chaotic disorder. The story of 'clothing' Abraham does not denote a fixed time. Will this event take place prior to the Judgment Day or after it? Islamic traditions indicate that God will appear on His Throne in the Day of Judgment after the intercession of Muhammad. Thus, the image of Abraham sitting facing the Throne after being covered with a dress from the Garden implies that this event occurs after the Reckoning. But the context of the story does not fit well with this reasoning, since it is connected with the Day of Resurrection. In Addition to the story of Abraham, Muhammad claims that he will be the second in line to be clothed; after that, he will sit at the right side of God "a place no one else will occupy but I; this will make the former and the latter envy me."[12] This tradition affirms that the episode of the 'clothing' will happen after the Day of Reckoning. But the sequence of events fails to provide us with a sequential order and we find ourselves in total confusion. Another *hadith* attributed to Muhammad and related by Um Salamah states,

194

She said, "I heard the Messenger of God saying: 'People will gathered together bare-footed and naked as they were (when) born'; Um Salamah said: 'Will we be looking at each other?' He said: 'people will be busy.' I said: 'With what will they be so busy?' He said: 'with the spreading of the scrolls that (contain) the weights of dust speck and the weights of mustard seeds.[13]

This tradition, provided it is authentic, hints that this salient event is not isolated from the Day of Judgment; but there is no mentioning of the anecdote of the 'clothing'. It is also interesting to notice that the identity of Muhammad's wives who related the *hadith* of 'the bare-footed and naked' differs from one tradition to another. Actually three names are mentioned: 'A'isha, Sawdah and Um Salamah. The three traditions are not exactly the same but they include variant additional information. That makes one wonder whether the three wives ask the same question at various times, or it is the same tradition related with some adaptation.

During the interval between the Resurrection and the Day of Judgment human kind will endure an unbearable time of toil and agony. People will experience two types of hardship: a physical anguish and a psychological ordeal. According to the Islamic Tradition, the Day of Assembly does not exempt any human being from the suffering and vicissitudes of the longest waiting period in human history. Islamic Traditions supply us with terrible images of that day. People will be very exhausted and thirsty under an extremely hot sun and will be drown in their own sweat. In a *hadith* attributed to Muhammad he said,

You will indeed stand waiting for seventy years[14] without being dealt with or judged.

You will weep until tears run dry, then you will be tearful with blood. You will sweat until (your sweat) covers (your mouths) and bridles you, or reaches your chins. Then you will raise your voices saying, 'Who will intercede for us with our Lord to issue (His) decree on us? [15]

Both al-Bukhari and Muslim indicate, "on the Day of Resurrection mankind will sweat so much that its sweat will penetrate the earth seventy cubits and it will cover their mouths, reaching to their ears."[16] They will be stricken by fear and agony and burned by the extreme heat of the sun. They will long for a drop of water to cool their unbearable thirst. It is a state of unimaginable torture. No one will be exempted from this anguish except the prophets, the saints, and the most devouts that God wills to spare them the excruciating pain of the Day of Reckoning.

People, then, will seek the intercession of the prophets. They will think that no one is worthier than their ancestor Adam, whom God created with his own hand, breathed in him from His spirit[17] and talked to him face to face. They will plead with him but he will decline saying: "I am not the right person for that."[18] Then they plead with the prophets one after another, but all of them refrain from accepting the task. The Messenger of God then said,

Until they come to me, so I proceed until I reach in front of the Throne. I bow down kneeling...till God sends an angel to me who will take hold of my arm and raise me up. He (God) says to me, 'O, Muhammad! I say: Yes Lord; here I am. He will say: - although He already knows - What do you want? I say: You promised me the intercession, thus let me intercede on behalf of your creatures (by asking You) to issue Your decree on them. He will say: I (accept) your intercession; I will come down to judge among you.[19]

In his dramatic and rhetorical style, the Ghazali addresses the human race by painting a depressive picture of dense fear that will grip the hearts and the soul of people, especially the evildoers. In the Day of Reckoning, *"a man shall flee from his own brothers, and from his own mother and his father, and from his wife and his children. Each one of them, that day, will have enough concern (of his own) to make him indifferent to others"* (Sura 80:33-37). In that day secrets things will be revealed, no master shall help another, the wicked are summoned towards the infernal fire and their faces are cast into hell, and their transgressions are divulged.[20] For the transgressors the picture is so bleak and there is no escape from the wrath of God.

As God descends from heaven to judge humanity, *jinns*, and animals, He will question them to expose their wickedness. In Sura 6:128, God interrogates the *Jinns* and humankind,[21]

One day He will gather them all together (and say): "O ye assembly of Jinns! Much (toll) did ye take of men." Their friends among men will say: "Our Lord! We made profit from each other, but (alas) we reached our term- which Thou didst appoint for us." He will say: "The fire will be your dwelling place; you will dwell therein forever, except as Allah willeth." Thy Lord is oft-wise, oft-knowing.

197

وَيَوْمَ يَحْشُرُهُمْ جَمِيعًا يَا مَعْشَرَ الْجِنِّ قَدِ اسْتَكْثَرْتُمْ مِنَ الْإِنْس
وَقَالَ أَوْلِيَاؤُهُمْ مِنَ الْإِنْس رَبَّنَا اسْتَمْتَعَ بَعْضُنَا بِبَعْض وَبَلَغْنَا
أَجَلَنَا الَّذِي أَجَّلْتَ لَنَا قَالَ النَّارُ مَثْوَاكُمْ خَالِدِينَ فِيهَا إِلَّا مَا
شَاءَ اللهُ إِنَّ رَبَّكَ حَكِيمٌ عَلِيمٌ .

The Qur'an suggests that the *Jinns* are subject to condemnation because, like humankind, they heard the message of God from messengers from among them but they rejected it because they were allured by the life of this world. Sura 6:13 states,

> O ye assembly of Jinns and men! Came there not unto you messengers *from amongst you* setting forth unto you My signs, and warning you of the meeting of this Day of yours? They will say: "We bear witness against ourselves." It was the life of this world that deceived them. So against themselves will they bear witness that they rejected faith.

يَا مَعْشَرَ الْجِنِّ وَالْإِنْس أَلَمْ يَأْتِكُمْ رُسُلٌ مِنْكُمْ يَقُصُّونَ عَلَيْكُمْ
آيَتِي وَيُنْذِرُونَكُمْ لِقَاءَ يَوْمِكُمْ هَذَا قَالُوا شَهِدْنَا عَلَى أَنْفُسِنَا
وَغَرَّتْهُمُ الْحَيَاةُ الدُّنْيَا وَشَهِدُوا عَلَى أَنْفُسِهِمْ أَنَّهُمْ كَانُوا
كَافِرِينَ.

Several events will take place in the Day of Reckoning. The destiny of each individual will be sealed. God's judgment will be absolute and final, and His justice will be impartial and fair. All nations will be summoned to the divine court to receive the unalterable verdict of God. But on what basis will God judge mankind? There are two areas God will utilize in determining the destination of each individual: his belief in one God and in His messenger

Muhammad, and one's ethical conduct. Man's creed had already been pre-determined when the two angels Munker and Nakir interrogated him as soon as he was buried. Now his beliefs and ethical conduct are brought forth publicly for the final verdict. The recording angels, who will confront him with all the details of his life, record all of man's deeds. The Qur'an sets the stage for the moment of recognition when the evidences are presented.

The first evidence is the books of record. There are two types of books: one book lists the good deeds and the right achievements of man, and the other one records all the bad deeds and evil intentions of his life. Those who will receive their books in their right hands are the blessed ones, but those who will receive their books in their left hands are the accursed that will be tormented in hell. In this day, some people will rejoice and be grateful for God's mercy. There are three places in the Qur'an that point to this act of forgiveness and compassion. Sura 17:71 says,

> The day in which We shall call together all human beings with *Imamihim*.[22] Those who are given their record book in their right hands, they will read their book; and those will not be treated with a single date-thread unjustly (my translation.)

يَوْمَ نَدْعُو كُلَّ النَّاس بِإِمَامِهِمْ فَمَنْ أُوتِيَ كِتَابَهُ بِيَمِينِهِ فَأُولَئِكَ
يَقْرَأُونَ كِتَابَهُمْ وَلاَ يُظْلَمُونَ فَتِيلاً

In Sura 84:7-9, the Qur'an indicates,

> But who is given his book of record in his right hand he will indeed receive an easy reckoning and will return to his own people delightfully (my translation.)[23]

199

فَأَمَّا مَنْ أُوتِيَ كِتَابَهُ بِيَمِينِهِ فَسَوْفَ يُحَاسَبُ حِسَابًا يَسِيرًا
وَيَنقَلِبُ إِلَى أَهْلِهِ مَسْرُورًا.

The unfortunate group will receive their books of records in their left hands or behind their backs. Those unbelievers were immersed in the pleasures of life without any regard for their eternal life. They defied the injunction of God's laws and rejected the faith. They were allured by the lustful desires of their hearts and feared not the wrath of God. But as they discover that the Day of Judgment is a reality, they will wish that they will be given a second opportunity to be reborn on this earth so as to live according to the teaching of the Qur'an and do good deeds. Such a wish will never come true. In Sura 69:25-26 we read,

> And whosoever is given his book of records in his left hand, will say: "I wish I had not been given my book of record and not known the outcome of my account" (my translation).

وَأَمَّا مَنْ أُوتِيَ كِتَابَهُ بِشِمَالِهِ فَيَقُولُ يَا لَيْتَنِي لَمْ أُوتِ كِتَابِيَه
وَلَمْ أَدْرِ مَا حِسَابِيَه

Another Qur'anic verse denotes that all the unbelievers will receive their dreadful books behind their backs. Actually, there is no difference between those who are given the books of records in their left hands or behind their back. They will face the same destiny. They are the people of hell. Sura 84:10-12 states,

> But whosoever given his book of record behind his back, will call for damnation and will be burned in a blazing fire.

200

وَأَمَّا مَنْ أُوتِيَ كِتَابَهُ وَرَاءَ ظَهْرِهِ فَسَوْفَ يَدْعُو ثُبُورًا
وَيَصْلَى سَعِيرًا

Al-Ghazali points to three types of people who will be present in the Day of Judgment, "Those who have not a single good deed to their credit; ...Those with not a single transgression..., (and) a third party, which constitutes the greater part of mankind...They have mingled good works with ill, and although it may not be plain to them, it is plain to God (exalted is He!) which of them are those whose good or evil deeds predominate."[24] It seems that Al-Ghazali suggests that those who will receive their record books, either in their right or left hand, are the ones whose right-eousness and wickedness have already been determined, based on their books of records. What remains is to decide the destiny of the majority who have lived on the threshold of the faith and mingled their good deeds with their bad deeds.

The Book of record is not the only criteria by which God will determine the eternal life of each individual in the Day of Judgment. There is also the concept of the balance or the scale. In his dynamic and dramatic style al-Ghazali explains,

> So the books and scroll which contain the good and evil deeds fly up, and the Scales are erected, and all eyes are upturned towards the books: shall they fall into the left scale or the right? Then they look to the Scales themselves: shall they tip in favour of the evil actions or in favour of the good? This state is fearsome indeed, and dazes the minds of all creatures.[25]

201

But another hadith related by Anas indicates that "each descendant of Adam will be brought on the Day of Arising and made to stand before the two sides of the Scale, to which an angel is assigned."[26] This *hadith* contrasts the aforementioned notion that only one party of the human kind will face the ordeal of the Scale. In her book *Qur'an and Woman,* Amina Wadud agrees with Anas's *hadith* as she stresses that all deeds of every individual will be weighted on a scale and "evil things are without merit: weightless. The weight of each good thing will be added and given multiple values."[27] The Qur'an, however, supports the idea of the Scale as the true and most reliable measure that God will employ in the Day of Judgment. After all, God is the one who sent down the Book and the Balance[28]. Thus, the Scale was created for a particular task as the final word in the process of reckoning. Only God, by His own mercy can forgive the wrongdoings of the people if He wished to do so. The Qur'an reiterates that

> The weighing that day is true; he whose scales are heavy - they are the prosperers, and he whose scales are light - they have lost their souls for wronging our signs (Sura 7:8-9, Arberry's translation).

وَالْوَزْنُ يَوْمَئِذٍ الْحَقُّ فَمَنْ ثَقُلَتْ مَوَازِينُهُ فَأُولَٰئِكَ هُمُ الْمُفْلِحُونَ وَمَنْ خَفَّتْ مَوَازِينُهُ فَأُولَٰئِكَ الَّذِينَ خَسِرُوا أَنْفُسَهُمْ بِمَا كَانُوا بِآيَاتِنَا يَظْلِمُونَ.

Smith and Haddad believes that when the Qur'an refers to the balance "in the singular it has been interpreted as the principle of justice and occasionally even the books through which the principles of justice are clarified."[29] But when the Qur'an uses the plural case for balances موازين it "has the clearer eschatological references of the scales by which deeds are weighted on the day of resurrection."[30] As

God weighs the deeds of every individual, He will deal with them justly and equitably; not the least of the good deeds will be missed:

> And we shall set up the just balances for the Resurrection Day, so that not one soul shall be wronged anything; even if it be the weight of one grain of mustard-seed We shall produce it, *and We are sufficient to count it* (Sura 21:47; Arberry's translation with the exception of the italics).[31]

وَنَضَعُ المَوَازِينَ القِسْطَ لِيَوْمِ القِيَامَةِ فَلاَ تُظْلَمُ نَفْسٌ شَيْئًا وَإِنْ كَانَ مِثْقَالَ حَبَّةٍ خَرْدَلٍ أَتَيْنَا بِهَا وَكَفَى بِنَا حَاسِبِينَ.

Some of the condemned will attempt to object or complain against the dreadful consequences of their bad deeds. They will try to justify their actions on the basis of their circumstances or ignorance, or even to deny them. They will make every endeavor to avoid God's wrath but to no avail. All their attempts will be hopeless, for God will silence them, but their faculties and body organs will bear witness against them:

> Today shall we set a seal on their mouths. But their hands will speak to Us, and their feet bear witness as to what they have been earning (Sura 36:65; Arberry's translation).

The Qur'anic episode of the Scale will finalize the drama of the Day of Judgment. God determines the destiny of each individual. It is true that Islamic Tradition alludes to the act of intercession and the role of Muhammad and other prophets in saving their followers from the torment of hell. But the bulk of these hadiths are questionable, if not deniable, at best. Besides, the concepts of the Book of

Record and the Scale contradict one of the major elements of the fundamentals of Islam; that is, the creed of the predestination. According to this Islamic creed, God has already preordained man's actions. That implies that man does not have the choice to determine his deeds. He lacks the free will to make his choices in life. Thus, how will God judge this man's deeds if He Himself has preordained his actions? This issue occupied the Islamic theological circles during the golden age of the Abbasid era. While the *Mu'tazilites*[32] had associated the concept of the free will of man and his ability to create his own deeds with the attribute of the justice of God, Islamic orthodoxy that endorsed the creed of predestination on the basis of the Qur'anic teaching, rejected this theology and encountered it.

This is an overview narrative of the Islamic Day of Judgment.

This narrative may instigate some questions in the mind of any inquisitive reader who seeks to discover the basic sources from which the idea of the Book of Records and the story of the Scale or the Balance had originated.

Several sources to which we can allude refer to the Book of Records. An early fictitious work entitled *The Testament of Abraham*, "written originally in Egypt some four hundred years before the Hegira and thence translated into Greek and Arabic,"[33] indicated that Abraham wished to see the wonders of heaven and the earth before his death. God granted that wish to him. As he ascended to the second heaven, he saw the Scale by which the angels weigh the deeds of humankind, then:

> Betwixt the two doors there stood a throne…and upon it was seated a wonderful Man…Before him stood a Table, like as of crystal, all covered with gold and linen. And

204

upon the Table a book lays, its length six fingers, and breadth ten fingers. On the right hand of it and on the left, stood two angels (with) paper(s) and ink and pen. In front of the Table sat a brilliant angel holding in his hand a Balance. On the left sat an angel, as if it were all of fire, merciless and stern, having in his hand a trumpet, in which was flaming fire, the touchstone of sinful men. The wonderful man seated on the throne was judging the souls and passing sentence upon them. And the angels on the right and on the left were writing down, the one on the right, righteous deed, and he on the left, sinful ones. And he that stood before the Table holding the Balance was weighing the souls, and the angel holding the fire, passing judgment upon them. And so Abraham asked Michael, the Captain of the Host, what is all that we see? He answered: That which thou seest, Holy Abraham, is the Judgment and Retribution.[34]

It was necessary to quote this long extract to show that the Islamic concept of the Book of Record and the Scale is not an original or even divine revelation but thoroughly borrowed from previous ancient fictitious literature. Moreover, this particular book informs us that every soul whose good deeds and bad deeds are balanced will be kept in place between paradise and hell, similar to the Qur'anic image that remarks, "between the two a veil and men upon the A 'raf" (Sura 7:46). Those who are placed upon the A 'raf (heights) are the ones whose fates have not yet been decided. These similarities did not happen accidentally but intentionally by the evidence of the predated material from which the Qur'an cited.

Another source that predated the Qur'an and mentioned the Scale is the *Book of the Dead*. Many copies of this book have been discovered in ancient Egyptian tombs. It was alleged that the god Thoth wrote this book. In that book, there is an illustration of the Judgment Hall of *Osiris*. A Scale is placed in the Hall and two deities stand, each on opposite side of the Scale. One of these deities placed a vessel containing a heart of a good man on one pan of the Scale to weigh it, while the other deity put an idol of *Ma* (the Truth) in the other pan. The great god was recording in heliography the fate of the deceased man: "Osiris the justified is alive; his balance is equal in the midst of the God's palace; the heart of Osiris the justified is to enter to its place. Let the great god, Lord of Hermopolis, say so."[35]

Some skeptic may wonder how Muhammad the illiterate, as Muslims claim became acquainted with these Egyptian, Persian and Christian tales and legends. In regard to the *Testimony of Abraham*, it was already translated into Arabic and most probably was narrated to him by his Egyptian concubine Mary who was a highly educated woman, one of his favorites who bore him a male child Abraham. It may also be that some of the former Christians who were converted to Islam narrated to him these apocryphal materials.

Another source from which Muhammad benefited was the Persian stories that were well known to the Arabs. In his book *Sirat al-Rasul* (The Life of the Prophet), Ibn Hisham indicates that the tales of Rustum, Isfandiyar, and other ancient kings of Persia were current in both al-Madina and Mecca. He relates a story about a man by the name of al-Nadr ibn al-Harith who came one day after Muhammad prayed and preached, warning the Qurishites 'of what in times passed had happened to the unbelieving nations.'[36] When Muhammad departed from the assembly, al-Nadr began to narrate to the people stories "of the great Rustum and of Isfandiyar and the kings of Persia." [37] Even he claimed that Muhammad had narrated to them stories from the past, which he "has written out, just as I have written mine out."[38] But this author believes that the greatest source from which Muhammad received much of his religious information about Zoroastrian eschatology must had been his knowledgeable companion Bilal al-Farisi (Bilal the Persian).

According to Zoroastrianism, the soul will journey to the place of judgment. Based on the person's deeds performed during his lifetime, the three angels Mitra, Sarosha, and Rashnu will judge the soul. The deeds will be balanced on a scale. If the bad deeds outweigh the good deeds, the soul will be bound to hell, but if the scale tips even slightly and the good deeds outweigh the bad deeds, the soul will soon be escorted to paradise.[39]

There are two other significant points that are worth mentioning in this respect. One of them is a verse found in the book of Daniel. It says: '*You have been weighted **on the scales** and found deficient*' (Daniel 5:27). That was God's verdict issued against king Belshazzar who defiled the vessels of God's Temple when he used them to drink wine with his nobles, wives, generals and concubines. Such an act was abominable in the eyes of God and thus, God condemned him. The other point is mentioned in the book of Revelation. It is remarked in chapter 20:12,

> And I saw the dead, the great and the small,
> standing before the throne, and books were
> opened; and another book was opened,
> which is the book of life; and the dead were

207

judged from the things which were written in the books according to their deeds.[40]

Here we have two types of record books. One of them is the book of life in which all the names of the believers are written as the only eligible people to be in the presence of God. That is, those who are redeemed by the blood of the Lamb. The other books are the records of non-believers; those who rejected the redemptive act of Christ on the cross and continued to be embroiled in sin. They were judged according to their own deeds that were recorded in these books.

Thus, the concepts of the Book of Records and the Balance had not originated with Islam. It could have been influenced by any of the aforementioned sources. But this author tends to believe that the Egyptian and Zoroastrian religions could be the original sources from which the Qur'an received a wealth of knowledge about the process of judgment without precluding some Christian fables of the time. According to the Islamic criteria, both these religions are not regarded as divine revelations.

As the biblical Day of Judgment is examined, there are distinctive characteristics that differentiate it from the Islamic Day of Reckoning:

1. The Bible refers to two resurrections. The first one is the resurrection of the dead believers and the rapture of the living Christians, which will take place upon the Second Coming of Christ.[41] The second resurrection occurs after the millennium.[42] This is the resurrection of the non-believers who will be judged according to their deeds. The term 'deed' here is associated with the belief in Jesus Christ and His redemptive act on the cross. The

208

non-believers are those who rejected the atoning power of the crucifixion and denied that Jesus is the Son of God. Their deeds, thus, echo their disbelief. There is no mentioning in the New Testament of the scale, for righteousness does not rely on human effort but reveals God's holiness as it is manifested in Jesus Christ. Unless righteousness meets God's standards, no one can enter into the presence of God. In Christianity, the believers are justified through the blood of Christ on the cross. The point here is very obvious. It is not our good deeds or our self-righteousness that make us qualified to go to heaven, but we only become acceptable to God through the merits of the Savior of the world. The good deeds will never wipe out the bad deeds as it is claimed in Islam (Sura 11:114).

2. In the Day of Judgment Christ, Who paid the price for our salvation, will be the Judge of the living and the dead. He is the One who gave His life to save us from the condemnation of God. Therefore, He is the One who has the right to judge His creatures. He paid the price and, thus, He owns us. In that day, from His *"presence earth and heaven fled away, and no place was found for them"* (Revelation 20:11). Only the redeemed will rejoice, waiting with great expectation, that joyful moment of glory.

3. Those whose names are listed in the book of life will not be subject to the judgment of God. But they will be classified according to the quality of their Christian life style. This is the moment of rewards in which God will award every Christian on the basis of his spiritual contribution, dedication and his service to the Lord. (1 Corinthians 3:11-15). All the believers are going to be saved but not all of them

will be rewarded: *"If any man's work is burned up, he will suffer loss; but he himself will be saved, yet so as through fire"* (1 Corinthians 3:15). The Bible states *"therefore there is now no condemnation for those who are in Jesus Christ* (Romans 8:1). Thus, salvation is not based on the merits of works but rewards are, for *"Behold I am coming quickly and My reward is with Me to render to every man according to what he has done* (Revelation 22:12).

4. Once the verdict is decreed, it becomes final and eternal. There is no appealing to a higher authority or intercession. The non-believers will be thrown into the Lake of Fire forever. None of them will harbor the slightest hope to be delivered from its torment. Their destiny is sealed for eternity. Besides, the Bible does not allude to a place similar to the *A'raf* (the high places), where, those whose good deeds and bad deeds weigh equally will be relocated as long as God wills, for He, by His mercy, will forgive them and allow them to enter Paradise. The Bible teaches that after death the gate of mercy and forgiveness is closed forever.

These distinctive characteristics distinguish the biblical Day of Judgment with certain traits that are lacking in other eschatological views. In the center stage, Christ sits on the throne, not as the loving savior of the world but as the righteous Judge whose wrath will fall on all those who reject His sacrificial act on the cross. His historical role has changed from a savior to a fearful judge. Actually, Jesus announced, before He ascended to heaven, *"All authority has been given to me in heaven and on earth"* (Matthew 28:18). As He sits on His throne, He will manifest all the glory, power, sovereignty, and unquestionable justice that He possessed before the foundation of the universe.

CHAPTER ELEVEN

Heaven, Paradise and Hell
السَّماء والفردوس، والجحيم

In Zoroastrianism, Judaism, Christianity and Islam, the Day of Judgment tends to deal with individuals. Every individual is inevitably accountable for his beliefs and deeds. Ahura Mazda, Jehovah, God in the person of Christ and Allah, will have the final unequivocal word that no one has the right to dispute. Zoroastrianism, Judaism and Islam employ the ethical criteria as standardized by their Revelations and Traditions. On the other hand, Christianity emphasizes the concept of redemption as the sole criteria by which God will judge people. The three former religions rely heavily on good works and the mercy of God as their means of salvation. Such ideology lacks the sense of certainty and the assurance that the eternal life is granted on the basis of the criteria of good deeds. When the ideology of ethics becomes the foundation of salvation, no one of the adherents of this ideology is sure that his pietistic deeds and virtuous motives are sufficient to please God or to obtain His favor and mercy. Abu Hurayra (one of Muhammad's companions) reported "Allah's Messenger...as saying: None amongst you would attain salvation purely because of his deeds. A person said: Allah's Messenger, even you also? Thereupon he said: Yes. Not even I, but that Allah wraps me in Mercy..."[1] To a certain extent, this *hadith* agrees with the biblical teachings but stop short of pointing to the redemptive act of Christ on the cross that grants everlasting eternity to all those who believe in Him as the savior of the world, and submit their life to Him. Thus, the way to Paradise in Islam depends, essentially, not on good deeds, but on God's mercy and His favors that He bestows on the believers. This ideology, in spite of its appeal, conflicts with the nature of God. God is just. His laws are just also and are not subject to change. God's mercy does not challenge and defy His justice or abrogate it. If His mercy overrules His justice, He will contradict His holiness and His nature. In this case, neither man's good deeds, nor the mercy of God – because where there is no redemption, there is not forgiveness and mercy - will be of any help to the sinner.

Once the ordeal of the Day of Judgment is over, the execution of God's verdict will begin. Every human being has to cross the *Sirat* (the bridge).[2] The term *Sirat* and its derivations are mentioned forty five times in the Qur'an.[3] In most cases they refer to the right path. Only in two places, Suras 36:66 and 37:23-24, they assumingly allude to the bridge:

> Did we will, we would have obliterated their eyes, then they would race to the path, but how would they see? (Arberry's translation).

وَلَوْ نَشَاءُ لَطَمَسْنَا عَلَى أَعْيُنِهِمْ فَاسْتَبَقُوا الصِّرَاطَ فَأَنَّى يُبْصِرُونَ.

> Assemble together the unjust, their wives and what they had worshipped, beside God, and guide them unto the path of hell. (No), stop them for they must be questioned (my translation).

احْشُرُوا الَّذِينَ ظَلَمُوا وَأَزْوَاجَهُمْ وَمَا كَانُوا يَعْبُدُونَ مِنْ دُونِ اللهِ فَاهْدُوهُمْ إِلَى صِرَاطِ الْجَحِيمِ وَقِفُوهُمْ إِنَّهُمْ مَسْئُولُونَ.

These two verses do not explicitly support the notion of the bridge, but the concept of a path. The idea that this Sirat is extended from one side to another over hell, and the inclination of Muslim commentators to interpret it as the bridge on which all mankind will walk over, either to the other side on their way to paradise, or they will fall down into the pit, suggest to them that this path is a sort of a bridge.

In his book *The Lives of Man,* Imam 'Abdullah Al-Haddad describes the bridge:

> It is related that it will be sharper than a sword, narrower than a hair, and that people will have to cross it with their deeds. Those whose faith is more perfect and who were quicker to obedience, will be light, and shall cross as [swiftly as] lighting [Others will be] like the wind, others like birds, others like the best of horses, others like riders, others like strong men burden by their deeds, others will go on hands and knees, some will be scorched by the Fire, and others will tumble into it.[4]

Al-Ghazali reiterates the same opinion as he attempts to warn humanity of the consequences of their sinful life:

> Mankind, after the terrors ... shall be driven to the Traverse, which is a bridge stretched over the gulf of Hell, sharper than a sword and thinner than a hair.[5]

This description of the Islamic Sirat, it seems, is a parallel to the Zoroastrian Chinvat, which is a wide easy

213

path for the pious that will lead him into heaven.[6] But for the wicked whose bad deeds outweigh their good deeds they will encounter a different experience. The bridge will "turn up on its edge and become as hard to walk on as the edge of a sword...and (the wicked) eventually falls off the bridge and into hell."[7]

The term *Sirat* "is not an original Arabic word and Muslim scholars such as as-Suyuti concluded that it was of Greek origin ... being derived from the Latin strata."[8] As a doctrine, it has undoubtedly derived its meaning as a bridge from the Persian *Chinvat*, and popular Islamic tradition relied on the Zoroastrian eschatology in their doctrine of the *Sirat*.[9]

The *Sirat* shall be stretched between the two opposite edges of the Inferno. This picture is similar to the image mentioned in the *Avesta* where the bridge extends from "the *Mount Alburz* to *Chakat Daitith*, reaching over the hole of hell."[10] Such parallelisms are irrefutable proofs of the impact of Zoroastrianism on Islamic eschatology.

Islamic sources indicate that the first to cross the Traverse with his faithful is Muhammad. "That Day none shall speak save the Prophets, whose prayers shall be, 'O God, deliver! O Lord God, deliver!'"[11] Such supplication reflects the fear that will seize the hearts of humanity, even the prophets, who are afraid that their feet may slip from the Traverse into the Inferno. It is obvious that no one is really sure that he will be able to cross the bridge safely. It is a moment dreaded even by the emissaries of God. As the faithful attempt to cross the *Sirat,* they will hear the shrieks of woe from the perils of hell sounding from the depth of the inferno out of the mouths of the cursed ones "who have already slipped from the Traverse."[12] These shrieks, the sight of the fire and the hooks that resembles the thorns of

214

Sa'dan bush* whose size is so large that it is only known to God,[13] create fear and disequilibrium which may lead the condemned to loose their balance and slip into hell.

Once the faithful cross the Bridge safely, they will gather together at the *Hawd*, the Pool of the prophet. There is a dispute among Muslim scholars whether this assembly around the Pool "will be after the Bridge and before entering the Garden or before the Balance and the Bridge."[14] Some *hadiths* denote that the Pool will be located before the Bridge and the Balance since some of Muhammad's acquaintances will be driven away from the Pool and taken to the left side. When Muhammad objected to that, he was told that after his death they deviated from the true teaching of Islam and "you do not know what they did after you".[15] Such *hadiths* suggest that the Pool will be located in the area where the Judgment will take place; otherwise how can these 'innovators' be able to cross the Bridge without slipping into the Inferno if they were not among the people of Paradise? But other traditions indicate that the Pool must be on the other side of the *Sirat*. It is indeed not an ordinary Pool because those who cross the Traverse successfully "will drink from it and their thirst will vanish."[16] Its water flows from the Garden's spring *al-Kawthar* through two channels: "Its water will be whiter than milk, more fragrant than musk, and sweeter than honey. Its breadth will be one month journey, its length likewise, and around it will be pitchers [as numerous] as the stars."[17] Apparently, such descriptions hint that the Pool ought to be located on the other side of the Bridge because during the aforementioned interval of fifty thousand years, waiting for the moment of reckoning, people were suffering from dehydration and they could not get a gulp of water. But as it is the case with the Islamic eschatology, there is lack of time sequence or systemized chronological order that sometimes creates an arbitrary chain of events that leave the reader totally confused.

The Pool, however, will be the assembly place for the fortunate faithful, who are now destined to enter and enjoy the bliss of the Garden. Some traditions remark that Muhammad made an appointment with one of his companions by the name of Anas bin Malik to meet with him either at the *Sirat* or beside the Balance or around the Pool.[18] The Pool is the last station before the gates of Paradise are opened to receive the righteous. But it seems that there will be another long interval before the blessed are allowed to enter into Paradise.

Contrary to the teaching of the Qur'an, popular Islamic traditions make many references to the process of intercession. This process will start at the time of the Day of Judgment as people suffer from the agony of stress, dehydration and the unbearable heat of the sun. Muhammad will be the only prophet among all the prophets who will be eligible to intercede with God and plead with Him to shorten this interval and descend to judge the people. But the intercession does not end here. At the Pool, two types of intercession will take place. One is for the people of the Garden who are waiting outside the gates of Paradise. Here the same story is repeated and Muhammad becomes the only eligible prophet to intercede with God for the people to enter into the Garden. God will accept Muhammad's intercession and give His permission for the faithful to enter the Garden. The Second type of intercession is the intercession of the angels, prophets, the martyrs, the faithful and even the Qur'an, on behalf of those who are condemned to hell or already in hell, who have an atom of faith in their heart, to be delivered from the fire. All the condemned will be delivered from hell by the abundant mercy of God. So as not to be outmatched, God

216

will say, 'I remained, (or it is My turn now) and I am the most merciful of all'. Then He stretches His hand down to hell and brings out formidable number of people from hell that no one can count but God. They look like burned wood, but God will plant them beside the river of life and they will be known as the free slaves of the Merciful.[19] Only the polytheists will be eternally consigned to hell.

As both the people of the Garden and the people of Hell are bound for their final and eternal abode, Death will be brought to a place between the Garden and hell where it will be slaughtered. This act will seal the destiny of both groups forever. The people of Paradise will be greatly rejoicing, whereas the people of Fire become more sorrowful.[20] Both groups will realize that there will be no end for their bliss or their suffering.

Before the nature of the Islamic Garden is examined, it is necessary here to discuss five significant points pertaining to our study. Unlike Islam, Christianity does not entertain the concept of the *Sirat* or the Bridge, nor accommodates for the notion of the *Hawd* or the Pool. These two images are lacking in the Christian eschatology. In the Day of Judgment, only the disbelievers will be judged, for Jesus Christ has already received those whose names are recorded in the Book of life before the second resurrection. In reality, they will join Jesus as He sits on His throne to decree his final verdict on all those who rejected Him as their personal savior. Thus, there is no *Sirat* or Bridge to cross and no Pool at which to meet. A third point of interest is the idea of intercession. Though the Qur'an does not endorse this precept, Islamic Tradition attributes a number of *hadiths* to Muhammad in which he asserts that he will be the first to intercede for the sake of his *ummat*. Actually, he claims that God has favored him from among all the prophets, to intercede three times for

217

his *ummat.* This bliss of intercession is not limited to the prophets, but was open to the angels, the saints, the martyrs, and the believers. These traditions intend to manifest that God's mercy is greater than His wrath. In this case, the mercy of God annuls His justice and the laws of God become dysfunctional or inapplicable. In Christianity, Christ is the only intercessor, but in the Day of Judgment His role as intercessor will be suspended, since He will assume the role of the judge of all humanity. It is too late for the people to hope for the mercy of God.

The concept of the river of life is not foreign to biblical language. It is the belief of this author that this phrase is borrowed from the Christian scripture. In Revelation 22:1, it is stated: *Then he showed me a river of the water of life as crystal, coming from the throne of God and of the Lamb.*[21] Most probably, this verse is the source of the Islamic river of water that will flow from beneath God's throne to revive the dead and bring them back to life in the Day of Resurrection. It could also be the river of life in which 'the freed slave of God' who will be delivered from the Inferno by His mercy, will bath.

Another biblical concept incorporated into the Islamic eschatology is the slaughtering of death. Revelation 20:14 remarks: *Then death and Hades were thrown into the lake of fire.* This is a clear indication that death will be abolished and annihilated. 1 Corinthians 15:26 clarifies this truth as it denotes: *The last enemy that will be abolished is death.* By abolishing or slaughtering death, there will no longer be any mourning, or crying, or pain for *"there will no longer be any death* (Revelation 21:4). These biblical quotations are irrefutable proofs that Christian eschatological teaching in more than one respect had left their mark on Islamic traditions.[22]

It is also noteworthy at this point to assert that the concept of heaven in Islam does not conform to the biblical eternal abode of felicity. It seems that there is a distinctive difference between what is called Heaven and what is regarded as Gardens. Heaven, symbolically, is where God and His angels are located; whereas the Gardens are the eternal haven of the faithful. It does not seem that the Qur'an is concerned to furnish enough specifics about Heaven. It is true that the Qur'an mentions the throne of God, the angels and even the prototype of the Qur'an, but it hardly provides detailed description of Heaven. Contrary to that, the Qur'an is interested in delineating a vivid picture of the Garden. It is the lost abode of Adam and Eve. Humankind is supposed to attempt "through moral action to win their original home…, which then onward would be their eternal home (S. 25:15)."[23] This is compatible with Muhammad's strategy to motivate the believers to obey God and His messenger, and to entice the non-believers to convert to Islam. They will become the righteous who will be the rightful heirs of Adam and Eve.[24]

The term Garden جنّة, as an abode of felicity is mentioned 62 times in the Qur'an, as dual gardens جنّتان three times, and as Gardens in the plural جنّات 56 times.[25] Also the term Paradise فردوس is stated twice (Sura 18:107 and 23:11). In some cases it is called Garden of Felicity (13 times), or Garden of Eden (11 times), or Garden of Immortality (one time). "Heavens are spread out over these gardens, but are separated from them by the kingdom (*malakut*) and the power (*jabaruut*).[26] The Qur'an mentions seven heavens (Suras 2:25; 17:44; 23:86; 41:12; 65:12; 67:3 and 71:15). Islamic traditions indicate that these seven heavens are:" (1) That which is of pure virgin silver and which is Adam's residence; (2) of pure gold, which is John the Baptist's and Jesus'; (3) of pearls, which is Joseph's; (4) of white gold which is Enoch's; (5) of silver, which is

Aaron's; (6) of ruby and garnet, which is Moses'; (7) which is Abraham's."[27] Obviously, this view is congruent with the seven spheres of Ptolemy, which are the spheres of Moon, Mercury, Venus, Sun, Mars Jupiter, and Saturn.[28] This view corresponds to the seven levels of hell.[29]

The Garden is as wide as that of heavens and earth (3:133; 57:21). There are four rivers flowing under the garden (2:25; 3:15, 136, 195, 198; 5:85; 4:15 etc...).[30] There are fountains and springs (76:6, 18). Some of these paradisiacal "springs have specific names: one is called *Kawthar* (108:1) implying abundance; another is called *Salsabil* (76:18); a third is called *Tasmin* (83:27)."[31] This fresh water and rivers bring forth countless fruit trees; under their deep shades recline the faithful (4:57; 13:35; 55:68; 56:28-32). This magnificent garden is an excellent recompense for those who strive for righteousness (3:136). Everyone (76:13) enjoys the temperate climate. There is neither excessive heat nor excessive cold (76:13). For those who are honored and brought near to God, gilded couches have been prepared, covered with costly cushions and expensive rugs (76:13; 88:15-16); they and their wives shall be in shades, reclining on raised couches (36:56). Pious Muslims wear heavy brocades and shining clothes made of green fine silk (18:31; 22:23; 35:33; 44:53; 76:12, 21). They are adorned with bracelets of silver, gold and precious pearls (76:21; 22:23; 35:33). The believers will drink from cups filled with wine mixed with ginger (76:17), or wine pure and holy (76:21) served by immortally youthful lads (52:24; 56:17-19; 76:19).[32] The Garden has guarded gates at each of its entrance (39:73) so that no one but the worthy can enter. There are eight gates among them: the Gate of Prayer, the Gate of Fasting, the Gate of Charity and the Gate of *Jihad*.[33] This echoes what is mentioned in the book of Revelation 21:12 about the New Jerusalem: "*It had a great and high wall, with twelve gates, and at the gates twelve angels."* Only the *"Blessed... have the right to the tree of life and may enter by the gates into the city"* (22:14).

In all the levels of the Garden there will be a haven of magnificent mansions (9:72; 35:35) to accommodate the believers and their families. The notion of the reunion of the believers with their families preceded the Islamic concept by more than one century. In some of his literary works, Saint Augustine of Hippo "asserts that in heaven saved souls will experience a great reunion with loved ones."[34] Most probably, the image of the mansion is taken from the saying of Jesus in John 14:2, *"In my Father's house are many dwelling places; If it were not so, I would have told you; for I go to prepare a place for you."*

The Garden is full of fruits such as dates and pomegranates; also, plenty of food and drinks will be available to the blessed ones. Meat (52:22), wine (76:5, 21; 83:25), and unspoiled milk and honey (47:15) are offered on dishes and cups of gold (43:71), or on silver and crystal dishes. This picture of heavenly banquets was not foreign to the Christian community of the sixth century. An Egyptian monk by the name of Cosmas Indicopleustes wrote a treatise on Christian eschatology in which he speculated that after the Day of Judgment, "virtuous spirits will be escorted into paradise to enjoy an eternal banquet hosted by God. This never ending feast will feature an abundance fruit, sweet waters, meats, and other harvests of 'earth's bounty.'"[35] Such striking similarities between Cosmas' imaginary description of the eternal banquet and the Islamic picture of the heavenly feast, implies that the Qur'an has relied heavily on such material in its paradisiacal images.

The Qur'an asserts that Paradise is the abode of bliss and happiness (36:55; 69:21-22; 88:8-10), everlasting life (15:48; 38: 50) in which all desires are granted and fulfilled (16:31; 41:31; 43: 71). It is a place that is free from fear, sorrow and grief (7:43, 49), weariness, vanity and deception (15:48; 35:35; 78:35), and the faithful relax and receive good rewards (89:27; 55:60). There is almost an identical description of the Islamic Paradise in the Yashts (9.9-10, 15.16-17, 17.29-30, 1932-33) as "a realm without heat or cold, snow or rain, without cares or suffering, tears or pain; a realm without dakness, sickness, old age, or death; a realm where labor and want are equally unknown."[36]

One of the interesting features of the Islamic Paradise is that its inhabitants are able to communicate with the inhabitants of Inferno (7:44). This concept is not new. In biblical context, as Jesus was relating the story of Lazarus and the rich man (Luke 16:20-31), he said, *"In Hades he* (the rich man) *lifted up his eyes, being in torment, and saw Abraham far away and Lazarus in his bosom. And he cried out and said, 'Father Abraham have mercy on me, and send Lazarus so that he may dip the tip of his finger in water and cool off my tongue, for I am in agony in this flame.' But Abraham said, 'Child, remember that during your life you received your good things, and likewise Lazarus bad things; but now he is comforted here, and you are in agony.'*

The dialogue between Abraham and the rich man ends when he realizes that his destiny is final and there is no hope for him to be delivered from Hades. This incident illustrates that there is conscious existence after death. The rest of the episode teaches also that there is no second chance after death. In addition, it shows that many of the

Islamic images and precepts are borrowed from non-Islamic religious literature especially Christianity.

In the Islamic Paradise, there is a feature that does not exist in Christianity or Judaism, though it certainly finds its roots in Zoroastrianism. That is the concept of the paradisiacal *Huris*. In the context of heavenly pleasures and rewards, there are four places in the Qur'an where the *Huris* are mentioned. Three of them are found in Suras revealed in Mecca and one in Madina:

> Even so; and we shall espouse them to wide-eyed houris (Sura 44:54; Arberry)
>
> كَذَلِكَ وَزَوَّجْنَاهُمْ بِحُورٍ عِينٍ.

> Reclining upon couches ranged in rows; and we shall espouse them to wide-eyed houris (Sura 52:20; Arberry).
>
> مُتَّكِئِينَ عَلَى سُرَرٍ مَصْفُوفَةٍ وَزَوَّجْنَاهُمْ بِحُورٍ عِينٍ.

> And wide-eyed houris like well guarded pearls (Sura 56:22-23; my translation).
>
> وَحُورٌ عِينٌ كَأَمْثَالِ اللُّؤْلُوءِ المَكْنُونِ.

> Houris confined to pavilions (Sura 55:72).
>
> حُورٌ مَقْصُورَاتٌ فِي الخِيَامِ.

Allah creates these heavenly *huris* as rewards for the faithful. They are perpetually young, virgin, and very beautiful, secluded in tents and shall never be vexed. They are eternal and never pass away.[37] They will be awarded as purified wives 'of menstruation, excrement, mucus, semen and childbearing.'[38] Ordinary Muslims will be given forty *huris*, but the martyrs who died for the cause of Allah will be recompensed with seventy -two of these heavenly *huris*. When Muhammad was asked if the people of heaven would

223

enjoy carnal relation, he replied, 'Every man therein shall be given in a single day the capacity of seventy of you.'[39] In another *hadith* ascribed to Muhammad he said,

> A single man in Heaven shall wed five hundred *houris*, four thousand virgins, and eight thousand deflowered women, and shall embrace each one of them for a period equal to his lifetime in the world.[40]

In his book *The Qur'an: The Scripture of Islam*, John Gilgrist suggests that the Arabic *huwr*, has probably its "origins in the Pahlavi word *hurust* which means 'beautiful' and is used in Pahlavi books to describe the beautiful damsels of Paradise (*Arda Viraf,* 4. 18)." He also adds, "In particular work the word is used to describe a graceful maiden of heaven, white-armed, strong with a striking face and well formed breasts (*Hadost Nask,* 2.23)."[41] Obviously, Zoroastrianism has greatly contributed to the images of the Islamic Paradise, or as Gilchrist say, "It is clear that it (Qur'an) ...has many origins in the legends of Zoroastrianism."[42]

It is obvious that the vivid imaginations of the narrators who related this tradition have invented these colorful sensual descriptions, to gratify the yearning of their audience. On the other hand, if it is true that such tradition originated from Muhammad, it was when he intended to motivate the Arabs to embrace Islam and the Muslims to fight for the cause of Allah unto death. In this case, martyrdom becomes the desire of a Muslim in order to enjoy the pleasures that are awaiting him in Paradise. Al-Ghazali cites a *hadith* ascribed to Muhammad addressed to his companions:

224

Ho! Is there anyone that will roll up his sleeves for heaven? Truly, Heaven is without rival. By the Lord of the Ka'ba, it is a light which sparkles, and sweet basil which waves, and a *lofty palace*, and a flowing river, and abundant ripe fruit, and a beautiful comely wife, in happiness and ease in an abode everlasting. It is a joy in a lofty residence, splendid and secure. And they said, 'We are the ones who will roll up their sleeves for it, O Emissary of God!' And he said, 'Say, "if God (Exalted is He!) so wills".' Then he made mention of the Holy War (*Jihad*), and recommended it.[43]

In another *hadith* attributed to Muhammad, he said,

"The lowliest of Heaven's people shall have eighty thousand servants and seventy-two wives..."[44]

These traditions, if authentic, are clear evidence that Muhammad had skillfully employed the allurement of Paradise to entice the believers to sacrifice their lives in order to enjoy the pleasures of Paradise. Thus, martyrdom in Islam is not only a matter of faith, but the sensual rewards prompt them to die for the cause of Allah. What a Muslim is expecting in the *Janna* motivates him to seek martyrdom in the cause of Allah. The Islamic Paradise is the abode of perpetual voluptuousness that gratifies man's desires, which are unlawful to him while he is alive on earth. Some Muslims have attempted to allegorize these physical descriptions of Paradise on the basis of a tradition which remarks, "And in Heaven there is that which no eye has seen, no ear heard, and which has never occurred to mortal mind."[45] But the majority of Muslims are inclined towards a literal interpretation of these paradisiacal images.

Muslims, however, anticipate to be favored by the vision of the Divine Countenance.This is called the Beatific Vision. It was related that as Muhammad was watching the moon with his companions, he said, "You shall behold your Lord just as you behold this moon. You shall not be obstructed from the vision of Him..."[46] This Beatific Vision is not ever-present in Islam but an occasional bliss from the Lord upon the people of Paradise. According to some traditions God and His angels will 'visit' the faithful in paradise on Fridays to bestow on them more blessings. Heaven or paradise, from the point of view of man, is the place where physical reality joins metaphy-sical reality.[47]

The Biblical Heaven

The Biblical heaven testifies to the spiritual nature of the final abode that God has prepared for the redeemed. There are many fundamental differences between the Islamic Paradise and the Christian heaven. After the resurrection of Jesus Christ and His ascension to heaven, the words paradise and heaven are used interchangeably.

In his book *Heaven Better by Far,* J. Oswald Sanders tries to summarize a few of the blessings and benefits of this eternal abode, among them: eternal life in the presence of God, holy life, unequal joy, spiritual prosperity, immunity from temptations from the world, the flesh and the devil, unlimited knowledge, freedom of the limitation of the body, enriched life, reunion with loved ones and the development of new everlasting relationships that will make heaven a delightful place of holy fellowship, heavenly music that surpasses the finest earthly performance, and complete satisfaction for all the holy longings and spiritual yearning.[48]

If these are some of the blessings and benefits that will be bestowed on the redeemed, then what is the description of the biblical heaven? The Bible teaches that the kingdom of God starts in the hearts of the believers on earth as soon as they accept Jesus as their redeemer and savior.[49] They will be filled with the power of the Holy Spirit and they sense the presence of the Lord. But this is a partial spiritual state that the believer experiences. The earthly body lacks the supernatural faculties to grasp the fullness and the dimensions of the kingdom of God, even in its allegorical presentation. When the apostle Paul was caught up to the third heaven, he joyfully declared, "(I) *heard inexpressible words, which a man is not permitted to speak*" (2 Corinthians 12:4). God has prepared for those who love Him "*Things which eye has not seen and ear has not heard and which have not entered the heart of man*" (1Corinthians 2:4). But all this will change as soon the believers receive the heavenly bodies after the resurrection or the rapture. These heavenly bodies that are free from the limitations of the earthly body will possess the spiritual faculties to comprehend fully the meaning of the kingdom of God and enjoy its blessings. This heavenly body is a "recognizable body, having identity that had been laid to rest."[50] Retaining the same human identity without its limitations and fragility explains how the redeemed who receive resurrected bodies, will recognize their righteous relatives and friends.[51]

But what are the characteristics of the Biblical heaven? The main source for examining the distinctive features of heaven is the Bible itself. Yet, it is very important to keep in mind that Biblical scholars may differ in interpreting these descriptions. Some may lean towards a literal explanation, while others may embrace an allegorical interpretation, but both schools agree that it is a place of uttermost happiness and holiness where God is ever-present.

Chapter 20 of the book of Revelation confirms the destiny of Satan. He is thrown into the lake of fire forever. That will be the disastrous end of the archenemy of God and man. At the same time, it ushers the beginning of the new world. Chapters 21 and 22 of Revelation portray "a breathtaking picture of what heaven will be like."[52] In his divine vision, the Apostle John saw a new heaven and a new earth (Revelation 21:1). This new universe will replace the first heaven and the first earth that passed away. These events entails a universal change in which the new order will be reshaped to accommodate a different type of life void of sorrow, anguish, death and misery. Some signifycant points need to be clarified here:

- The phrase "pass away" does not mean that the entire old universe will be eradicated. It should be causiously interpreted as "a change or rearrangement of order."[53]
- The rearrangement of the old order of the universe is to be incurred by means of fire. 2 Peter 3:10-12 dramatically describes the process by which the purging will take place. The reason for this purification is the removal of all traces of evil that blemished the old order.[54]
- The righteous will be protected from this supernatural process by divine intervention and the new heaven and the new earth will become the perfect abode for the redeemed.
- The earth will undergo a drastic change. One of the distinctive features is the elimination of the sea (Rev.21:1). The entire earth will become the new

Garden of Eden, as it used to be before it was defiled by the sin of man. All barriers will disappear and there will be one holy Kingdom of God.

- The restoration of the purity of the earth and the removal of the curse imposed on it because of man's sin will provide an atmosphere of delight and productivity and a magnificent society.
- Revelation 21:2 talks about the Holy City, the new adorned Jerusalem that will descend down from heaven. This city will be the seat of the eternal Kingdom of God. The literal description of this city must be interpreted metaphorically. The usage of the physical description is an acknowledgement of the failure of the human language to manifest the splendor and the grandeur of the greatness and the beauty of this city. Or, as Leon Morris says, "He (John) is describing a complete transformation of all things, but he uses the language of heaven and earth for he has no other language."[55] This is the city whose architect and builder is God, Who prepared it for the redeemed (Hebrews 11:10, 16).
- The residents of the new city will consist of the triune God, "with the visible manifestation in the Lord Jesus Christ,"[56] the angels, the church, Old Testament saints, the redeemed, and the tribulation martyrs and saints. The city will be filled with the glory of God (Revelation 21:11).
- The presence of God will dwell among man. This is the beatific vision of God, which is the ultimate joyful bliss the Christians experience as they see the face of God in Jesus Christ. The holiness of God will permeate the city. Sensual attraction, sex and other human activities that reflect the lust of the flesh, will not have place in the eternal kingdom of God (Matthew 22:30).[57]

- There will be no temple in it *"for the Lord God almighty and the Lamb are its temple."* (Rev. 21:22) It also will not need a sun or a moon to shine on it, *"for the glory of God has illuminated it, and its lamp is the Lamb."* (Rev. 21:23)

- It will be an open city because its gate will never be closed, for there will be no night there (21:25). People of all races will be like one nation under the sovereignty of God and the Lamb. Peace, security, prosperity and happiness will fill the new transformed world. The throne of God and the Lamb will be in the midst of the city.

- The redeemed will serve their savior and will be delighted in seeing His loving face, *"and His name will be on their foreheads"* (22:4). This is the holy mark of ownership and belonging, and the zenith of spiritual fulfillment and joy. The believers will be serving their Lord with worship and praises, for He is only worthy of all glory. Thus, "heaven will be a worshiping community"[58] in which the redeemed will express their adoration, love and gratitude, to the triune God who, through the provision of the plan of salvation, has saved them from the Lake of Fire.

Hell جَهَنَّم In Islam

As the Islamic heaven or paradise is made of seven levels, hell, likewise, consists of seven fixed regions. According to the speculations of Muslim commentators, each level will be the habitation of a particular group of people. The first region is called *Jahannam*, the purgatorial hell that all Muslims will pass through. Sura 19:72 indicates that,

Not one of you there is, but he shall go down to it (hell), for thy Lord is a thing decreed, determined (Arberry).

وَإِنْ مِنْكُمْ إِلاَّ وَارِدُهَا كَانَ عَلَى رَبِّكَ حَتْمًا مَقْضِيًّا.

The term *Jahannam* is listed seventy-seven times in the Qur'an.[59]

The second level or region is called *Laza* (لظى). It is mentioned only once in Sura 70:15-18

Nay, it is a furnace (*Laza*) snatching away the scalp, calling him who drew back and turned away, who amassed and horded

كَلاَّ، إِنَّهَا لَظَى، نَزَّاعَةً لِلشَّوَى، تَدْعُوا مَنْ أَدْبَرَ وَتَوَلَّى.

This level will be the abode of Christians.

The third level is *Al-Hutama* (Crusher). It is repeated twice in Sura 104:4-7,

Nay! He is surely thrown into the Crusher; and what do you know what is the Crusher? It is Allah's blazing fire that is roaring over the hearts (my translation).

كَلاَّ لَيُنْبَذَنَّ فِي الْحُطَمَةِ، وَمَا أَدْرَاكَ مَا الْحُطَمَةُ؟ نَارُ اللهِ الْمُوقَدَةُ الَّتِي تَطَّلِعُ عَلَى الأَفْئِدَةِ.

This place of an intense fire is designated for the Jews who resisted Muhammad's claim of prophethood.

The fourth level is called *Al-Sa'ir* (Blaze). Sura 4:10 reiterates, [60]

Those who devour the property of orphans
unjustly, devour Fire in their bellies, and
shall assuredly roast in a Blaze (Arberry).

إِنَّ الَّذِينَ يَأْكُلُونَ أَمْوَالَ الْيَتَامَى ظُلْمًا إِنَّمَا يَأْكُلُونَ فِي
بُطُونِهِمْ نَارًا وَسَيَصْلَوْنَ سَعِيرًا.

The *Sa'ir* is the place prepared for the Sabeans.[61]

The fifth place is called *Saqar* (scorching hell). Saqar is
repeated in the Qur'an four times; three of them in Sura
74.[62] It is the region where the Magis or Zoroastrians will
endure the scorching fire. Sura 54:48 remarks: "The day
when they are dragged on their faces into the fire: 'Taste
now the touch of Sakar'

يَوْمَ يُسْحَبُونَ فِي النَّارِ عَلَى وُجُوهِهِمْ، ذُوقُوا مَسَّ سَقَر .

The sixth level is *Al-Jahim* (inferno) where the
idolaters who associated other gods with God, will spend
their eternity. *Al- shirk* (polytheism) is one of the grave sins
in Islam. *Al-Jahim* is mentioned 26 times in the Qur'an. It
calls its inhabitants the people of the inferno أَصْحَابُ الْجَحِيم.

The last region is the *Hawiya* (the bottomless pit or
Hades), whose tenants are the hypocrites. Muhammad had
suffered the most from these people. It is mentioned only
once in the Qur'an in Sura 101:9,

But he whose deeds are found light, his
Mother (final place) is a bottomless pit...It
is a fiercely blazing fire.

وَأَمَّا مَنْ خَفَّتْ مَوَازِينُهُ فَأُمُّهُ هَاوِيَةٌ...نَارٌ حَامِيَةٌ.

The Qur'anic teaching does not support the claims
of Muslim expositors, who assigned each region to a

specific party. It is the idea of correlation with the seven realms of heaven and the vivid fancy of the commentators that incited them to develop this structure with its hellish tenants. Thus, the Qur'an does not furnish a detailed description for each realm but delineates a general picture for hell as a whole and the different sorts of retribution the non-believers will endure.

The topography of hell in the Qur'an reveals the existence of a dreadful place. The inhabitants of hell are the evildoers who will be covered with fire over and beneath (39:16), and hell is enclosed with sparks as large as castles (77:32). Al-Ghazali denotes that "the evil-doers are whelmed in shadows pierced by sheets of flame, as a flaming blaze overspreads and they hear it sighing and gurgling from the violence of its wrath and fury."[63] The unbelievers and stones will be its permanent fuel (2:24) and it will never be gratified (50:30). Hell has seven gates, "for each of those gates is a (special) class of sinners assigned" (15:44). The fire of hell will torment the sinners and will perpetually roast their skins (2:10; 3:178). Torturers and relentless angels, who do not flinch from executing God's command (66:6), and do not accept any intercession (40:49-50) guard hell. They will fetter the newly arrived condemned with shackles around their necks, then will drag them along by chains into the fitted fluid and will throw them "in the fire...(to) be burned" (40:71-72). Many are fettered together (25:34); others will be dressed with garments of fire, and over their heads boiling water will be poured out (22:19). Their food is made of filth (69:36), thorny bushes (88:6) and the leaves of the *zaqqume tree* that is planted in the deepest bottom of hellfire; whose shoots of fruit-stalks are the devils' heads (37:62-68). When they cry out of thirst, they will be given water of pus to drink (14:16-17).

Abu Hamid al-Ghazali declares that the torment will be so excruciating that the condemned will cry from every side, direction and place calling upon Malik, the chief guardian of Hell,

> O Malik! The threat has come true for us! O Malik! We are weighted down with iron! O Malik! Our skins have become roasted! O Malik! Release us from here, for we shall not return [to our former sins]! But the Guardians of Hell shall say, 'What folly! There is no place of safety, and for you there shall be no escape from the abode of degradation! *Fall back therein, and speak not*' (23:108).[64]

Al-Ghazali also adds,

> Each time they shriek out in grief and lamentation scalding water is poured over their heads, '*melting away their skin and what is in their bellies. There are iron rods for them*' (22:20-21)...'*As often as their skins are consumed We shall exchange them for fresh skins*' (4:56).[65]

It seems that some images of the Islamic hell echo Zoroastrian description of its inferno. Humans will be punished in hell by demons to which they subjugated their will in life. These demons will attack them from the front except the backbiter and the slanderers. These will be attacked from behind. In general, the punishment is congruent with each person's grave sin.[66] Souls in hell will be forced to eat brimstone, lizards, snakes' poison and venom, scorpions and other noxious creatures; blood and filth, bodily refuse and excrement, impurity and menstrual discharge, dust and human flesh, and dirt and ash.[67] The fires of hell will burn and never consume.[68]

Once we examine the Islamic Tradition, we encounter a number of *hadiths* appertain to chastisement of Hell. At the same time, there is lack of certainty about the authenticity of most of them. Most narrators and commentators try to magnify the description of Hell to urge Muslims to live a moral life according to the laws of Islam. Such exaggeration was a calculated design to impact the society that deviated from the teaching of Islam and indulged in the sensuous pleasures of life. In a *hadith* attributed to Muhammad, he said, "The least tormented of Hell's denizens shall, on the Day of Arising, wear sandals of fire, the heat of which will cause his brains to boil."[69]

Both the people of hell and the people of Paradise will live immortally, for death will be no more. In one of the *hadiths,* it is indicated that Muhammad remarked, "On the Day of Arising, death shall be brought in the form of a white ram, which is then slaughtered between Heaven and Hell. And it shall be announced, 'O people of Heaven, eternity, and no death!' and 'O people of Hell, eternity, and no death!'"[70]

Who will be the occupants of the Islamic hell? They are the infidels (Suras 8:36; 9:49, 68, 73; 17:8; 18:100,102,106; 29:54, 68; 35:36; 39:32, 71; 50:24; 67:6; 98:6), the polytheists (17:39; 21:29, 98), the unbelieving in the existence of hell and resurrection (55:43), those who rejected the Allah of Muhammad and his prophethood, including Christians and Jews (9:63; 72:23: 85:10), the apostates, the despisers, the proud (16:27; 39:59; 40:60, 70; 72:23), the hypocrites (9:69, 73), the deceivers (8:36, 37), the criminals and blasphemers (19:86; 20:74; 43:74; 55:43-44). There is also in hell Muslims who killed unjustly and intentionally, other Muslims (4:93), the unfaithful in their tithing (72:14-15), the non-Muslim jinns (11:119; 19:68; 32:13),[71] and all those who failed to live according to the laws of Islam. One interesting point is a *hadith* attributed to Muhammad that hints that most of the occupants of Hell are women. This tradition is in full contrast to the above discussion.

Hell in Christianity

Christianity asserts that those who are condemned to go to hell are indeed unable to escape the everlasting judgment of God. Through the course of church history, different interpretations are hotly debated among theologians and eschatological schools of thought. Some believed in the concept of restoration; that is, "someday the doors of hell will be opened and all or some of its occupants will be received into heaven."[72] This concept echoes the Islamic view of the *Hadith* that at the end of time God will unfold His mercy and, through the intercessions of the angels, prophets and other pious Muslims, most residents of hell will be released, except the polytheists. Then there are those who teach the theory of annihilation. This theory denotes that the wicked will be annihilated immediately after their deaths or will first be severely punished in hell, then, will be annihilated.[73] These two theories are biblically baseless. The Scriptures teach of an everlasting punishment in *Gehenna* for all who sinned against God.

The term *Gehenna* is originally a Greek word. The Hebrew word is *Gehinnom,* which means 'valley of Hinnom, a geographical place located outside Jerusalem. It is also called *Jahannam* in Arabic. In Judaic, Christian and Islamic religious language, this term has become a symbol of the final place of retribution. Jesus and the apostles used this meaning in the New Testament.

The Bible clearly talks about hell as the dwelling place of the wicked, who are condemned to be separated from the presence of God. There is no mention of regions or levels in the Christian hell. The evildoers will be cast into the Inferno where the fire is never quenched and its worms never die (Mark 9:47-48). It is a fiery hell (Matthew 5:22), a furnace of blazing fire, weeping and gnashing of teeth (Matthew 13:40-50), eternal fire that is prepared for the wicked, the devil and his angels (Matthew 25:41, 46), an outer darkness where its inhabitants endure all types of suffering (Matthew 25:41) and eternal destruction, away from the presence of the Lord and the glory of His power (2Thessalonians 1:9). It is an abyss (Revelation 20:3), a fire and brimstone "And the smoke of their (the wicked) torment goes forever and ever; they will have no rest all day and night...(Revelation 14:10-11)," a Lake of fire where the Beast, the False Prophet and the Devil will be thrown to "be tormented day and night forever and ever (Revelation 20:10)."

But who will be thrown into the lake of fire beside the Beast, the False Prophet and the Devil? Revelation 21:8 provides a list of the condemned parties. They are,

> The cowardly and unbelieving and abomina-
> ble and murderers and immoral persons and
> sorcerers and idolaters and all liars, their
> part will be in the lake that burns with fire
> and brimstone, which is the second death.

Even *Hades* and death will be cast into the lake of fire. The Bible calls the lake of fire the second death (Revelation 20:14). The significance of casting death into the lake of fire is to assert that the righteous will immortally enjoy all the blessings and the glory of the Lord, and the condemned will be tormented in the lake of fire forever. There is no more death to cause cessation of life or termination of their torture. On the other hand, it is an indication that "death and Hades are ultimately as powerless as the other forces of evil. Finally, there is no power but that of God. All else is completely impotent."[74]

CHAPTER TWELVE

The Qur'an and Biblical Eschatological Language and Images

ألقرآن والتَّعبيرات والتَّشابيه الكتابيَّة
الإسكتالوجيَّة

This chapter intends to examine the biblical expressions, images, figures of speech and formalism that have impacted the Islamic eschatological language. A corpus of biblical allegorical images and similes that found their ways into Islamic literature and Qur'anic texts had created a mosaic of pictures that, most often, lack harmonious shades, logic and sensibility. It seems also that during the pre-Islamic era, several trends of Christian eschatological interpretations had been in circulation among the Arabs who became acquainted with some Christian sects, and thus, acquired some knowledge of these trends. Besides, a large amount of the Islamic Tradition had been collected in the second Islamic century after the Islamic conquest. That opened the door wide for Muslims outside Arabia, who became preoccupied with interfaith dialogues with Christian religious scholars, to acquire better understanding of the Christian faith and Hellenistic philosophy. Consequently, Muslim scholars became more acquainted with the Christian eschatology of the time. On the other hand, Muslims who were familiar with the Persian literary heritage and faith benefited from the Zoroastrian legends. Thus, whenever they failed to interpret a Qur'anic verse appertaining to the end of times, they resorted either to the

Judeo-Christian literatures or to Zoroastrian religious tenets and works to expound what the Qur'an vaguely tried to communicate. That implies that many of the apocalyptic and eschatological traditions ascribed to Muhammad may not be authentic, but the creation of a much later time. Even the Qur'an, it seems, had reflected this phenomenon in different ways. In this chapter, I am partially indebt to the work of Abu Musa al-Hariri, *Quss wa Nabi*, "A Priest and a Prophet."

In previous chapters, we alluded, explicitly or implicitly, to a number of the borrowed images and meanings that are extracted from the aforementioned sources. But this chapter will comprehensively show how the Qur'an, in many cases, has copied directly its eschatological expressions, vocabulary and figures of speech, the Torah, the Gospels and some of other Christian traditions.

The description of the signs of the end of times, the last Day, the portrayal of Paradise and Hell, the belief in the Day of resurrection, and the Day of Judgment,[1] are almost the same. But before attempting to prove that the Qur'an had indeed borrowed from the Bible, specially the apocalyptic book of Revelation and other Christian sources, it is necessary to answer an essential question. Since the book of Revelation did not enjoy in the East a canonical status until a later time, and since we have no evidence that an Arabic translation of this book was available to Muhammad,[2] how could then Muhammad become familiar with the apocalyptic imagery and forms? There are three possibilities to be taken into consideration:

1. Enough information was in circulation among the Christian communities of the time with which Muhammad had an intimate relationship. Christian figures like Waraqa ibn Nawfal, Mary the Coptic,

Muhammad's concubine, and other *Nasara* must have exchanged knowledge or responded to his inquiries and, thus, provided him with the information after which he sought.

2.   Since Muhammad was not acquainted with foreign languages, it seems he had to rely "upon oral information given to him in response to his inquiries."[3] Most of the information he obtained are borrowed, either from apocalyptic or apocryphal sources.[4] In reality "so far as the descriptions of the end of the world are concerned, almost every detail of them can be paralleled in well-known books of apocalyptic."[5] Moreover, the book of Revelation, as Brady remarks,

> "May have doubtful status in Arabia; this does not imply its non-availability as apocryphone and it is possible that as such it might be alluded to in the Qur'an. After all, there are apocrypha enough else-where in the Qur'an."[6]

3.   Among his entourage, there were a number of *Nasara* who were converted to Islam. Some of them were literate and possessed or had an access to apocalyptic and apocryphal material. They undoubtedly shared with him the information they acquired. Besides, different Islamic Tradition denoted that Muhammad encouraged few of his companions to learn Hebrew and Syriac in order to acquaint themselves with their religious literature.

This rationale may explain how the biblical expressions and imageries have left their marks on the Qur'anic style and similes, and even on the meaning. The following comparative study is just a paradigm, showing these striking similarities as a proof that Muhammad was, consciously or unconsciously, not immune from the influence of the biblical diction. This statement stands against the general Islamic belief that the Qur'anic revelation is independent of the influence of any existing source. It is a direct *tanzil*, pure and divine.

The Qur'an confirms that Muhammad was familiar with three main books of scriptures: the Torah (the books of Moses), the *Zubur* (Psalms), and the Gospel of *'Isa* (Jesus).[7] It also refers to the scrolls of Abraham and other prophets such as Ishmael, Isaac, Jacob and the tribes (the twelve children of Jacob) 4:41, of which none are included or mentioned in the Bible. Some of these scrolls are regarded as apocryphal literature.

The Last Day

The Qur'an affirms that the Last Hour:	The Bible says that Jesus will come:
Will come suddenly;[8] the Hour will "certainly come;"[9] it is "like the twinkling of the eye;"[10] and it is nigh.[11]	"At an hour when you do not think He will;"[12] at an hour which no one does know;[13] "like a thief in the night;"[14] "He is near, right at the door"[15] "In a moment, in the twinkling of the eye."[16]
The Qur'an denotes that only God has "the knowledge of the Hour;"[17] "The knowledge of the (Hour) thereof is with my Lord;"[18] "Its knowledge is with Allah;"[19]	The same idea is reiterated in Christianity, "But of that day and hour no one knows, not even the angels, nor the Son, but the Father alone."[20]

The Qur'an vividly and dreadfully describes the features of that fearful Day in which the order of the astral and universal phenomena will be changed: "The sky is rent asunder,"[21] or "cleft asunder,"[22] or "unveiled,"[23] or "will be like molten brass,"[24] or "heaven will be in violent commotion,"[25] or it becomes "red like the ointment,"[26] or "be rent asunder with clouds,"[27] or when it rolled up "like a scroll rolled up for books."[28] When "the moon is eclipsed. And the sun and the moon are joined together,"[29] or "the sun is rolled and stars fall,"[30] or "the planets are scat-tered,"[31] or "the oceans burst forth."[32]

The Bible also presents a striking portrait as a prelude to the second coming of Christ. In that Day "the sun will be darkend, the moon will not give its light and the stars will fall the sky, and the powers of heaven will be shaken."[37]
" But the Day of the Lord will come like the thief, in which the heavens will pass away with aroar and the elements will be destroyed with intence heat and the earth and its woks will be burned up"[38]
"And all the hosts of heaven will wear away, and the sky will be rolled; all their hosts will wither away..."[39]
"Then the moon will be abashed away and the sun ashamed."[40]

In that day the earth will experience turmoil. " The earth and thr mountain will be violently shaken and the mountains become a heap of sands,"[33] plains,[34] the earth and the mountains will be lifted up and crushed with a single blow,[35] and the earth will be changed to a new different earth.[36]

As the end of time draws nigh there will be terrible earthquakes,[41] and "every mountain and island were moved out of their place,"[42] also "a great mountain burning with fire was thrown to the sea."[43] There will be also a new earth for, the first earth passed away.[44]

*In that day the trumpet will sound,[45] and the blast of resurrection will be heard,[46] *It is a day in which there will be successive blasts that make the hearts throbbing and the eyes be humbled[47] *It is a day in which a suckling woman shall forget the child she has suckled, and every pregnant woman shall deposit her burden,[48] and children's hair will turn hoary.[49] *It is a day in which no one will intercede for another.[50] *God comes in canopies of clouds.[51]	*In that day God will sent his angels with the ram horn and trumpet (Matthew 24:31; 1Corinthians 15:52) and with a shout (1Thessalonians 4:16). *All the tribes will mourn (Matthew 24;30; and woe to those who are pregnant and to those who are nursing babies in those days (Ibid., 24:19). *It is a day in which God will come with many thousands of His holy ones (Jude 14).
*The Day whereon neither wealth nor sons will avail.[52]	*Riches do not profit in the day of wrath.[53]
*In that day men will proceed in companies sorted out.[54] God will sort out the companions of the right from the companions of the left.[55] *Every one will give an account.[56]All deeds and intentionswill be revealed.[57] Good and bad deeds will be recorded in one's book.[58]	*All the nations will be gathered before Him and He will separate them from one another…He will put the (righteous) on His right, and the (wicked) on His left.[59] *Every man will receive recompense according to his deeds.[60] Each one will give an account of himself.[61] Names will be written in the book of life.[62]

Heaven and Paradise

As it is indicated above, Islamic paradise retains some characteristics of the Zoroastrian paradise, as well as other features mentioned in the writings of the church fathers. But it seems that Islam also borrowed from a poem entitled "Paradise' composed by Saint Aphraem the Syriac, who lived in the fourth century. In his book *Quss wa Nabi* "A Priest and a Prophet", Abu Musa al-Hariri presents a comparative study between the Qur'anic Garden and Saint Aphraem's Paradise in which he rightly points to a number of basic similarities.[63] He also alludes to some Talmudic and apocryphal materials.[64] But this chapter will continue to deal with the biblical imageries and expressions apart from other sources.

The Qur'nic paradise remarks that:	The Bible indicates that:
*The faithful will be having lofty mansions.[65]	*Houses will await the righteous in heaven.[69]
*The Paradise has gates opened to the believers only.[66]	*The heavenly Jerusalem has 12 gates, only the righteous can enter into it.[70]
*The ultimate happiness is to enjoy the beautific vision and to obtainGod's favor, for nothing of the earthly pleasures is compared to the eternal pleasures.[67]	*The righteous should not store up forthemselves treasures on earth, where moth and rust destroy and...thieves break in and steal; but store up in heaven...[71]
*There is neither excessive heat nor bitter cold.[68]	*Nor will the sun beat down on them, nor any heat.[72]
*Peace be upon you. You have done well, so enter here to abide therein. Sura 40:73.	*Well done, good and faithful slave... enter into the joy of your master,(Matthew 25:21; Luke 19:17).
*It has four rivers of pure water, milk, wine and pure honey.[73]	* Similar to the Garden of Eden from which four rivers flow.[74]

Hell

As it was denoted above, hell of Islam is divided into seven regions of terror. Most probably, this compartmentalization is borrowed from the Talmud.[75] The Qur'anic hell has seven gates, similar to the Jewish hell, though the latter has only three gates: one is opened towards the desert, the second towards the sea and the third towards Jerusalem.[76] The Bible alludes to the gates of death or the shadows of death and the gates of hell in both the Old and the New Testaments.[77] Apparently, each gate leads to a certain region designated to a specified group of the condemned, who will suffer in accordance to their deeds. In Christianity, the Bible does not refer to compartmentalizetion, though it, like the Qur'an, emphasizes that hell is a place of suffering and torture.[78] Also, as the wicked will be chained into fetters and punished, likewise in Christianity, God cast the evil angels "into hell and committed them to pits of darkness,[79] reserved for judgment."[80] These sinful angels are "kept in eternal bonds under darkness for the judgment of the great day."[81]

Another striking similarity that arrests our attention is the notion of 'one death' the faithful endure. The Qur'an reiterates this notion:

Nor will they there taste Death, except the first death; and He will preserve them from the penalty of the blazing fire (Sura 44:56).

لاَ يَذُوقُونَ فِيهَا المَوْتَ إلاَّ المَوْتَة الأُولى وَوَقَاهُمْ عَذَابَ الجَحِيم

This same notion is repeated in the Qur'an several times.[82] However, in reality it echoes what is mentioned in Revelation 20:6:

Blessed and holy is the one who has a part in the first resurrection; over these the second death has no power...

246

That means the righteous will die once only and after that they will be resurrected to be in the presence of God; contrary to the wicked, whose fate is to be thrown into the lake of fire which is "the second death."[83]

Another Qur'anic picture that reflects a similar biblical image is the portrayal of the fetters and chains that surround the necks of the evildoers by which they will be dragged to hell for torturing.[84] The Gospel of Matthew refers to a similar situation when it remarks, "Then the king said to the servants, 'Bind his hand and foot, and throw him into the outer darkness; in that place there will be weeping and gnashing of teeth'" (22:13).[85]

There are other biblical images that impacted the Qur'anic eschatological expressions, among them:

*The Qur'an says: "The inhabitants of the fire will call to the inhabitants of the Garden 'Pour on us water or of that Allah has provided you.' They will say: 'Allah has forbidden them to the unbelievers.'" (7:50)	*In the story of Lazarus and the rich man the Bible states that the rich man pleaded with Abraham to send Lazarus 'so that he may dip the tip of his finger in water and cool off my tongue, for I am in agony in this flame.' But Abraham said, 'Child, remember that during your life you received your good things; and likewise Lazarus bad things; but now he is being comforted and you are in agony.'(Luke 16:24-25)
*Upon that day when the unbelievers are exposed to the fire: 'You dissipated your good things in your present life, and you took your enjoyment in them; therefore today you shall be recompensed with the chastisement of humiliation for that you waxed proud in the earth without right, and for your ungodliness.' (46:20)	
*The dwellers of the Heights will call to certain men whom	*In Hades (the rich man) lifted up his eyes, being in torment, and saw Abraham far away and Lazarus in his bosom... (Luke 16:23) * Abraham said (to the rich man),

they will know from their marks... (7:48) *They (the unbelievers) have sworn by Allah the most earnest oaths if a sign comes to them they will believe in it... Even if We had send down the angels to them, and the dead had spoken with them, had We mustered everything before their very eyes they would not believe. (6:109-111) *Then the fire whose fuel is men and stones which is prepared for the unbelievers. (2:24)	'If they do not listen to Moses and the Prophets, they will not be persuaded even if someone rises from the dead. (Luke 16:31) *Then He will say to those on His left, 'Depart from Me, accursed ones, into the eternal fire which has been prepared for the devil and his angels. (Matthew 25:41)

Many apocalyptic Islamic images are also borrowed from apocryphal, pseudepigraphal, non-biblical Christian material and Talmudic resources such as Sibylline Oracles, Apocalypse of John, Apocalypse of Thomas, Testament of Levi, 1 and 2 Enoch, St. Ephraem's Paradise, the books of the Talmud, Apocalypse of Paul, and many other sources.[86] The borrowed data have undoubtedly enriched the apocalyptic description of the Qur'an, but, at the same time, have constituted an historical evidence of the Christian influence that helped shape the Islamic view of the apocalypse.[87] For instance, in regard to the scene of the chains and the fetters that shackle the hands and the feet of the condemned, it is reported that the tormenting angels carry with them chains and clubs of iron. In other Christian sources, we read, "the wrath of God fetters the perished to a pole and the angels will descend carrying in their hands resplendent clubs and chains of fire."[88] Therefore, Christian biblical or apocalyptic literature provided the Qur'an and Islamic Tradition with ample data that would not be available to Islamic apocalyptic imageries without the abundant supply of Christian resources.

Conclusion

Obviously, this study raises at least some serious questions about two or more significant areas in Islamic studies. One of them revolves around the concept of revelation in Islam. The other is related to the intricate problems of the *Hadith*. Furthermore, to what extend can a researcher rely on the Islamic data if they are not supported by external historical and archeological evidence? How can he reconstruct the chronological order when there is no such order? Or how can we trust the *Hadith* when the al-Bukhari the greatest and the most trusted collector of the Islamic Tradition recognized only about seven thousand *hadith* or a little more, out of six hundred thousand and disregarded the rest as unsound or spurious? To a researcher, these enigmatic issues and questions seem to be problematic and irreconcilable.

Attempting to examine and answering these questions and ambiguities are regarded as derogatory and a threat to the faith of Islam, and may have dangerous consequences. Thus, Muslims, in general, believe any critical study of the Qur'an posits a poignant confrontation against the very sacredness of their scripture, and to question its validity perpetrates anger, rejection and unsolicited accusations. Through the course of the Islamic history, those who dared or tried to criticize the Qur'an, even on a scholarly level, were considered as the enemy of Islam. There is no place for an objective study of the Qur'an in the light of history or factual data. A scholarly dialogue with its pros and cons about the revelatory of the Qur'an and its veracity is not permitted in any Islamic society. Taha Husayn and Faraj Fuda,[1] who were bold enough to employ reason and logic in their analytical study of the Qur'an, were subjected to jail, persecution, exile and death. These Muslim scholars and writers lived in the twentieth century. I am not here to advocate their views or to oppose them, but rather to prove a salient point that there is no room in Islamic societies for the free thinkers who do not fully conform to the Islamic ideology of the Qur'anic revelation.

One of the basic difference between Christian and Islamic eschatology starts with their respective outlooks upon their views of the concept of eschatology. In Christianity, the crucifixion of Jesus and his resurrection are the focal points in systematic theology, including the events of the end of time. The redemptive act of Christ on the cross that reconciled man and creation with God and recovered the lost relationship, restored also the eschatological hope of all the redeemed. The second coming of Christ as the Lord of all creation and the Redeeming King has always been the hope of the church and the fulfillment of its eschatological salvation.

Islam, however, is fundamentally a theology of deeds and not of redemption. There is no Jesus Who atones for the sins of man to free them from the bondage of their old nature. Their salvation depends on their deeds and the Mercy of God. Actually, Islamic theology advocates a reward-based eschatology where man's eternal life is determined by his human effort.[2] It is true that the *Hadith* refers to the grace of God for the salvation of man, but that grace is based on the sovereignty of God Who, if He wills, does not hesitate to contradict His nature. The lack of a redemptive act entails unjustifiable divine decision.

This comprehensive study has already documented that the eschatological data the Qur'an borrowed from various authentic sources, whether revealed, apocryphal, or legendary, are in a direct contradiction to the Islamic claim of revelation. The high esteem by which Muslims regard the Qur'an is based on its infallibility and verbatim revelation as it was exactly preserved in the Mother of the Book from eternity.[3] The cogent historical facts as well as other documented material are irrefutable testimony against the Islamic claims of the source of the Qur'an. There are two points Muslims always articulate: first, that any similarity between the Qur'an and the Bible is a proof that the source is one and not by virtue of copying. Second, that the Qur'an has the final word in settling all the differences between the Biblical and the Qur'anic ideologies. Both claims are baseless and irrational because it is not difficult to demonstrate that the origin of these similarities is the verbal transmission of the biblical and apocalyptic material that Muhammad obtained through different means, and, thus, revelation has nothing to do with it.

Employing euphemistic expressions, in this case, are not helpful in affirming the truth. Objectivity, not prejudice, is the path that is conducive to the truth. This fact has led the author to be honest with himself in presenting his findings, since some of these findings have a fateful impact on the views and lives of many radical Muslims, thus having tragic consequences on the world. To illustrate, the suicidal activities of radical Muslims are basically inspired by the rewards the Islamic paradise offers that are not available to them in this life. This incentive was and is still the force behind these suicidal impediments, as Muslims believe in a literal description of the Qur'anic paradise; the utopia that is yet to come. Yet, the majority of Muslims do not realize that the images of their paradise are reflections of the Zoroastrian paradise and the appealing of the sensual pleasures inflames their desire to die for "the cause of Allah."[4] What will be the reaction of these radical Muslims if they realize that their paradise is just an echo of the Zoroastrian paradise? Would they sacrifice their lives for a mirage or an illusion? Undoubtedly there is a heaven, but of a different type. It is a righteous and not a sensual heaven that perpetually enkindles the passions and the desires of the flesh.

On the other hand, Islamic eschatological events mentioned in the Qur'an or the *Hadith* have failed to prove their originality or even authenticity, due to the intriguing imagination of the storytellers who masterly created their own world of fantasy to thrill their folkic audiences.The borrowed apocalyptic Qur'anic material has been colorfully woven into the fabric of the storytellers fantasy, forming a corrupted heritage that neither the Qur'an nor Muhammad intended.

Islamic eschatology also has diminished the role of Christ in His second coming from the Judge of the world to a mere follower of Muhammad. Obviously, Islamic Tradition refuses to acknowledge the divinity of Jesus, which, consequently, elevates Him above Muhammad, and even makes Muhammad accountable to Him. This does not respond well to the teaching of the Islamic Tradition, which regards Muhammad as the seal of the prophets and the master of the messengers of God. خاتم الأنبياء وسيّد المرسلين. It is true that Jesus will come to free the world from the tyranny of the Antichrist. He will also be instrumental in destroying the people of Gog and Magog through His supplication, but what is more important to Muslims is that Jesus will eradicate all the various religions of the world including Christianity, and will revive the faith of Islam as the true religion of God. In this case, Jesus will be in the service of Islam and one of its followers. This view will strip Jesus from His divinity, authority and power, and turn Him into an ordinary man, endowed only with the prophethood. By that, the Christian view of Jesus Christ as King of Kings and Lord of Lords will fade as a shadow from the past. Accordingly, this becomes the real message that Jesus is commissioned to accomplish in His second coming. This Islamic perception is in full congruent with the Qur'anic teaching about Jesus' humanity.

The Antichrist in Islam is a mythological figure. His basic characteristics are derived from the Biblical teaching and other foreign legends. Nevertheless, the imagination of Muslim narrators created of him a formidable Cyclops endowed with supernatural powers. The Islamic episodes that surrounded his life intended to present him as a symbol of evil with distinctive physical description to warn the faithful Muslims against his deceptive claims. God will permit him to perform miracles as a trial from God to test the faith of the believers. This notion is borrowed from Revelation in which God allowed the Beast to perform supernatural deeds to deceive the people. The biblical Antichrist does not have a face or any physical description. He could be the hidden power behind a political and socio-economical system, or a head of a state or a religious regime. Certainly, he is not a deformed figure.

The Islamic Antichrist, as it seems, will be the embodiment of the Jewish hope and longing. The bulk of his army is recruited from the Jews. What is interesting is his ability to reconcile between the Jews and the renegade Muslims who will be allured to follow him. At this point, Islamic Tradition is chaotic. There is nothing mentioned about the end of these apostates. We are told about the destiny of the Jews who adhere to his cause, but there is nothing reported about the destiny of the Muslims who betray their faith and their prophet, when Jesus encounters the *Dajjal*. Whereas the Bible condemns whosoever receives the mark of the Beast to be thrown into the Lake of Fire.

The Bible asserts that the beatific vision through Christ is ever-present in the new heaven and new earth. Though the Qur'an hints to the beatific vision but it does not seem that it is omnipresent. The Islamic paradise is not a spiritual habitat in which its denizens are occupied with worshipping and glorifying their Lord day and night. They are busy in gratifying their blazing desires. The presence of the beatific vision is occasional and does not appear to be a top priority in the Islamic hereafter, though the Qur'an testifies that the beatific vision is better than all the pleasures of paradise. But in reality, this Qur'anic emphasis is not reflected in the total Islamic paradisiacal picture. The Qur'an is more concerned in describing the physical and sensual rewards than in the spiritual aspects of paradise.

In the Shi'ite's theology and expectation, the messianic *Mahdi* replaces Jesus. His messianic role at the end of time is a mirror that reflects most of the Christian views about the second coming of Christ. Apparently, the *Mahdi* will bear most of the marks of the future savior who will free the world from the forces of evil and rule as the only righteous judge, supported by God and His angels. It is true that Jesus will advent during his time but Jesus' role will be the role of a supporting actor and for a short period only. Based on Shi'ite sources, the *Mahdi*, not Jesus, is the one who will debate with Christians and Jews to convert them to Islam.[5] This claim contradicts the Sunnis views and is incompatible with the biblical teaching. Undoubtedly, the Shi'ites benefited from the Christian apocalyptic sources and attempted to apply the messianic images to the *Mahdi*.

255

The belief that he did not die and disappeared at a very early age, his appearance by the end of time, his glorious advent from his long occultation proclaimed by the archangel Gabriel, his miraculous annihilation of all his renitent enemies, and his reign over the entire world, are faithful imitation of the Messiah of the end of time.

But if the Shiʿites regard their *Mahdi* as the savior of the world and bestow on him some messianic characteristics, it is not in his power to claim any divine origin. He is not even a prophet, or the Word of God born of the Holy Spirit. He is not the one who died to save the world from the bondage of sin. He is not the one who will judge the dead and the living, and he is not the One whose reign will last for eternity. Shiʿite sources assert that he will be killed at the hand of a women. Despite that, the *Mahdi* is revered by the Shiʿites more than Jesus.

In the final analysis both Sunnis and Shiʿites distorted the image of the Christian Christ and reduced his role in the Day of Judgment from the Lord of all creatures to a mere ordinary human being who did not find himself worthy to intercede on behalf of the people. They transformed his person from a divine being into a mere human character, who will be a follower of the Tradition of Muhammad.

End Notes

Introduction

[1] *Funk & Wagnalls Encyclopedia*, vol. 18, p. 233.

[2] Ibid., p. 232.

[3] Lewis M. Hoppe, *The religions of the World*, 4th ed. (New York: MacMillan Publushing House, 1987), pp. 263-271.

[4] This story will be examined in chapter three.

[5] Islamic sources as we see in the context of this study, indicate that Jesus is the one who will destroy the cross and eradicate the unbelieving Jews.

[6] Each major Shiʻite sect claims a different Mahdi, but they all agree that he must be from the lineage of Ali and his wife Fatima, Muhammad's daughter.

[7] William C. Chittick, *Muslim World,* Death and the World of Imagination: Ibn Al-ʻArabi's Eschatology, (The Duncan Black Macdonald Center), January 1988, #1, pp. 51-52.

[8] Ibid.

[9] Among the few books available in English are *The Islamic Understanding of Death and Resurrection,* by Jane Smith & Yvonne Haddad, (Albany: State University of New York Press, 1981), and *Muslim Eschatology and the Missiological Implication; A Thematic Study,* by Emmanuel Sudhir Isaiah (Ann Arbor: UMI, 1989).

[10] All standard studies in Islamic theology have designated a section on Islamic eschatology. Refer to *Islam, Muhammad And His Religion,* Arthur Jeffery, editor, (New York: The Liberal Arts Press, 1958) p. 138.

[11] Gershom Gorenberg, *The End of Days,* (New York, NY: Oxford University Press, 2002), pp. 185-189.

[12] Ibid.

[13] This list is not a comprehensive list by any means and does not include the books of Islamic Tradition which attribute most of the eschatological hadiths to Muhammad.

Chapter 1

[1] The six canonical collections of Sunni Hadith are: (1) *The Sahih* of al-Bukhari (d.870 A.D.); (2) *the Sahih* of Muslim (d. 875 A.D.); (3) *Jami'* of al-Tirmidhi (d. 892 A.D.); (4) *the Sunan* of Abi Dawud (d. 888 A.D.); (5) *the Sunan* of Ibn Maja (d. 886 A.D.); (6) and *the Sunan* of al-Nisa'i (d. 915 A.D.). Also the Shi'ites have their own collections of the Hadith. They are: (1) *Al-Kafi* of al-Kulaini (d. 939); (2) *Man La Yahduruhu al-Faqih,* Ibn Babuya (d. 991-2); (3) *Al-Istibsar fi ma 'ukhtulifa min al-Akhbar,* Abu Ja'far Muh. B. al-Hasan al-Tusi (d. 1283); (4) *Tahdhib of al-Ahkam,* al-Tusi (d. 1283). The two sets of collections may interchangeably include some of the same hadiths.

[2] Muhammad A. Shah al-Kashmiri *Al-Tasrih bima Tawatara fi Nuzul al-Masih,* (Halab: Maktabat al-Matbu'at al-Islamiya, 1965), footnote 5, p. 289.

[3] Jeffery, *Islam, Muhammad and His Religion,* 138.

[4] Sura, 45:27.

[5] Sura 45:27. See also 14:10; 18:81; 21:18.

[6] Refer also to Suras 15:45; 18:21; 20:20; 22:7; 40:59; 41:47; and 45:32.

[7] See also Suras 43:66; and 47:18. It is in vain to believe after its occurrence (47:18).

[8] Sura 79:7-12.

[9] Sura 79:34-46; 25:11.

[10] Sura 4:136.

[11] Sura 31:34; 33:63; and 43:85. There are five things that are only known to God: the time of the Hour, the sex of the embryo in the womb of the mother, the land in which a person may die, when it will rain, and how much money a person may gain in the morrow (31:34).

[12] Sura 19:75. The Christian's belief is that God is delaying the arrival of the doomsday to provide more opportunities for people to repent and be saved.

[13] See also Mark 13:32. Jesus here is referring to himself as the Son of Man.

[14] Abu Dawud, *Sunan of Abi Dawud,* 'Alim CD-ROM, hadith #1054.

[15] See Rom. 13:13-12; 1 Thess. 5:1-11; 1 Cor. 15:50-53; (cf. 2 Pet. 3:8-9).

[16] Jane Idleman Smith & Yvonne Y. Haddad, *The Islamic*

Understanding of Death and Resurrection, (Albany: State of New York Press), footnote of chapter 3, p. 212.

[17] Book of Acts 17:32.

[18] Ibn Sa'd, *Tabaqat of ibn Sa'd,* (Beirut: n. p. 1957), vol. 5, p. 543.

[19] We will discuss in chapter twelve the impact of the biblical data on the Islamic eschatology.

[20] The school of the post-millennium believes in one general resurrection for both the righteous and the evil-doers.

[21] William MacDonald, *Believer's Bible Commentary,* Nashville: Thomas Nelson Publishers, 1990), p. 854.

[22] 'Alim, *Sahih of Muslim,* #1370.

[23] Dalton Galloway, *Moslim World,* The Resurrection and Judgment in the Qur'an, (vol. 17, 1922), p. 348.

[24] Taha Husayn, *Fi al-Shi'r al-Jahili.* 1ˢᵗ ed., (Cairo: Egypt: Matba'at Dar al-Kutub al-Misriyah, 1926), p.48.

[25] Sura 2:136.

[26] From Christian point of view we cannot compare between Muhammad and Jesus. Jesus in the Christian faith is more than a prophet.

[27] W. St. Clair Tisdall, *The Sources of Islam,* (Edinburg, Scotland: T. & T. Clark, n.d.), pp. 69-83.

[28] This fact will be examined when the person of the *Dajjal* is discussed.

[29] The term *Nasara* was applied to the Jewish Christians at first, then it became a title for all the Christians in Arabia.

Chapter 2

[1] Al-Bukhari, *Sahih*, edit Mustafa Deeb al-Bugha, (Damascus-Beirut: Dar ibn Kathir-Dar al-Yamama, 1408H./1987AD), 6: 2590 (Arabic Version).

[2] 'Alim, *Sunan of Abi Dawud,* # 232.

[3] 'Alim, *Sahih of al-Bukhari,* 2:663.

[4] Ibid 9:232. This is the idol of Dus tribe which they used to worship before Islam.

[5] Ibid 8:800a.

[6] 2 Timothy 3:1-5; 2 Peter 3:3.

[7] 'Alim, *Sunan of Abi Dawud,* #1992.

[8] Louis Sheikho, *Shu'ara' al-Nusraniya qabla al-Islam,* (Beirut:

Manshurat Dar al-Mashriq, 3th. Ed. 1967), pp. 219-237.

[9] Ibid; p.211. A pre-Islamic Christian preacher and hermit.

[10] Ibid. 211.

[11] Ibid, 211. Most recent studies suggest that Waraqa belongs to the Ebionite sect.

[12] *Sahih of al-Bukhari,* trans. Muhammad M. Khan, (New Delhi: Kitab Bahavan, 1994), 9:286 (English version).

[13] Ibid, 1:162,167; 9:288. Some Muslim scholars explain this phenomena by claiming that these women are four wives and the rest are sisters, mother, aunts and grandmothers etc.

[14] Ibid, 1:56.

[15] Ibid, 6:300.

[16] 'Alim, *Sunan of al-Tirmidhi,* # 1436. People of very humble origin.

[17] *Sunan of al-Nisa'i,* (Egypt: Al-Tab'at al-Misriya, (1348H./1929), 3:22.

[18] *Sahih of al-Bukhari,* 1:47.

[19] *Muwatta' of ibn Malik,* 54:14; the Arabic version.

[20] 'Alim, *Sahih of al-Bukhari,* 9:421 (English version). It is interesting that during the life of Muhammad these two nations were still dominants and they were not yet the 'previous' nations.

[21] Ibid, 4:806 and 9:69.

[22] Ibid, 9:233.

[23] C. L. Geddes, *The Muslim World,* The Messiah in South Arabia, p. 314.

[24] *Musnad of Ahmad* 5: 395.

[25] 'Alim, *Sunan of Abi Dawud,* #2031, 2032 and 'Alim, *Sahih of al-Bukhari* 4:806.

[26] *Musnad of Ahmad,* 2:349.

[27] Isma'il ibn Kathir al-Shafi'i, *al-Fitan wa al-Malahim,* (Damascus-Beirut: Dar Ibn Kathir, 1414H.-1993 A.D.), 90, #180.

[28] Ibid. 78, #148.

[29] 'Alim, *Sunan of al-Tirmdhi,* #1435.

[30] Ibid, #1236.

[31] The writer believes that such a tradition was developed at a later time.

[32] 'Alim, *Sunan of Abi Dawud,* #1045.

[33] 'Alim, *Sunan of al-Tirmidhi,* #1552.

[34] *Sahih of Muslim,* # 1353. These are ancient locations in the suburbs of the Medina.

[35] Ibn Kathir, *The Signs Before the Day of Judgment;* trans. Huda Khattab, (London: Dar Al- Taqwa, LTD), 2000.

[36] *Sahih of al-Bukhari* # 3557-3588; also #3590 (Arabic version).

[37] Ibn Maja, *Sunan of ibn Maja*,(Egypt: Tab'at 'Isa al-Babi al-Halabi, 1372H.-1952 A.D.), #4094 (Arabic version).

[38] *Al-Ffitan wa al-Malahim*, 82, #156.

[39] *Musnad of Ahmad*, 2:537-538; and *Sahih of Muslim*, #2949 (Arabic version).

[40] *Al-Fitan wa al-Malhim*, 183-184 and 185-187.

[41] Ibid.

[42] *Musnad of Ahmad*, 2:220. Also, *Sahih of al-Bukhari*, #1595 (Arabic version).

[43] *Al-Fitan wa al-Malahim*, 187.

[44] 'Alim, *Sunan of al-Tirmidhi*, #1236.

[45] The anecdote of Gog and Magog will be discussed in chapter five.

[46] 'Alim, *Sunan of al-Tirmidhi*, #1446.

[47] Ibid., #1450.

[48] *Sahih of Muslim*, v. 8, p.174, (English translation}.

[49] *Sahih of al-Bukhari*, v. 9, p. 73, (English translation).

[50] Refer also to Isaiah 11:15 ff.

[51] Refer to pages 244-253.

Chapter 3

[1] *Al-Tasrih bima Tawatara fi Nuzul al-Masih*, p.102.

[2] 'Alim, *Sahih of Muslim*, # 1352.

[3] *al-Fitan wa al-Malahim*, 152 quoting Ahmad ibn al-Abbar, one of the guardian of the Hadith.

[4] Ibid., p. 152.

[5] Ibid., p. 152

[6] Ibid., p. 82.

[7] Ibid., p. 152-53; see also 'Alim, *Sahih of Muslim* # 1374 and *Hadith of al-Tirmdhi*, # 1453

[8] Ibid., p. 153.

[9] Ibid., p. 153.

[10] Ibid., p. 153.

[11] One of Muhammad's companions.

[12] *Sahih of al-Bukhari*, 2:626 and 4:574. It is said that Muhammad even spelled it as k-f-r.

[13] 'Alim, *Sahih of al-Bukhari*, 4:553, 4:554; 5:685, 7:789, 7:795, 9:128, 9:153, 9:241, 9:242. More other similar traditions are dispersed in

the collections of the Hadith.

[14] *Musnad of Ahmad,* 3:79.

[15] Ibid., op. cit.

[16] 'Alim, *Sahih of Muslim,* #1370. Ibn Qatan is a man from the tribe of Khuza'a who died in pre-Islamic time. But in another tradition it is indicated that he was present when Muhammad narrated this description; Ibn Kathir, p. 157.

[17] 'Alim, *Sunan of Abi Dawud,* #2024.

[18] *Sahih of Muslim,* 18:50; (the Arabic version).

[19] This issue will be discussed in the following pages.

[20] Refer to pp. 43-50.

[21] The Bible, *Book of Revelation,* 13:17-18.

[22] 'Alim, *Sahih of Muslim,* #1373.

[23] In *Sunan of Abi Daud,* # 4327, (Arabic version) the Jassasa told them to go to a palace where they found the *Dajjal* shackled with iron leaping between heaven and earth.

[24] Another *hadith* indicates that the *Dajjal* looked very sad and was ever complaining; *al-Fitan wa al-Malahim,* 100.

[25] 'Alim, *Sahih of Muslim,* # 1373.

[26] *Al-Tasrih bima Tawarara fi Nuzul al-Masih,* op. cit. p. 157.

[27] *Sahih of Muslim,* 17:84-85 (the Arabic version).

[28] *Al-Fitan wa al-Malahim,* Op. cit., p.102.

[29] *Sahih of Muslim,* 17:84 (The Arabic version)

[30] Ibid., 17:85.

[31] 'Alim, *Sunan of Abi Dawud,* #2026.

[32] *Al-Tasrih bima Tawatara fi Nuzul al-Masih,* footnote 2, p. 131.

[33] *Al-Fitan wa al-Malahim,* p. 145-146.

[34] 'Alim, *Sunan of al-Tirmidhi,* #3072.

[35] The literate or illiterate will read the word *infidel* on the forehead of the *Dajjal.* That would convince some to denounce him.

[36] Abdullah Yusuf Ali, *The Meaning of the Qur'an,* Betsville, Maryland: Amana Publications, 9th ed., 1997, p.341.

[37] Refer to the Book of Revelation and to the second epistle of Paul to the Thessalonians.

[38] See the Book of Daniel 7.

[39] 'Alim, *Sunan of Abi Dawud,* # 2024.

[40] Ibid., #2013.

[41] Ibid., #1982.

[42] 'Alim, *Sahih of Muslim,* #278.

[43] 'Alim, *Al-Muwatta',* 33:15.

[44] Ibid., 4:12.

[45] This interpretation is undoubtedly borrowed from Revelation 13 which repeatedly emphasized that the Beast "was given to him" to perform miracles.

[46] 'Alim, *Sunan of Abi Dawud*, #2023.

[47] *Sahih of Muslim*, 9:194, 195 (the Arabic version).

[48] *Musnad of Ahmad*, 5:221.

[49] *Ibid.*

[50] 'Alim, *Sahih of Muslim*, # 1370.

[51] Ibid., 8: 192; also *Sahih al-Bukhari* 4:164 (the Arabic versions).

[52] *Ibid,.* #1374.

[53] Ibid., vol. 18, p 73 (Arabic version).

[54] Ibid,. op. cit.

[55] Ibid., op. cit. It seems that the story of this believer is influenced by a Christian tale implies that Elijah would appear and denounce the Antichrist, and thus he will be put to death for his claims.

[56] *Sunan of Abi Dawud*, # 2482 and *Musnad of Ahmad*, 2:199.

[57] *Musnad of Ahmad*, 3:292.

[58] Ibid., op.cit.2:67.

[59] Ibid., op.cit. 3:292.

[60] *The Signs Before the Day of Judgment*, p.57.

[61] *Al-Fitan wa al-Malahim*, p. 131.

[62] *Sahih of al-Bukhari*, 18:66, (the Arabic version).

[63] *Gospel of Mark* 13:22; *Matt.*, 24:24.

[64] F.F.Bruce, *1 and 2 Thessalonians*, (Waco, Texas: World Publisher, 1982), p. 179.

[65] Refer to 1:8-9.

[66] *Book of Acts* 21:8-11.

[67] F. F. Bruce, op. cit., 179.

[68] *Book of Revelation*, 11:7; 13:1-2; 11-19.

[69] Ibid., 13:2.

[70] Ibid., 13:13.

[71] Ibid., 13:14.

[72] Ibid., 13:16-17.

[73] As quoted by F. F. Bruce, p.179.

[74] Op. cit.

[75] Ibid., p. 183.

[76] Ibid,. p. 184.

[77] Op. cit.

[78] Bernard McGinn, *Anti-Christ*, (N.Y.: Harper Collins, 1996), p. 9.

[79] As quoted by McGinn, p. 61.

[80] Ibid,. p. 66.

[81] Ibid,. pp. 68, as quoted by MacGinn from *The Testament of the Lord*, translated by James cooper and Arthur L. Mclean. (Edinburgh: Clark, 1902), 57-58.

[82] Ibid., 69, as quoted by McGinn from *Vision of the End,* trans. by James Tabor, p.55.

[83] The Islamic sources indicate that the *Dajjal* will appear from Asfahan or Khurasan or from a road between Syria and Iraq.

[84] *Musnad of Ahmad,* 3:367-368.

[85] Matthew 24:16.

[86] *Musnad of Ahmad ,* 1:374.

[87] As quoted by Bernard McGinn, p. 69.

[88] *Musnad of Ahmad,* 1:374. In another hadith it is described as curly.

[89] As quoted by McGinn, p. 69.

[90] *Hadith Literature: Its Origin, Development and Special Features,* edited and revised by abdul Hakim Murad; (Cambridge, UK: Islamic Texts Society, 1993), p. 35.

[91] 'Alim, 9:242. This story is repeated in several places of *Sahih of al-Bukhari,* 9:128, 9:158; 7:789; 4:650 and 4:649, with slight variation

[92] Ibid, 4:462.

[93] *Musnad of Ahmad,* 1:374.

[94] Mark 13:19.

[95] *Al-Fitan wa al-Malahim,* p 149-150.

[96] Ibid, p.150.

[97] Ibid.

[98] This is the topic of chapter four.

Chapter 4

[1] Sura 4:157-158.

[2] Sura 43:61.

[3] Sura 4:159.

[4] *The Meaning of the Holy Qur'an,* p. 263, footnote # 665.

[5] *Tafsir of Ibn Jarir,* 6:18.

[6] Op. cit.

[7] *Al-Tasrih bima Tawatara fi Nuzul al-Masih,* p. 94.

[8] Sura 61:6.

[9] Ibid.

[10] The reader should remember that the Byzantine empire and its army do not exist any more and Constantinople is now an Islamic city in Turkey. This is evidence that the author of this *hadith* was bound to the historical era of his time before Constantinople was conquered by the Ottoman.

[11] This plain is called the Ghuta of Damascus of Syria.

[12] We have already discussed the contradictions that surround this story in chapter two.

[13] *Musnad of Ahmad*, 1:384-385; 'Alim, *Sahih of Muslim*, #1350.

[14] Ibid.

[15] *Al-Tasrih bima Tawatara fi Nuzul al-Masih*, footnote # 2, p. 129.

[16] *Musnad of Ahmad*, 3:367-368.

[17] *Al-Fitan wa al-Malahim*, p. 111.

[18] *Musnad of Ahmad*, 4:216.

[19] Al-Bazzar, *Kasf al-Astar*, #3387; as quoted by Ibn Kathir, p.140.

[20] 'Alim, *Sahih of Muslim*, #1348.

[21] *Musnad of Ahmad*, #367-368.

[22] 'Alim, *Sahih of Muslim*, #1370.

[23] *Al-Fitan wa al-Malahim*, p. 139-149.

[24] *Musnad of Ahmad*, 4:216-217.

[25] "Alim, *Sahih of Muslim*, # 1373.

[26] *Musnad of Ahmad*, 4: 216-217.

[27] *Sahih of Muslim*, 18:21 (Arabic version).

[28] Ibn Khathir, pp. 139-140. When Jesus descends he will have with him two swords; refer to *Sunan of ibn Maja*, # 4081 and *Musnad of Ahmad*, 1:375.

[29] Ibid. p. 154.

[30] *Musnad of Ahmad*, 3: 367-368.

[31] Al-Suyuti, *al-Hawi lil Fatawi*, (Egypt: al-Muniriya Pub., 1352H. / 1933 A.D.), 2:81. There is no indication about the identity of this Mahdi.

[32] Ibid. p. 111.

[33] Ibid.

[34] *al-Tasrih bima Tawatara fi Nuzul al-Masih*. p. 117.

[35] Ibid., p.119.

[36] F.F. Bruce, p.183.

[37] *Musnad of Ahmad*, 4:214-215.

[38] *Sunan of Abi Dawud*, 4:117; *Musnad of Ahmad*, 2:437.

[39] *Sunan of Abi Dawud*, 4:117; *Musnad of Ahmad*, 2:437; Ibn Jarir al-Tabari, *Tafsir of the Tabari*, (Egypt: Bulaq, 1323H. /1905 A.D), 6:16; Ibn Hajar al-Asqalani, *Fath al-Bari bi Sharh Sahih al*

Bukhari,(Egypt:Bulaq,1300H./1911 A.D.), 6:357; al-Suyuti, *al-Durr al-Manthur fi Tafsir al-Qur'an bi al-Ma'thur*, (Egypt: al-Maymaniya edition, 1315H./1896 A.D.), 2:242.

[40] *Sahih of al-Bukhari,* 4: 402; see also *Sahih of Muslim,* 1:106, 107 (English translation).

[41] Ibid., 4:608

[42] Ibid.

[43] *Sahih of Muslim* # 2938.

[44] Ibid. #2940.

[45] 'Alim, *Al-Muwatta',* 2:49.

[46] 'Alim, *Sahih of al-Bukhari*, 9:242.

[47] Ibid., 9:153.

[48] Yahya M. Hendi, *The Descent of Jesus son of Mary at the End of Tme,* M.A. Thesis, (Hartford Seminary, Hartford, Connecticut, 1993), pp. 18-19.

[49] Al-Barzanji, *al-Isha'a li Ashrat al-Sa'a,* (Egypt: Sa'ada Publishing, 1325H. 1907 A.D.), p.240; al-Suyuti. *al-Hawi lil Fatawi,* (Egypt: al.Muniriya Publishing 1352H./ 1933 A.D.), 2:89.

[50] Philippians 2:10-11.

[51] Matthew 24:30-31.

[52] Revelation 17:19.

[53] Revelation 17:14.

[54] Ibid., 19:20.

[55] Ibid., 19:21. The word breath is also interpreted as the word of God or His Spirit.

[56] Ibid., 14:10-11.

[57] The Acts of the Apostles 1:10-11.

[58] Ibid.

[59] Zechariah 14:4; Revelation 1:7 and 19:11. Mount Olives is in the environ of Jerusalem.

[60] Mark 13:7-8.

[61] Ibid., 13:24-25.

[62] It is not clear what is the sign of the Son of Man will be, but it will be the prelude for His second coming.

Chapter 5

[1] Or dam.

[2] It should be translated as, "Bring me, that I may pour over it molten

lead."

[3] This is my translation.

[4] *The Meaning of the Holy Qur'an,* tr. A. Y. 'Ali, appendix 5 for chapter 18, p. 738. Most probably this king is the biblical Melchizedek.

[5] Ibid., p. 739.

[6] Ibn Hisham, *The Life of the Prophet,* trans. by A. Guillaume, 9th ed., (Oxford: New York, Karachi impression, 1990).

[7] Al-Baydawi, *Anwar al-Tanzil wa Asrar al-Ta'wil,* (Beirut: Lebanon: Dar al-Jil, no date).

[8] *Fafsir of al-Fakhr al-Razi,* 3th ed., vol., 21, (Beirut: Lebanon: Dar al-Fikr, 1985), p. 165.

[9] *Tafsir of Ibn Jarir al-Tabari,* 8th ed.. vol., 8, part 17, (Egypt: al-Matba'a al-Amiriya, 1328 H./1910 A.D.), pp.7-23.

[10] *Kitab of al-Kash-shaf,* edited Mustafa Husayn Ahmad, (Beirut: Dar al-Kitab al-'Arabi, 1986), pp.742-749. He cites the fables of the former authors concerning *Dhu al-Qarnayn.*

[11] 'A. Y. Ali, App. VI, p. 740.

[12] Op.cit., pp. 738-739.

[13] *Funk & Wagnall's New Encyclopedia,* vol. 1, under Alexander.

[14] Ibid., p. 369.

[15] Ibid., p. 370.

[16] This book is published by the Medieval Academy of America, Cambridge, Massachusetts, 1932.

[17] P. 3.

[18] Ibid.

[19] Ibid.

[20] Book of Daniel, chapter 7.

[21] Anderson, p. 3

[22] Ibid.

[23] This legend is translated into English by E. A. Wallis Budge, *The History of Alexander the Great* (Cambridge: 1889), pp. 144-161.

[24] As quoted by Anderson, p.23.

[25] Ibid.

[26] Ibid., p.24.

[27] H.A.R. Gibb and J.H. Kramers, *Shorter Encyclopaedia of Islam,* (Leiden: E. J. Brill, 1974), p. 76.

[28] Cyril Glasse, *The Concise Encyclopedia of Islam,* (San Francisco: Harper and Row, 1991), p. 32.

[29] Ibid., pp. 24-25.

[30] Ibid. p. 25.

[31] Refer to chapter five of Anderson's monograph.

[32] Ibid. p. 97.

[33] Qur'an 18:82ff.

[34] Ezekiel 38:2.

[35] *Ryrie Study Bible,* Expanded Edition, (Chicago: Moody press, 1995), p.1323; footnotes on Ezekiel 38:2.

[36] *The New Bible Commentary,* edited, F. Davidson, A. M. Stibbs, & E. M. Kevan, (London: The Inter-Varsity Fellowship, ed., 1962), P. 662-663. Yamauchi indicates that Meshech and Tubal are located in central and eastern Asia; Gomer "is to be identified as the ancestor of the Akkadian Gimmirrai, the classical Cimmerians." Refer to E. Yamauch review article entited *Meshech, Tubal, and Company,* Jets 19, (76), pp.239-347.

[37] Some scholars believe that Beth-togarmah is part of Turkey near the Syrian border; refer to *Ryrie Study Bible,* p. 1323, footnotes on 38:5-6.

[38] *New Bible Commentary,* p. 663.

[39] *The New International Commentary, Book of Ezekiel,* chapters 25-48, (Grand Rapids, Michigan / Cambrigde - U. K., 1998) p.443. Phrases between brackets are mine.

[40] Ibid., pp. 443-444.

[41] *New Bible Commentary,* p.663.

[42] *Ryrie Study Bible.* Footnotes on Revelation 20:8, p. 2041.

[43] *The New International Commentary,* p. 444.

[44] 'Alim, *Sahih of al-Bukhari,* 9:181.

[45] Ibid.

[46] 'Alim, *Sahih of Muslim,* # 1372.

[47] Ibid.

[48] Ibid.

[49] Ibid.

[50] Ibid.

[51] Ibid.

[52] *Musnad of Ahmad,* 3:77; and *Sunan of ibn Maja,* 2:1363.

[53] *Tafsir of ibn Kathir,* 3:105.

[54] *Al-Tasrih bima Tawatara fi Nuzul al-Masih,* p. 159.

[55] Ibid., 204. See also *Sahih of Muslim,* 18:61 (Arabic version); Ibn Hajar, 6:450.

[56] *Musnad of Ahmad,* 2:482, 483.

[57] Ibid., 2:406.

[58] Ibn Hajar, *Fath al-Bari,* 6:357; see also *Sunan of Abu Dawud* 4:117; *Musnad of Ahmad,* 2:437; and *Tafsir of Ibn Jarir,* 6:16.

[59] Al-Maqrizi, *al-khutat,* (Beirut: Matba'at al-Sahil al-Janubi, 1379H./1979 A.D.), vol. 2:350. Muslims believe that the tribe of *Judham* is the tribe of *Jethro,* the father-in-law of Moses.

[60] al-Suyuti, *al-Hawi,* 2:89.

[61] As quoted by Charles L. Holman, p. 91.

[62] Al-Muttaqi al-Hindi, *Kanz of al-'Ummal,*(India: Tab'at Haydar Abad al-Dakn, 1312 H./1894 A.D.), 7:276.

[63] *Sahih of al-Bukhari,* 4:343, 6:356; *Sahih of Muslim,* 2:189 and 192; *Sunan of Abi Dawud,* 4:117; *Sunan of Ibn Maja,* 2:1363; *Musnad of Ahmad,* 2:406, 411 and 494; al-Suyuti, *al-Durr al-Manthur,* 2:241-242.

[64] al-Suyuti, *al-Hawi,* 2:90.

[65] al-Barzanji, *al-Isha'a li Ashrat al-Sa'ah,* p. 240 and *al-Hawi,* 2:89.

[66] Ibid.

Chapter 6

[1] Hassan Ahmad Ibrahim and Ibrahim M. Zein, *The Muslim World,* Vol. LXXXIII, Islah and Tajdid – The Case of the Sudanese Mahdiyya 1881-1898, Jan. 1997, p. 35.

[2] Mustafa Jiha, *Mihnat al-'Aql fi al-Islam,* 2nd ed., (Beirut, Lebanon: 1982), p. 396. Many Western Islamicists and Middle Eastern scholars favor this view, among them Vloten, Goldziher, Ahmad Amin, Taha Husayn and Ahmad al-Kasrawi.

[3] The theory of the Imamate revolves around the twelve Imams, 'Ali (d. 661) the son in law of Muhammad, being the first Imam, then al-Hasan (d. 670); al-Husayn (d. 680); 'Ali ibn al-Husayn (d. 712-13); Muhammad al-Baqir (d. 731-2); Ja'far al-Sadiq (d. 765); Musa al-Kazim (d. 799-800); 'Ali al-Rida (d. 817-18); Muhammad al-Jawad (d. 835); 'Ali al-Hadi (d. 868); Hasan al-'Askari (873-74); Muhammad al-Mahdi who disappeared in the year 873-74.

[4] Some of the Shi'ites assert that the Qur'an has alluded to the Mahdi. They refer to Suras 24:55; 43:61; 21:105 and 9:33. See Muhammad Jawad al-Mahdi, *al-Muslih al-'Alami,* (Toledo: Ohio, Muslim Group in US and Canada,) pp. 8-10.

[5] Riffat Hassan, *Journal of Ecumenical Studies,* Messianism and Islam, 22:2, Spring 1985, pp.277-279.

[6] Muhammad al-Husayn Al Kashif al-Ghita', *Asl al-Shi'a wa 'Usuluha,,* (Beirut, Lebanon: Dar al-Bihar,1960) p. 103.

[7] Ibid.

[8] Ibid.

[9] *Al-Muslih al-'Alami*, p. 9.

[10] *Messianism and Islam*, p. 262.

[11] Ibid., p.263.

[12] Abdulaziz Abdulhussein Sachedina, *Islamic Missianism, The Idea of Mahdi In Twelver Shi'ism*, (Albany, N.Y: State University Press, 1981,) p. 1.

[13] Ibid., pp. 1-2.

[14] Ibid., p. 2.

[15] Ibid., p.2.

[16] Sayyid Muhammad Husayn Tabataba'i, trans. Sayyid Husayn Nasr, *Shiite Islam*, (Houston, Texas: Free Islamic Literature, Inc., 1971), p. 214.

[17] David Pinault, *The Shiites: Rituals and Popular Piety in a Muslim Community.* (New York: St. Martin's Press, 1992), pp. 8-9.

[18] Al-Suyuti, *al-Hawi*, 2:241.

[19] Ibid., 2:235. This account differs from the account that is mentioned on page 106.

[20] Kamel Sulayman, *Yawm al-Khalas fi Zilli al-Qa'im al-Mahdi* (Beirut: Dar al-Kitab al-Lubnani, 1991,) p.66.

[21] Ibid., p.73.

[22] Op. cit.

[23] Mustafa al-Kazimi, *Bisharat al-Islam*, (al-Najaf, Iraq, 1382 H. /1962 A.D), p. 77 and 82.

[24] Al-Saduq, *'Uyun Akhbar al-Rida,* (al-Najaf, Iraq, 1970), vol. 1, p. 36.

[25] Lutfalla al-Safi, *Muntakhab al-Athar fi al-Imam al-Thani 'Ashar,* (Tahran: 1373 H./1953 A.D.), p. 341. He is likened to Jesus who spoke in his cradle according to the Qur'an.

[26] Al-Qanduzi, *Yanabi' al-Mawadda*, vol. 3, (Istanbul: 1301 H./ 1883 A.D.), p.53.

[27] Ibid., p.136; *Bisharat al-Islam*, p.253.

[28] 'Ali al-yazdi al-Ha'iri. *Ilzam al-Nasib fi Ithbat Hujjiyat al-Gha'ib,* (Tahran Press, 1351 H./1952 A.D.), p.228.

[29] Ibid., p. 229.

[30] Al-Majlisy, *Bihar al-Anwar*, section 52, (Tahran, Iran: Matba'at Tahran, 1385 H./1965 A.D.), p.192.

[31] Al-Hasan al-Arbali, *Kashf al-Ghamma fi Ma'rifat al-A'imma*, vol. 3, (Iran edition, 1382 H./1962 A.D.), p. 259.

[32] *Yawm al-Khalas,* p. 331.

[33] *Bihar al-Anwar,* vol. 51, p. 84.

[34] *Ilzam al-Nasib,* p. 208.

[35] Ibid., pp. 139,140, 227, and 239.

[36] Ibid,. p. 10.

[37] Ahmad Kasravi, *On Islam and Shi'ism*, trans. M.R. Ghanooparvar, (Costa Mesa, CA: Mazda Publishers, 1990,) p. 140.

[38] *Yawm al-Khalas,* p. 384.

[39] *Ilzam al-Nasib,* p. 245.

[40] Ibid., p. 190.

[41] *Islamic Messianism,* p.172.

[42] *Al-Hawi lil Fatawi.* Vol. 2, p. 134.

[43] *Kasf al-Ghamma,* vol. 3. p. 279.

[44] *Yanabi' al-Mawaddat.* vol. 3, p. 90.

[45] See *Yawm al-Khalas,* pp.343-347.

[46] *Ilzam al-Nasib.* p. 229.

[47] *Yawm al-Khalas,* pp. 348-355.

[48] Ibid., p.352.

[49] P. 165, note 49. As quoted from H. G. Kippenberg, *Garrizin und Synagoge,*(Berlin, 1971), p.131.

[50] Ibid. See also p. 354 in which the author quotes Revelation 6:15-16; he comments: "Isn't this what is related in our narratives that describe the fear of the Jews of the sword of the Overlord (the *Mahdi*) and their hiding in the shades of every tree and rock?"

[51] Ibid. Modern translations of the Bible suggest, on linguistic basis, a different translation such as, 'and they will come with the wealth of the nations' (NIV).

[52] *Yawm al-Khalas,* p. 350.

[53] Ibid., p.546.

[54] Ibid., pp. 404-406.

[55] Ibid., p.550.

[56] Sa'id Ayyub, *'Aqidat al-Masih al-Dajjal fi al-Adyan,* (Beirut, Lebanon: Dar al-Hadi, 1991,) pp. 44-47. But this sort of quotation and interpretation permeates the entire book.

[57] Ibid., pp. 86-89.

[58] Ibid ., refer to pp.48-89.

[59] Ibid., p. 98.

[60] Ibid., p.100.

[61] Op. cit. 100-101.

[62] *'Aqidat al-Masih al-Dajjal,* p. 293; footnote 6.

[63] Ayatollah Ibrahim Amini, trans. Abdulaziz Sachedini, *Al-Imam al-Mahdi the Just Leader of Humanity,* (Qum, Iran: Ansaryan Publications, 1997), p. 44.

271

[64] Ibid., pp.44-45.

[65] Refer to *Yawm al-Khalas* in which the author emphatically indicates in different place that the Imams have predicted the invention of these modern weapons.

[66] Amini, pp. 318-319.

[67] Ibibd., p. 313.

[68] Ibid., p. 314.

[69] Ibid., pp. 314-315.

[70] Ibid., p. 315.

[71] Gorden D. Newby *Studies in Islamic And Judaic Tradition,* The Drowned Son: Midrash and Midrash Making in the Qur'an and Tafsir (commentary), 1:20. See also Newby, *A History of the Jews of Arabia,* (University of South Carolina Press, 1988), pp.49-77.

[72] Ibid.

[73] Ibid.

[74] Al-Dhahabi, *Tath-karat al-Huffaz,* (India. n. p.; n.d.), v.1:27.

[75] *Studies in Islamic and Judaic Tradition.* 1:20.

[76] Ibn Kathir, 4:17.

[77] Jawad Ali, *Tarikh al-' Arab Qabla al-Islam,* (Iraq: al-Majma' al-'Ilmi al-'Iraqi, 1956), 6:99, 101.

[78] *Studies in Islamic and Judaic Tradition,* 1:21.

[79] Ibid.

[80] Ibid.

[81] Ibid.

[82] For more information about the Judeo-Christian influence, refer to Abraham Geiger, *Judaism and Islam,* (Ktav: NY, 1970), ori. 1853; Abraham Katch, *Judaism in Islam: Biblical and Talmudic Background of the Koran and its Commentaries,* (Bloch Pub., 1954); Charles Torrey, *The Jewish Foundation of Islam,* (Ktav: NY, 1967), orig. 1933; Mordechai Nisan, *The Identity and Civilization: Essays on Judaism and Islam,* (Lanham, New York: University Press of America, 1999).

[83] Ramzi Na'na'a, *al-Isra'iliyat,* (Beirut, Lebanon and Damascus, Syria: Pub. Dar al-Qalam and Dar al-Diya', 1970), p.111.

[84] Ibid., 113.

[85] Ibn 'Abd Rabbih, Ahmad ibn al-Qurtubi, al-'*Aqd al-Farid,* (Cairo: Egypt, Lujnat al-ta'lif wa al- tarjama wa al-Nashr, 1940-1953), 1:269

[86] *Al-Isra'iliyat,* p. 115.

[87] *Haggarism,* p. 27.

[88] In his article *The late Sasanian Economic Impact on the Arabian Peninsula,* Michael Morony documented that there were a number of

Zoroastrian communities in Arabia who contributed to the economy of the Peninsula; refer to *Name-ye Iran-e Bastan*, vol.1, No 2, pp. 25-37. This fact demonstrates that the Arabs were acquainted with some aspects of the social and religious life of the Zoroastrians.

[89] Though the term *saoshyant* is sometimes translated to mean redeemer, it does not carry the concept of a savior from sin and guilt but "he who will bring benefit", a benefactor; (as quoted by Edwin Uamauchi, *Persia and the Bible*, 444, from J. R. Hinnells, *Zoroastrian Saviour Imagery and Its Influence on the New Testament*, (Numen 16, 1969), 164.

[90] *On Islam and Shi'ism*. p. 128.

[91] *'Aqidat al-Masih al-Dajjal*, p. 277-343.

[92] *Yawm al-Khalas*, p. 711.

[93] Ibid.

[94] Ibid. p. 724.

[95] *Islamic Messianism*, p. 171.

[96] Ibid. p.172.

[97] Ibid. p. 173.

[98] Ibid.

[99] *'Aqidat al-Masih al-Dajjal*, p. 363.

[100] Ibid.

[101] Ibid., p.276.

[102] The black color will be the color of the Shi'ites and the Imam as it was in the past.

Chapter 7

[1] Sura 27:82.

[2] Ibid., v. 81

[*] A.Y. Ali translates the pronoun as 'he'; but the phrase 'speak to them' uses the feminine verb form for the subject Beast. Grammatically, it is true that the word Beast could be treated as either masculine or feminine, but in this case the Qur'an used the feminine verb 'tukallim' to indicate that the Beast here is feminine.

[3] A. Y. 'Ali, *The Meaning of the Holy Qur'an*, footnote 3313, p. 956.

[4] Ibid.

[5] Ibid.

[6] Al-Sha'rani, *Mukhtasar Tatdharat al-Qurtubi*, (Cairo, Egypt: Subayh

edition, 1354 / 1935 A.D.), p. 147.

[7] *Al-Isra'iliyat*, pp. 265, 266.

[8] *Tafsir of Ibn Kathir*, 3:374; footnote 1.

[9] Al-Alussy, *Ruh al-Ma'ani fi Tafsir al-Qur'an al-'Azim wa al-Sab' al-Mathani*, (Cairo, Egypt: Bulaq print, 1303/1885 A.D.), 6:314.

[10] Al-Tayalisi, *al-Musnad*, (India: Haydar Abad Print, 1321/ 1903 A.D.), p. 334.

[11] *Musnad of Ahmad*, 2:295 and 491.

[12] *Sunan of al-Tirmidhi*, 12:63 (Arabic version).

[13] *Sunan of Ibn Maja*, 2:1351 (Arabic version).

[14] *Ruh al-Ma'ani*, 6:314. He adds that this information about the Beast is more acceptable and sensible than the others.

[15] Pp. 189-191.

[16] *Al-Isra'iliyat*, p. 265 as quoted from the *Tafsir of al-Baghawi*, which is printed on the margin of *Tafsir of al-khazin*. Refer also to p. 266.

[17] *Al-Malahim wa al-Fitan*, p. 189.

[18] Ibid., p. 190-191.

[19] Leon Morris, *Tyndale New Testament Commentary: The Revelation of John*, (Grand Rapids, Michigan: William E. Eerdmans Publishing House, 1976), p. 166.

[20] Ibid. 167.

[21] *The Meaning of the Holy Qur'an*, p. 1284, footnote 4696.

[22] Ibid.

[23] *Al-Malahim wa al-Fitan*, p. 202.

[24] *Al-Tasrih bima Tawatara fi Nuzul al-Masih*, p. 133, footnote 1.

[25] Heribert Busse, *Islam, Judaism, and Christianity: Theological and Historical Affiliations*, trans. Allison Brown, (Princeton, New Jersey: Markus Weiner Publishers, 1998), p.27. Umayya died two years before Muhammad, and most probably, both of them used the same sources, p.27. This notion may be detrimental to many Muslims who insist that the entire Qur'an was revealed verbatim to Muhammad.

[26] Ibid. p. 129.

[27] *Al-Tasrih bima Tawatara fi Nuzul al-Masih*, p. 136.

[28] According to the Shi'ite resources, the Sufyani belongs to the 'Ummayyad clan, the traditional enemy of the family of "Ali ibn Abi Talib. His maternal uncles belong to the Christian tribe of Kalb. Mu'awiya, the first 'Umayyad caliph, married from this tribe. She begot him Yazid who became the second 'Umayyad caliph. This Yazid is the one whose army killed al-Husayn ibn 'Ali. According to the Shi'ite account, the Sufyani's name is 'uthman ibn'Anbasa. Refer to *Yawm al-Khalas*. P. 670, footnote 2.

[29] 'Ali Muhammad 'Ali Dakhil, *al-Imam al Mahdi*, (Najaf, Iraq, n.d.), p.71.

[30] Wilferd Madeulung, *Journal of Near Eastern Studies,* 'ABD ALLAH B. AL-ZUBAR AND THE MAHDI, 40, # 4, (1981), p. 293.

[31] Ibid.

[32] Ibid.

[33] Ibid., pp. 293-94.

Chapter 8

[1] *Sahih of al-Bukhari*, 6:73.

[2] *Musnad of Ahmad*, 3:31.

[3] *Sahih of Muslim*, 1:196; *Musnad of Ahmad*, 2:455.

[4] *Sahih of al-Bukhari*, # 7424 and *Sahih of Muslim* 159 (English version)

[5] *Musnad of Ahmad*, 2:201.

[6] *Al-Fitan wa al-Malahim*, p.197. It is related on the authority of 'Abdullah that the Prophet said, 'When the sun rises from the West the Devil will prostrate calling in a loud voice: O my God ! Command me to prostrate to whoever you will.' He ('Abdullah) said, 'His demons will gather around him saying: our Master, what is this imploring?' He will say, 'I had asked my Lord to spare me until the appointed time.' He ('Abdullah) said, 'Then the Beast of the earth will emerge out of the cleave of a rock and its first step will take place in Antioch. The Devil then will come (to it) and it (the Beast) will slap him.

[7] Ibid. p. 198-199. Ibn Khathir acknowledges that the above *hadith* is one of the strangest news, p. 198.

[8] Ibid., p. 198.

[9] Ibid. See notes 1 and 2.

[10] *Fi al-Shi'r al-Jahili*, p. 92.

[11] *Al-Fitan wa al-Malahim*, pp. 196-199.

[12] *The Signs before the Day of Judgment*, p. 87.

[13] Between brackets are mine.

[14] A.Y. A., *Qur'an.* P. 732, footnote # 2430.

[15] *Al-Fitan wa al-Malahim*, pp. 194-200.

[16] The three signs are: The Beast of the earth, Gog and Magog, and presumably, Jesus son of Mary.

[17] *Al-Fitan wa al-Malahim*, p.197.

[18] *Gospel of Matthew* 24:29-30. See also, Ezekiel 32:7; Joel 2:10, 31; 3:15f; Revelation 6:12-17; 8:12 and Isaiah 34:4.

[19] Pseudo-Callisthenenes, *The History of Alexander the Great,* trans., Ernest A. Wallis Budge from five Syriac manuscripts, (Amesterdam: Apa-philo Press, first published 1889, reprint 1976, Cambridge University press), p. 148.

[20] *Al-Fitan wa al-Malahim*, p. 257.

[21] It seems that this first *hashr* is not the same assembly after the resurrection. This implies that there are two types of *hashr*, one before the Hour and the other after the day of resurrection; refer to *al-Fitan wa al-Malahim*, pp. 260-261. Some Muslim scholars reject the notion of two *Hashrs*, Ibid.

[22] *Musnad of Ahmad*, 3:271.

[23] *Al-Fitan wa al-Malahim*, p. 162.

[24] *Musnad of Ahmad*, 2:354.

[25] Ibid.

[26] Ibid.

[27] Eden or Aden is a city at the sea cost of Yemen.

[28] *Sahih of al-Bukhari*, # 6522 (English version).

[29] Exodus 13:21.

[30] *Musnad of Ahmad*, 2:210

[31] Op. cit 1:454. Refer also to *Musnad of Ahmad*, 1:435; *Sahih of Muslim*, #2949.

[32] *al-Fitan wa al-Malahim*, PP. 216-218.

[33] Refer to p.

[34] *Musnad of Ahmad*, 5:3. The term Syria (al-Sham) here includes what is regarded as the greater Syria.

[35] Op. cit., 2:199.

Chapter 9

[1] We have briefly alluded in chapter two to the concept of resurrection; but in this chapter we will examine in-depth this basic creed and discuss the events that will accompany this universal incident which will end the current history f the world.

[2] Refer to the previous chapter, section of the Assembly.

[3] Abu Hamid al-Ghazali, *The Remembrance of Death and Afterlife, trans.* T. J. Winters, (Cambridge,Uk: The Islamic Texts Society,1989,) p. 123.

[4] Ibid., p. 124.

[5] Ibid., p. 125.

[6] Ibid., p. 126.

[7] *Sahih of Muslim*, 17:204; (4: #6863) of the English translation.

[8] Ibid., 17:206; (4: #6868) of the English translation.

[9] Ibid., 17:200; (4: #6857) of the English translation

[10] The Jewish Rabbinic eschatological material points to the trial of the grave. The soul is believed to encounter after death the *Hibbut hakever*, the pains of the grave; Dumah, the angel of silence; the angel of death, (http://en.wikipedia.org/wiki/Jewish_eschatology).

[11] *The Remembrance of Death and After Life*, p.135

[12] Refer to pp. 49-53. These problems which are cited from different Islamic sources reflect the dilemma that face the researcher as he tries to find his way through the jungle of these conflicting hadiths.

[13] Ibid. p.136.

[14] Op. cit. This statement asserts the concept of predestination in Islam.

[15] Ibid. pp. 136-37.

[16] *The Islamic Understanding of Death and Resurrection*, p. 32.

[17] Ahmad H. Sakr, *Death and Dying,* (Lombard, Illinois, 1995,) p. 16, fn. 4. Barzakh is translated in English as isthmus.

[18] *The Islamic Understanding of Death and Resurrection*, p. 64.

[19] Ibid. p. 39.

[20] Ibid. p.50. For more detail about the events that will take place between death and resurrection refer to chapter two of this source.

[21] A. Guillaum, *Life of Muhammad*, pp. 95-98.

[22] As quoted by Sadiq 'abdul-Haq in *Al-Islam: Is it Reasonable?* (n. place, n. publisher, n. date,) p. 125.

[23] George William Carter, *Zoroastrianism and Judaism,* (New York: AMS Press, 1970,) p. 96.

[24] Op., cit.

[25] Farnaz Ma'sumian, *The After Death: A study of the afterlife in world religion,* (Oxford: England: One Word Publication, 1995, reprint 1996), p. 19.

[26] *Zoroastrian and Judaism*, p.96.

[27] *The After Death*, p. 19.

[28] *Hadhokt Nask, 9;* as quoted in *the After Death*, p. 20.

[29] Ibid., 25; as quoted in *The After Death*, P.26.

[30] Ibid., p. 20. See also J. D. C. Pavry, *The Zoroastrian Dctrine of a Future Life,* (New York: AMS, 1965, reprint of 1929 edition), p.34, 41.

[31] These issues will be discussed below.

[32] *Al-Malahim wa al- Fitan*, p. 228.

[33] *Musnad of Ahmad*, 1:326.

[34] Israfil is the Arabic name of Seraphiel.

[35] *Al-Fitan wa al-Malahim*, pp. 244-245.

[36] Some Islamic traditions ascribed to Muhammad the claim that he said when Israfil blows the trumpet, the angel Gabriel will be at his right hand and the angel Michael will be at his left hand; see *Musnad of Ahmad* 3:10.

[37] There are several verses in the Qur'an that refer to the trumpet: Suras 6; 73; 10:48-54; 18:99-100; 16: 88; 20:102; 23:101; 38: 15; 39: 68-70; 54:50; 69:13-18; 74:8-10; 78:18-20; 79:13-14.

[38] *Al-Fitan wa al-Malahim*, p. 245

[39] Ibid., p. 246.

[40] As it is quoted by Smith and Haddad, footnote 29, p. 214, from Macdonald, "The Day of Resurrection," *Islamic Studies* 5, (19655), p. 148.

[41] *The Islamic Understanding of Death and Resurrection*, p. 73.

[42] Ibid., p. 246.

[43] *Sahih of al-Bukhari*, 6: #6705 (Arabic version).

[44] *Gospel of Matthew* 24:15-19, 40-41 and *Gospel of Luke* 17:35-36.

[45] Suras 14:48; 20:107.

[46] *Al-Fitan wa al-Malahim*, p. 246. *'Ukaz* is a place in Arabia.

[47] As quoted by al-Ghazali in *The Remembrance of Death*, p. 178.

[48] Al-Ghazali hints at two trumpets only (refer to the *Remembrance of Death and Afterlife,* p. 176) though the Qur'an, it seems, differentiates between the trumpet of terror and the trumpet of *al-Sa'qa* as explained above.

[49] John of Damascus asserts that "the God who created our bodies from earth can raise them once again incorruptible, and reunite them to our souls…The first reason for the resurrection, he argues, is that it is required by God's justice: if the soul does not realize vice and virtue apart from the body, the body must share in its punishment and reward." See Brian E. Daley, *The Hope of The Early Church,* (New York - Port Chester – Melbourne – Sydney: Cambridge University Press, 1958), p.203.

[50] *Death and Dying*, p. 18.

[51] *Al-Fitan wa al-Malahim*, p. 246. al-Ghazali says '4 cubits'.

[52] As quoted in *The Islamic Understanding of Death and Resurrection,* p. 72, from *al-Durra*, by al-Ghazali, p.41.

[53] Muhammad indicates that "everything in the human body will decay except the coccyxes bone and from that bone Allah will reconstruct

the whole body." Refer to *Sahih of al-Bukhari*, 6:319.

[54] Phil Parshall, *Understanding Muslim Teaching and Traditions*, (Grand Rapids: MI, 2002), p. 130.

[55] Does this mean that the spirits somehow survive the absolute annihilation of the universe?

[56] *Al-Fitan wa al-Malahim*, pp.246-247; or seize them.

[57] It seems that later Islamic traditions and commentaries denote that "some elements would be exempt (sic) from the complete annihilation or the *fana'*, included in that category were the Throne, the Guarded Tablets, the Pen, sometimes the Garden and the fire, the prophets (along with the martyrs, who are assured a place in the Garden in the Qur'an), and the *hur* or the maidens of the Garden. Later theology even posited that human spirits will not perish at the *fana'*, but will remain, along with the top of the spine, from which the resurrected body begins its growth." Refer to Smith and Haddad, footnote 30, p. 214.

[58] *Al-Malahim wa al-Fitan*, p. 247.

[59] John Gilchrist, *The Qur'an the Scripture of Islam*, (Mondeor, South Africa: MERCSA, 1995), p. 96

[60] This topic will be discussed when we examine the concept of Paradise.

[61] In Christianity God will Judge the world through Jesus Christ.

[62] Suras 7: 34; 16: 61.

[63] Suras 30: 55; 30: 30; 46: 35.

[64] Suras 6: 31, 40; 7: 187; 12: 107; 15: 85; 16: 77; 18: 21, 36; 19: 75; 20: 15; 21:49; 22:1, 7, 55; 25: 11 (twice); 30: 12, 14; 31: 34; 33: 63 (twice); 34: 3; 40:46, 59; 41: 47, 50; 42: 17, 18; 43: 61, 66, 85; 45: 27, 32, ; 47: 18; 54: 1, 46 (twice); 79: 42.

[65] Matthew 24: 36, 42; 25: 13; Luke 12:40; John 5: 32.

[66] Sura 23:100. *Munkar* and *Nakir* are not mentioned in the Qur'an.

[67] Herman A. Hoyt, *The End of Times*, 4th print, (Chicago: IL, 1976).

[68] Sheol-Hades in Christianity are the equivalent of the Barzakh in Islam. Sheol is a Hebrew word, while Hades is a Greek term. Both give the same meaning.

[69] Ibid., p. 37.

[70] Ibid.

[71] Ibid., p. 37-38.

[72] Ibid., p. 38.

[73] Ibid. I am indebt, in the above discussion, to the study of Herman A. Hoyt in his book, *The End of Times*, chapter 3.

[74] Ibid,. pp. 38-43.

[75] It is important to note here that Hoyt believes that after the death of Jesus He went down to Hades and made an announcement to the righteous, a message of finished redemption. But for those who were in the lowest Sheol it was a message that sealed their doom. Also, at His resurrection and ascension, He transferred Paradise to the third heaven, including the spirits of the Old Testament saints (pp 45-46).

[76] *Al-Malahim wa al-fitan*, pp.244-245; see also Sura 81:1-14.

[77] Revelation, chapters 6-18.

[78] Ibid., chapter 21.

[79] John 5:28, 29; and Acts 24:15.

[80] 1 Thessalonians 4:15-17.

[81] Revelation 20:11-15.

[82] This issue has been discussed at the beginning of this chapter.

[83] There is a heated debate within Christian circles whether these 1000 years are actual years or symbolic years. It is not the concern of this study to discuss the different interpretations since its main interest is to present a comparative eschatological study between Islam and Christianity. For more information about the Millennium refer to *The Meaning of the Millennium*, edited by Robert G. Clouse, (Downers Grove, Illinois: InterVarsity Press, 1977).

Chapter 10

[1] *The Remembrance of Death and Afterlife*, p. 182.

[2] Ibid.

[3] *Sahih of Muslim*, # 2278 (Arabic version).

[4] *Al-Tasrih bima Tawatara fi Nuzul al-Masih*, p. 241.

[5] *Al-Fitan wa al-Malahim*, pp. 290-291.

*According to Islam The Day of the Tur is the day when God was angry at the people of Israel so He lifted mount Sinai as a canopy over them to smash them with it and made them all die for a while.

[6] *Sunan of al-Tirmidhi*, # 3669. Here we sense the implication of politics.

[7] Ceasar E. Farah, *Islam,* seventh ed., (Hauppauge: New York, Barron's 2003), p.115.

[8] *Musnad of Ahmad*, 6:90. Refer to Sura 80:37; my translation).

[9] *Sahih of Muslim*, 17:194 (Arabic version).

[10] Most of the rationales for why Abraham was selected to be the first to be clothed are mere speculations. In his book *al-Tadh-karat* 1:352,

al-Qurtubi claims that because Abraham was the first to wear the *sirwal* (underpants), and was stripped of it when he was thrown into the furnace, and 'God knows better.'

[11] *Musnad of Ahmad*, 1:398.

[12] Ibid. Undoubtedly this concept of sitting at the right hand of God is borrowed from Christianity. The Bible repeatedly reiterates that Jesus will be sitting at the right hand of God.

[13] *Al-Fitan wa al-Malahim*, p. 297. This means the records of bad deeds and the good deeds are opened.

[14] In other places it is mentioned that this interval will be fifty thousand years.

[15] *Al-Fitan wa al-Malahim*, p. 247.

[16] *Sahih al-Bukhari*, 8: 539 (English version).

[17] In the story of creation Muslims do not differentiate between breath and spirit.

[18] *Al-Fitan wa al-Malahim*, p. 247.

[19] *Al-Fitan wa al-Malahim*, p. 247.

[20] *The Remembrance of Death and Afterlife*, p. 186-187.

[21] In Islam there are two types of *jinns*: the good *jinns* and the bad *jinns*. The *jinns* are spirits created from fire. The *jinns* here are the evil spirits.

[22] This word is rather vague in this text. Muslim scholars claim it means leader. In this case it could mean their holy book, or the record book or their leaders who will bear witness to their virtues or vices (refer to *The Meaning of the Holy Qur'an*, footnote 2266, p. 694.) But this word can be read as nations *umamihim*, بامهم as it is figured in the Qur'an since the vocalization system was not yet invented when the Qur'an was codified. Thus the meaning may be 'with or by their nations.'

[23] See also Sura 69:19-25.

[24] *The Remembrance of Death and Afterlife*, p. 195-196.

[25] Ibid., p.196.

[26] Ibid.

[27] Amina Wadud, *Qur'an and Women*, (Oxford, New York: Oxford University Press, 1999), p.48.

[28] Sura 42:17. The scale here is the principle of justice which will be manifested in the Day of Judgment.

[29] *The Islamic Understanding of Death and Resurrection*, p. 77. Refer also to footnote 49 of chapter three, p. 216 of their book.

[30] Ibid.

[31] See also Suras 18:105; 23:102-103; 101:6-11.

[32] The *Mu'tazilites* were a scholastic movement that flourished during the time of the caliph al-Ma'mun who adhered to their theology that stressed the notion, among many, of the free will of man. They were the free thinkers of the age.

[33] *The Sources of Islam.* P. 68.

[34] Ibid., pp.68 and 69.

[35] Ibid., p.70. See also E. A. Wallis Budge, *The Book of the Dead*, (Arkana: Benguin Croup, 1989), pp.22-30 and 149-151.

[36] Ibid., p.73.

[37] Ibid.

[38] Ibid.

[39] *Zoroastrianism and Judaism*, p.98.

[40] See also verse 13.

[41] Revelation 20:4-5.

[42] Ibid., vv. 12-13.

Chapter 11

[1] *Sahih of Muslim*, 7:159; (4: 1472, English version). In another *hadith*, Muhammad said: "Unless God gets hold of me with a favor and mercy".

[2] It is also pronounced *Surat.*

[3] Muhammad Fu'ad 'abdul-baqi, *Al-Mu'jam al-Mufahras li Al-Faz al-Qur'an*, (Beirut, Lebanon: Dar al Fikr, 1987), p. 407, under صراط.

[4] *The Lives of Man*, (Louisville. KY: Fons Vitae, 1991), p.63.

[5] *The Remembrance of Death and Afterlife*, p. 206.

[6] *Religions of the World*, p. 269.

[7] Ibid.

[8] *The Qur'an the Scripture of Islam*, p. 96.

[9] Ibid., p.96-97. See also Sura 37:23.

[10] Ibid., p. 97.

[11] *The Remembrance of Death and Afterlife*, p. 207

[12] Ibid., p. 206.

* A desert thorny shrub that pricks and wounds the feet of anyone that treads upon it.

[13] Ibid., p.207.

[14] *The Lives of Man*, p. 64.

[15] *Sahih of Muslim*, 17:194, (Arabic version).

[16] *The Lives of Man*, p. 63.

[17] Ibid.

[18] Ibid., p. 65. The Islamic Tradition also suggests that for every prophet a Pool is assigned, and the prophets shall boast with each other 'about which (one) is reached by a larger number of people,' see *The Remembrance of Death and the Afterlife*, pp. 217-219.

[19] *Al-Fitan wa al-Malahim*, pp. 250-253; *The Remembrance of Death and the Afterlife*, pp. 210-216.

[20] *The Lives of Man*, p. 69.

[21] Refer also to Revelation 7:17 and 21:6.

[22] Chapter twelve will reflect the impact of biblical language on the Islamic eschatology.

[23] Muntasir Mir, *Dictionary of Qur'anic Terms and Concept*, (NY and London: Garland Publishing, Inc. 1987), p. 91.

[24] Ibid.

[25] Refer to Muhammad Fu'ad 'Abd al-Baqi, *Al-Mu'jam al-Mufahras li Al- Faz al-Qur'an*, under the word Jannat, pp.180-182.

[26] Abd Al-Masih, *The Gosel Questions the Qur'an*, (Villach, Austria: Light of Life, 1998), p.57.

[27] Jane Dammen McAuliffe, *Encyclopedia of the Qur'an*, (Leiden, the Netherlands: Koninklijke Brill NV, 2001), p.170. In another tradition the fourth heaven is assigned to Jesus.

[28] Ibid.

[29] This topic will be discussed below.

[30] See also 5:119; 9:89; 10:9; 16:31; 57:12; 61:12. There is over 30 references to these rivers in the Qur'an. The rivers are: one of 'fresh water,' one of 'milk' whose flavor does not change, one of 'wine' that is a delight to any one that drinks from it, and one of 'pure honey.' It seems that the idea of the four rivers that flow through the Garden is taken from the book of Genesis 2:10-14.

[31] Thomas Patrick Hughes, *Dictionary of Islam*, Library of Religious and Philosophic Thought, (Clifton, New Jersey: Reference Book Publisher, Inc. 1965), p. 283.

[32] In the Meaning of the Holy Qur'an, footnote 5849 points that S. 76:5-6 and 13-22, provide a description of a royal feast which is appropriate to such a kingly banquet which the blessed will "receive at the royal and Divine Banquet. The words in the next verse express the sort of speech which make the Guest a denizen of Heaven." P.1574. The idea of the royal banquet is a salient characteristic of the heavenly celebration when Christ receives the church, which is symbolically described, as the bride. Only the redeemed will participate in this feast (Revelation 20:7-9). This author believes that

the idea of the royal banquet is an echo of what is recorded in Revelation. It also reminds us of the parable that Jesus narrated about the kingly feast in Matt. 22:2-14.

[33] *The Remembrance of Death and Afterlife*, p. 235.

[34] Miriam Van Scott, *Encyclopedia of Heaven*, first edition, (NY, NY: Thomas Dunn Books, an imprint of St. Martin Press, 1999), p. 67.

[35] Ibid., p. 73.

[36] As quoted by Yamauchi from B. Lincoln, On the Imagery of Paradise, *Indogermanische Forschungen* 85 (1980). P.159.

[37] *The Remembrance of Death and Afterlife*, p. 244.

[38] Ibid., p. 245. A Pahlavi Rivayat indicates that in Paradise "there is sex satisfaction without procreation." Quoted by Yamauchi as cited by S. Shaked in Notions *menog and getig* in the Pahlavi Texts and their relation to Eschalogy, *Acta Orientalia* 33 (1971), p. 86.

[39] Ibid.

[40] Ibid. Quoted by al-Ghazali from Ahmad ibn al-Husayn al-Bayhaqi, *Kitab al-Ba' th wa al-Nushur*, ed. A. A. Haydar, (Beirut, 1986), p. 244.

[41] P. 98.

[42] Ibid.

[43] *The Remembrance of Death and Afterlife*, P. 347 as cited by al-Ghazali from *Sunan of Ibn Maja, Book of al-Zuhd*, 39.

[44] Al-Tirmidhi, *Janna*, 23;

[45] *The Remembrance of Death and Afterlife*, p. 248. This statement is quoted verbatim from 1Corinthians 2:9.

[46] *Sahih al-Bukhari*, Tawhid, 24; *Sahih of Muslim*, Masajid, 211 (Arabic version).

[47] Cyril Glass, *The New Encyclopedia of Islam*, rev, ed., (Lanham, N.Y.: Rowman and Littlefield Publishers, 2001), p. 175.

[48] J. Oswald Sanders, *Heaven Better by Far*, (Grand Rapids, Michigan: Discovery House Publishers, 1994), p. 22-23.

[49] Luke 21:17.

[50] *Heaven Better by Far*, p.89.

[51] In his book *A History of Heaven*, Jefferey Burton Russell explains that "Traditional Jewish and Christian thinkers recognized that metaphor expresses a deeper reality than can be attained through the overt sense. This manner of thinking can be called 'metaphorical ontology.' Ontology is the study of 'being' as such and in itself...Metaphor is the use of words overtly denoting one kind of object or idea in place of another to suggest an analogy between them

284

or a deeper meaning beneath them." p. 12, (Princeton University Press).

[52] *Heaven Better by Far,* p.132.

[53] *The End of Time,* p. 224.

[54] Ibid.

[55] Leon Morris, *The Revelation of Saint John,* (Grand Rapids, Michigan: Eerdmans, 1976), p. 243.

[56] *The End Time,* p. 225.

[57] See also Mark 12: 25; Luke 20:35.

[58] *Heaven Better by Far,* p. 102.

[59] Refer to *al-Mu'jam al-Mufahras, under Jahannam,* pp.184-185.

[60] The term *Sa'ir* occurs in fifteen other places in the Qur'an and in some cases attached to the definite article 'the'; refer to Suras: 22:4; 31:21; 34:12; 35:6; 42:7; 67:5, 10, 11. Without the definite article 'the' see Suras: 4:55; 17:97; 25:11; 33:64; 48:13; 76:4; 84:12.

[61] The information about the Sabeans is very meager, but it seems that the Qur'an regarded them among the People of the Book. Refer to Sinasi Gunduz, *The knowledge of Life,* (Oxford University Press, 1994), pp.15-29.

[62] 54:48; 74:26, 27, 42.

[63] *The Remembrance of Death and Afterlife,* p.220.

[64] Ibid., p. 220.

[65] Ibid., p. 221.

[66] Maneckji Nusservanji Dhalla *Zoroastrian Theology from the Earliest Times to the Present Day,* (New York: AMS Press Inc., reprint of 1914), p. 280.

[67] Ibid., p. 283.

[68] Ibid., p. 282.

[69] *Sahih of al-Bukhari,* Riqaq, p.51; *Sahih of Muslim,* 'Iman, p. 365, as quoted in *The Remembrance of Death and the Afterlife,* p. 224.

[70] As quoted in *The Remembrance of Death and Afterlife,* p. 229. This *Hadith* contradicts many other traditions of intercessions of the prophets and the acts of God's mercy on most of those who inhabit hell.

[71] Abd al-Masih, *The Gospel Questions the Qur'an,* pp.51-52.

[72] *The End Times,* p. 234-235.

[73] Ibid., p. 235-238.

[74] *The Revelation of St. John,* p. 242.

Chapter 12

[1] Abu Musa al-Hariri, *Quss wa Nabi* , (Diar 'Aql. Lebanon: Dar li Ajli al-Ma'rifa, 1985), p. 158.

[2] David Brady, *Journal of Semitic Studies*, The Book of Revelation and the Qur'an: Is there a Possible Literary Relationship? (Manchester: Manchester University Press, vol. 23, 1978), p. 216.

[3] *The Origin of Islam in its Christian Environment*, p.104.

[4] *The Sources of Islam*, pp. 45-75.

[5] *The Origin of Islam in its Christian Environment*, pp.104-105.

[6] *Journal of Islamic Studies*, The Book of Revelation and the Qur'an. P. 216.

[7] Muslims believe that the four Gospels of the N.T. are similar to the collections of the Tradition. They are not the book that was revealed to Jesus, but narratives about him. The real gospel of Jesus, they claim, was lost or destroyed or was lifted up with Jesus when God took him to heaven.

[8] 6:31; 7:187; 12:107; 21:40; 22:55; 29:53; 47:18.

[9] 15:85; 20:15; 22:7; 40:59.

[10] 16:77.

[11] 33:63; 42:17.

[12] Matthew 24:45

[13] Ibid., 24:50.

[14] 1 Thessalonians 5:2; 2 Peter 3:10; Revelation 3:3; 16:15.

[15] Mark 13: 29.

[16] 1 Corinthians 15:52.

[17] 43:85.

[18] 7:185.

[19] 33:63.

[20] Matthew 24:36.

[21] Suras 25:25; 55:37; 69:16; 84:1.

[22] Ibid., 82:1; 73:36.

[23] Ibid., 81:11.

[24] Ibid., 70:8.

[25] Ibid., 52:9.

[26] Ibid., 55:37.

[27] Ibid., 25:25

[28] Ibid., 21:104.

[29] Ibid .,75:8-9.

[30] Ibid., 81:1-2.

[31] Ibid., 82:2.
[32] Ibid., 52:6; 81:6; 82:3.
[33] Sura 37:14; 99:1.
[34] Sura 84:3.
[35] Sura 69:8.
[36] Sura 14: 18.
[37] Mathew 24:29.
[38] 2 Peter 3:10.
[39] Isaiah 34:4; Revelation 6:13.
[40] Ibid., 24: 23;13:10; Joel3:15; Revelation 6:12
[41] Matthew 24:7; Revelation 11:13.
[42] Revelation 6:14.
[43] Ibid,. 8:8.
[44] Ibid., 21:1.
[45] Sura 74:8; 6:73.
[46] Sura 50:42; 79:6-9.
[47] Sura 79:6-9.
[48] Sura 22:2.
[49] Sura 73:17.
[50] Suras 2:48.
[51] Sura 2:210.
[52] Sura 26:88.
[53] Proverbs 11:4.
[54] Sura 99:6.
[55] Ibid., 56:8-9, 38,41.
[56] Ibid., 84:8.
[57] Ibid., 69:18.
[58] Ibid., 78:18; 82:10-12; 36:11; 21:94.
[59] Matthew 25:32-33
[60] Ibid., 16:27.
[61] Romans 15:12.
[62] Revelation 20:12-15.
[63] Al-Hariri, p. 163-171.
[64] Ibid.
[65] Sura 39:20.
[66] Ibid., 38:50.
[67] Ibid., 3:15; 9:21,72, 100; 58:22; 5:119; 98:8; 93:4-5; 57:20.
[68] Ibid., 76:13.
[69] John 14:2.
[70] Revelation 21:12.
[71] Matthew 6:19-20.

[72] Revelation 7:16.

[73] Sura 47:15.

[74] Genesis 2:10-14.

[75] As quoted by al-Hariri, p. 172.

[76] Ibid., p. 173.

[77] Job 38:17; Isaiah 38:10; Matthew 16:18.

[78] Matthew 3:12; 18:8; 25:31, 46; Mark 9:44.

[79] Or underground pits. The word "pits" here is of some significance since it points to more than one place in Hell.

[80] 2 Peter 2:4; Revelation 20:1ff.

[81] Jude 6.

[82] Sura 44:35; 37:58-59.

[83] Revelation 21:8.

[84] Suras 38:8; 40:61; 69:30-32; 76:4; 73:12.

[85] See also 8:12; 25:30; Luke 13:28. Apparently the outer darkness is a symbol of hell. Refer also to David Brady's study, 'The Book of Revelation and the Qur'an'.

[86] Al-Hariri, pp. 158-184.

[87] Al-Hariri remarks, "I do not say that the Arabic Qur'an has directly copied St. Ephraem the Syriac or others, and I do not claim that Muhammad was acquainted with the irregularities of the Christian paradise and all its descriptions...But the ideas of St. Aphraem was in vogue in the Christian Syriac church and well known among its fathers and writers. Also the relationship between the Qur'an and the writings of the Syriac church was not only the result of a general environ in which Muhammad lived and been influenced, but it was through teachings and texts he knew, both orally and in writing. He became familiar with them through his personal acquaintances and direct contact with the literary works of the Syriac authors..." p.171.

[88] As quoted by al-Hariri, p.181.

Conclusion

[1] Among those who were ostracized in the twentieth century are Sheik Mustafa Abdul Razzaq, Sheik Badwan of Suhaj, Hassan al-Hallaq of Iran, the journalist Taslima Nasreen of Bangladesh, Naser Abu Zayd and his wife Ibtihal, Sa'd Ibrahim, Anis Mansour, Nobel Prize

recipient Najib Mahfuz, 'Adel Hammouda, Salman Rushdie, Mustafa Jiha, Nawal Sa'dawi, Tahmina Miladi from Iran, Toujan al-Faysal from Jordan, and Rashad Khalifa.

[2] Abd Al-Masih, *The Gospel Questions the Qur'an,* p.21.

[3] Suras 3:7; 13:39; 43:4.

[4] Moderate Muslims harbor a different idea about the concept of martyrdom in Islam. They differentiate between the act of suicide of 9/11 and dying for the cause of Allah in a just war, led by a caliph who is the Imam of the nation.

[5] Refer to chapter six.

Cited Bibliography

Important Notice

For the names of the authors that start with the definite article 'Al', the article 'Al' is disregarded and inserted between two brackets. The reader should look for the name under the first letter of the author's family name or surname.

A and 'A (ع)

Alussi (Al), *Ruh al-Ma'ani fi Tafsir al-Qur'an al-'Azim wa al-Sab' al-Mathani,* (Cairo, Egypt: Bulaq Print, 1303H/1885 A.D.), vol. 6.

Amini, Ayatollah Ibrahim, trans. Abdulaziz Sachedina, *Al-Imam Al-Mahdi the Just Leader of Humanity,* (Qum, Iran: Ansaryan Publications, 1997).

Arbali, (Al), Al-Hasan, *Kashf al-Ghamma fi Ma'rifat al-A'imma,* (Iran edition, 1382H,/1962 A.D.), vol.3.

Ayyub, Sa'id, *'Aqidat al-Dajjal fi al-Adyan,* (Beirut, Lebanon: Dar al-Hadi, 1991).

'Abddul Baqi, Muhammad Fu'ad, *Al-Mu'jam al-Mufahras li Alfaz al-Qur'an,* (Dar al-Fikr, 1987).

'Abdul Haq, *Al-Islam: Hal Huwa Ma'qul?* (n. place, n. date).

'Ali, Jawad, *Tarikh al-'Arab Qabla al-Islam,* (Iraq: Al-Majma' al-'ilmi al-'Iraqi,1956).

'Asqalani (Al), Ibn Hajar Abu al-Fadl Ahmad ibn Ali, *Fath al-Bari bi Sharh Sahih al-Bukhari,* (Egypt: Matb'at Bulaq, 1300H./1911 A.D.), vol.6.

B

Barzanji (Al), *Al-Isha'a li Ashrat al-Sa'a,* (Egypt: Sa'ada Pub., 1325H./1905 A.D.).

Baydawi (Al), 'Abd Allah ibn 'Umar, *Anwar al-Tanzil wa Asrar al-Ta'wil,* (Beirut, Lebanon: Dar al-Jil, n. d.).

Bayhaqi (Al), Ahmad ibn al-Husayn, *Kitab al-Ba'th wa al-Nushur,* ed. A.A. Haydar, (Beirut,1986).

Bradly, David, *Journal of Semetic Studies,* The Book of Revelation and the Qur'an: Is there a Possible Literary Relationship? (Menchester: Menchester University Press, 1978), vol. 23.

Bruce, F. F., *1and 2 Thessalonians,* (Waco, Texas: Word Pub., 1982).

Budge, Ernest A. Wallis, *Pseudo Calisthenenes, The History of Alexander the Great,* (Amesterdam: Apaphilo Press, first published 1889, reprint 1976, Cambridge University Press).

_____, *The Book of the Dead,* (Arkana, 1989).

Busse, Heribert, *Islam, Judaism, and Christianity: Theological and Historical Affiliation,* trans. Alleson Brown, (Prinston, New Jersey: Markus Weiner pub., 1998).

C

Carter, George William, *Zoroastrianism and Judaism,* (New York: AMS, 1970).

Chittick, William C. *Muslim World,* Death and the World of Imagination: Ibn al-'Arabi's Eschatology. (The Duncan Black MacDonald Center, January, 1988).

Clouse, Robert G., editor, *the Meaning of the Millennium,* (Downers Grove, Illinois: InterVarsity Press, 1977).

292

D

Dakhil, 'Ali Muhammad 'Ali, *Al-Imam al-Mahdi*, (Najaf, Iraq: n..p, n.d.).

Dhahabi (Al), Muhammad ibn Ahmad Shams al_Din, *Tadh-karat al-Huffaz*, (India:, n.p., n.d.),vol. 27.

Dhalla, Maneckli Nusservanji, *Zoroastrian Theology from the Earliest Times to the Present Days,* (New York: AMS press, Inc., reprint of 1914).

Daley, Brian A., *The Hope of the Early Church*, (New York, Port Chester-Melbourn-Sydney: Cambridge University Press, 1958).

G

Galloway, Dalton, *Moslim World*, The Resurrection and Judgment in the Qur'an, (Vol. 17, 1922).

Ghazali (Al), Abu Hamid Muhammad Ibn Muhammad, *The Remembrance of Death and Afterlife*, trans. T. J. Winters, (Cambridge. UK: The Islamic Text Society, 1989).

Geddes, C. L., *The Muslim World*, The Messiah of South Arabia

Geiger, Abraham, *Judaism and Islam*, (Ktav, New York: reprint 1970 from the original, 1853).

Gibb, H. A. R. and J.H. Krammers, *Shorter Encyclopedia of Islam*, (Leiden: E. J. Brill, 1974).

Gilchrist, John, *The Qur'an the Scripture of Islam*, (Mondeor, South Africa: Mercsa, 1999).

Glass, Cyrill, *The Concise Encyclopedia of Islam*, (San Francisco: Harper and Raw, 1991).

____, *The New Encyclopedia of Islam,* rev. ed., (Lanhaw, New York: Rowman and Littlefield publishers, 2001).

Gorenger, Gershom, *The End of Days*; (New York, New York: Oxford University Press, 2000).
Gunduz, Sinasi. *The Knowledge of Life*. Oxford University Press, 1994).

H

Haddad (Al), 'Abdullah, *The Life of Man*, (Louisville, KY: Fons Vitae, 1991).
Ha'iri (Al), Ali al-Yazdi, *Ilzam al-Nasib fi Ithbat Hujjiyat al-Gha'ib*, (Tahran: Tahran Press, 1351H./1952 A.D.).
Hariri (Al), Abu Musa, *Quss wa Nabiy*, (Diar 'aql, Lebanon: Dar li Ajli al-Ma'rifa,1985).
Hassan, Riffat, *Journal of Ecumenical Studies*, Messianism and Islam, 22:2, Spring 1985.
Hindi (Al) Al-Muttaqi, *Kanzu al-'Ummal*, (India: Matba'at Haydar 'Abad al-Dakn, 1312H./1894 A.D.).
Hoppe, Lewis M., *The Religions of the World*, 4th edition, (New York: Macmillan publishing House, 1987).
Hoyt, Herman A. *The End of Time*, 4th print, (Chicago, IL, 1976).
Hughes, Thomas Patrik, *Dictionary of Islam: library of religious and philosophical thought*, (Clifton, new Jersey: Reference Book Publisher, inc., 1965).
Husayn, Taha, *Fi al-Shi'r al-Jahili*, 1st ed., (Cairo, Egypt: Matb'at Dar al-Kutub al-Misriya, 1926).

I

Ibn 'Abd Rabbih, Ahmad ibn Muhammad al-Qurtubi, *al-'Iqd al-Farid*, (Cairo: Lujnat al-Ta'lif wa al-Tarjama wa al-Nashr, 1940-1953).
Ibn Hanbal, Ahmad Ibn Muhammd, *Musnad ibn Hanbal*,

Ibn Hisham, *Al-Sirat al-Nabawiya* (Arabic version), Mustfa al-Saqqa et la, ed., (Cairo:Mustfa al-Babi al-Halabi, 1936).

_____, *The Life of the Prophet*, Trans. A. Guillaum, 9th ed., (Oxford-New York-Karachi impression,1990).

Ibn Kathir, Isma'il, *Al-Fitan wa al-Malahim*, (Damascus-Beirut: Dar Ibn Kathir, 1414H./1993 A.D.).

_____, *The Signs before the Day of judgment*, Trans. Huda Khattab, London: Dar al-Taqwa, LTD, 2000).

Ibn Sa'd, *Tabaqat ibn Sa'd,* (Beirut, n.p., 1957).

Ibrahim, Hassan Ahmad and Ibrahim M. Zein, *The Moslim World*, Islah and Tajdid: The Case of the Sudanes Mahdiyyah, vol. Lxxxll, January 1997.

Isaiah, Emmanuel Sudhir, *Muslim Eschatological and Missiological Implication: A thematic Study,* (Ann Arbor: UMI, 1989).

J

Jeffery, Arthur (ed.), *Islam, Muhammad and His Religion*, (New York: The Liberal Art Press, 1958).

Jiha, Mustafa, *Mihnat al-'Aql fi al-Islam*, 2nd edition, (Beirut, Lebanon: 1982).

K

Kazimi (Al), Mustafa, *Bisharat al-Islam*, (al-Najaj, Iraq: n. p., 1382H./1926 A.D.).

Kamil, Sulayman, *Yaym al-Khalas fi Zilli al-Qa'im al-Mahdi*, (Beirut: Dar al-Kitab al-Lubnani, 1991).

Kashmiri (Al), Muhammad Anwar Shah, *Al-Tasrih bima Tawatara fi Nuzul al-Masih*, (Aleppo, Syria: al-Matba'a al-Islamiya, 1965).

295

Kasrawi, Ahmad, *On Islam and Shi'ism*, trans. M.R. Ghanooparvar (Cost Mesa, CA: Mazda Publishers, 1990).

Katch, Abraham, *Judaism in Islam: Biblical and Talmudic Background of the Koran and its Commentaries*, (Block pub. 1954).

L

Lincoln, B., *Indogermanishe Forschangen*, On the Imagery of Paradise 55, (1980).

M

Mahdi, Muhammad Jawad, *Al-Muslih al-'Alami*, (Toledo, Ohio: Muslim Group in US and Canada, n.d.).

Majlisi (Al), Mulla Muhammad Baqir, *Bihar al-Anwar*, (Tahran, Iran: Matba'at Tahran, 1385H./ 1985 A.D.), part 52.

Ma'sumian Farnaz, *The After Death: A Study of the Afterlife in World Religions*, (Oxford, England: One World Publications, 1995, reprint, 1996).

Madenlung, Wilferd, *Journal of Near Eastern Studies*, 'Abd Allah B. Al-Zubair and the Mahdi, 40, # 4, (1981)

Maqrizi (Al), *Al-Khutat*, (Beirut: Matba'at al-Sabil al-Junubi, 1379H./1979 A.D.).

Masih (Abd), *The Gospel Questions the Qur'an*, (Villach, Austria: Light of Life, 1998).

McAuliff, Jane Dammen, *Encyclopedia of the Qur'an*, (Leiden, The Netherland: Konninklijk Brill-NY, 2001).

MacDonald, William, *Believer's Bible Commentary*, (Nashville: Thomas Nelson Publishers, 1990).

McGinn, Bernard, *Anti-Christ,* (New York: Harper Collins, 1996).

Mir, Muntasir, *Dictionary of Qur'anic Terms and Concepts,* (NY and London: Garland Publishing, Inc., 1987).

Morony, Michael G., *Name-ye-e-Bastan,* The Late Sasanian Economic Impact on the Arabian Peninsula, vol. 1, No. 2.

Morris, Leon, *The Revelation of Saint John,* (Grand Rapids, Michigan: William E, Eardmans Publishing House, 1976).

_____, *Tyndale New Testament Commentary: The Revelation of John,* (Grand Rapids, Michigan: Eerdman, 1976).

N

Na'na'a, Ramzi, *Al-Isra'iliyat,* (Beirut, Lebanon-Damascus, Syria: Dar al-Qalam and Dar al-Diya', 1970).

Newby, *A History of the Jews in Arabia,* (University of South Carolina Press, 1988).

Nisan, Mordachai, *The Identity and Civilization: Essay on Judaism and Islam,* (Lanham, New York: University Press of America, 1999).

P

Parshall, Phil, *Understanding Muslim Teachings and Traditions,* (Grand Rapids, Michigan: Eerdman, 2001).

Pinault, David, *The Shi'ites: Rituals and Popular Piety in a Muslim Community*, (New York: St. Martin's Press, 1992).

Pavry, J.D.C., *The Zoroastrian Doctrine of Future Life*, (New York: AMC, 1965, reprint of 1929 edition).

Q

Qanduzi, *Yanabi' al-Mawaddah*, (Istanbul, n.p., 1301H./1883 A.D.).

R

Razi (Al), Fakhr al-Din ibn Diya' al-Din 'Umar, *Al-Tafsir al-Kabir*, (Beirut, Lebanon: Dar al-Fikr, 1985), 3rd edition, vol. 21.

Russell. Jefferey Burton, *A History of Heaven*, (Princeton: Princeton University Press, 1997).

S

Sachedina, Abdulaziz Abdulhussein, *Islamic Messianism: The Idea of th Mahdi in Twelver Shi'ism*, (Albany, New York, State University Press, 1981).

Saduq (Al), *'Uyun Akhbar al-Rida*, (Al-Najaf, Iraq: n.p., 1970), vol.1.

Safi (Al), Lutfalla, *Muntakhab al-Athar fi al-Imam al-Thani 'Ashar*, (Tahran, n.p., 173H./1953 A.D).

Sakr, Ahmad H. *Death and Dying*, (Lombard, Illinois,!995).

Sanders, Oswald, *Heaven Better by Far*, Grand Rapids, Michigan: Discovery House Publishers, 1994).

Scott, Miriam Van, *Encycopedia of Heaven*, 1st. ed, (New York, NewYork: Thomas Dunn Books, an imprint of St. Martin's Press, 1999).

Sha'rani (Al), *Mukhtasar Tadh-karat al-Qurtubi*, (Cairo, Egypt: Subayh edition,1354H./1935 A.D.).

Sheikho, Louis, *Shu'ara' al-Nusraniya Qabla al-Islam*, 3rd. ed. (Beirut, Lebanon: Dar al-Mashriq, 1967).

Smith, Jane and Yvonne Haddad, *The Islamic Understanding of Death and Resurrection*, (Albany, New York: State University of New York Press, 1981).

Suyuti (Al), Jalal al-Din Ibn 'Abd al-Rahman, *Al-Durr al-Manthur fi Tafsir al-Qur'an bi al-Ma'thur*, (Egypt: Tab'at al-Maymaniya, 1315H./1896 A.D.), vol.2.

_____, *Al-Hawi lil Fatawi*, (Egypt:Tab'at al-Muniriya, 1352H./ 1933 A.D.), vol.2.

T

Tabari (Al), Abu Ja'far Muhammad ibn Jarir, *Tafsir al-Tabari*, 8th ed., vol. 8, part 17, (Bulaq, Egypt: Matba'at al-Amiriya, 1328H./1910 A.D.).

Tabataba'i, Muhammad Husayn, *Shi'ite Islam*, Trans. Sayyid Husayn Nasr, (Houston, Texas: Free Islamic Literature, Inc., 1971).

Tayalisi (Al), *Musnad al-Tayalisi*, (India: Haydar Abad print, 1321H./1903 A.D.)

Tirmidhi (Al), Muhammad ibn 'Isa al-Dahhak, *Sunan of al-Tirmidhi*, (Egypt: Al-Matba'at al-Misriya, 1350H./1931 A.D.).

Tisdall, W. St. Clair, *The Sources of Islam*, (Edinburg, Scotland: T. and T. Clark, n.d.).

Torry, Charles, *The Jewish Foundation of Islam*,(ktav, New York: 1967, original edition 1933).

W

Wadud, Amina, *Qur'an and Women*, (Oxford, New York: Oxford
University Press, 1999).

Y

Yamauchi, Edwin M., *Persia and the Bible*, (Grand Rapids, Michigan: Baker book House, 1990).
_____, *JETS*, Meshech, Tubal, and Company: A Review Article, 19 (1976).

Z

Zamakh-shari (Al), Mahmud ibn 'Umar, *Al-Kash-shaf fi Haqiqat al-Tanzil,* ed. Mustafa Husayn Ahmad, (Beirut, Lebanon: Dar al-Kitab al-'Arabi, 1986).

GLOSSARY

'Ad and Thamud, two extinct pre-Islamic tribes.

A'raf, the heights at the edge of the bridge on which the people will try to cross after the day of judgment.

Ahiram, the god of evil in the Zoroastrian religion.

Ahl al-Bayt, the family of the prophet Muhammad.

Ahura Mazda, the god of goodness in the Zoroastrian religion.

Allah, the Arabic name for God.

Antichrist, the English name of the eschatological imposter who deifies himself to deceive the people of the earth.

Apocalypse, various Jewish and Christian writings (c.200 B.C.-c. 300 A.D.) that revolve around the end of time.

Apocryphal, Jewish or Christian literature of doubtful authenticity or authorship; or, the fourteen non-canonical books rejected by the protestant church.

Apostasy, the act of relinquishing the faith of Islam and embracing any other religion.

Athenians, the residents of Athens.

Beast, an ambiguous being that will appear in Islamic eschatology at the end of time to distinguish between the righteous and the wicked people.

Buwayhids, a Persian dynasty that ruled the Abbasid Empire from the tenth to the eleventh centuries.

Caliph, the title assumed by Muhammad's successors as secular and religious heads of the Islamic community.

Caliphate, the reign of the Caliph.

Chivnat, an eschatological bridge on which the people will cross from one end to another in the Day of Judgment according to the Zoroastrian religion.

Dajjal, the Islamic Antichrist.

Day of the Hashr (the), the day of the assembly prior to the Day of Judgment in Islamic eschatology.

Dhu al-khulasa, a pre-Islamic idol worshipped by the tribe of Dus.

301

Doena, the conscience of the deceased person in the Zoroastrian religion.

Dragon, a title for Satan.

Dus, a pre-Islamic tribe that later converted to Islam.

Eschatology, the study of the events of the end of time.

Faithful Spirit (the), one of the titles of the archangel Gabriel in the Qur'an.

Gilgamesh, a legendary Babylonian hero of the Gilgamesh epic.

Gog an Magog, biblical nations from the north who will invade the East and will be miraculously destroyed by God as prophesied in the book of Ezekiel.

Hades, (from Greek origin) the lowest part of the pit or abyss.

Hadith, the collection of the sayings and deeds of Muhammad.

Hajj, the pilgrimage to Mecca.

Hanifs, a minor monotheistic sect that believed in one God and abstained from offering sacrifices to the idols of Mecca.

Hawd (the), a pool that is located in front of the gates of paradise according to Islamic eschatology.

Himyarite's era, the era of the reign of the Himyarite tribe that lived in Southern Arabia before Islam.

Hour (the), the day of resurrection and judgment according to the teaching of the Qur'an.

Imam (sunni), the religious leader in any given mosque.

Imam (shi'ite), a position ordained by God to the descendents of 'Ali, Muhammad's son-in-law, and his wife Fatima. They exert a great authority over their followers.

'Isa, The Qur'anic Arabic name for Jesus.

Jassasa, a legendary beast associated with the Antichrist according to the Islamic Tradition.

Jehovah, the name of God in the Hebrew Old Testament.

Jinns, genies; some of them are good Muslims, while others are bad. They are created from smoke.

Ka'ba, the most holy shrine in Islam, located in Mecca.

Khadir, according to Islamic Tradition, he is a prophet, divinely empowered, who lived during the time of Moses.

302

Kawthar, the name of one of the rivers in paradise.

Mahdi (the), the expected deliverer and savior of the Shi'ites who will return from his occultation at the end of time.

Mamluks, a class of slaves who distinguished themselves, and later ruled Egypt from 1250–1515 A.D., and remained powerful until 1810 A.D.

Masih ad-Dajjal, the deceiver Christ.

Mecca, The religious capital of Islam, located in Saudi Arabia.

Medinites, the citizens of al-Madina, the city to which Muhammad immigrated and was buried. It is located in Saudi Arabia.

Messianic (adj.) anything related to the Messiah, the deliverer and savior.

Millennium, the period of one thousand years in which the pre-millenniumists believe that Christ will reign on earth at the end of time.

Millenarian, one who believes in the millennium.

Munkar and Nakir, the two angels whose role in Islam is to interrogate the deceased Muslim in order to determine whether he was true Muslim or not.

Muq'ad, a man designated by Christ to succeed Him in administering the affairs of Muslims after His death.

Night journey of the Mi'raj, the night in which Muhammad claims that he ascended to heaven by way of Jerusalem to meet with God.

People of the Book, a Qur'anic reference to Christians, Jews and the Sabeans.

Polytheists, those who associate any god with the God.

Pseudo-canonical literature, Christian religious literature whose authors are anonymous.

Pseudepigraphal, a corpus of early writings not included in the biblical canon or the apocrypha, some which erroneously attributed to biblical characters.

Qur'an, the Holy Book of Islam.

Qurayshites, members of the tribe of Quraish who inhabited Mecca and were Muhammad's relatives.

Rafida, the dissenters. A radical branch of the Shi'ite sect.

Rukn and Maqam, the court of the holy shrine and the mosque of Abraham located in Saudi Arabia.

Salsabil, the name of one of the rivers of paradise.

Sa'qa, the blast of the trumpet that causes the death of all the creatures in the universe before the Day of Resurrection.

Scale (the), an eschatological scale by which God will weigh the good and the bad deeds of the people on the Day of Judgment.

Seraphiel, An angel whose task is to blast the trumpet of death and resurrection.

Sham (al), greater Syria.

Shari'a, Islamic law.

Sheol, (of Hebrew origin) the lowest part of the pit or the abyss.

Shi'ites, the partisans of 'Ali, the son-in-law of Muhammad, and the second largest sect in Islam who separated themselves from the Sunnis.

Sidrat al-Muntaha, a tree located in the seventh heaven at the right side of God's throne.

Sirat, the straight path, or the bridge.

Smoke Mountain, Mount of Harmon in Lebanon.

Soshyant, a deliverer from the race of Zoroaster, according to Zoroastrianism.

Sufism, an Islamic mystic movement that reacted against the formalism of Islam and sought to be united with God as their uttermost goal in life.

Sufyani (the), the archenemy of the Mahdi who will be defeated by the forces of the Mahdi at the end of time.

Suljuks, a Turkish dynasty that reined in Baghdad during the 12th and 13th centuries.

Sunnis (the), the major sect of Islam that regarded themselves as the orthodox followers of the faith adhering to the Tradition of Muhammad.

Sur, a ram's horn.

Sura (s), a Qur'anic chapter.

Tradition, the saying and the deeds of Muhammad

Traditionists or Traditionalists, those who adhere to and are knowledgeable of Islamic Tradition.

Talmud, the collection of writings instituting the Jewish civil and religious laws, as well as commentaries.

Tasmin, the name of one of the rivers of paradise.

Ummat, the nation or community of Islam.

'Ukaz, an ancient market in the suburb of Mecca where poets, preachers and orators would compete in their rhetorical skills.

Valley of Hinnom, a geographical place located outside of Jerusalem, called Jahannam in Arabic.

Yathrib, the ancient name of the Madina in Saudi Arabia.

Zakat, Islamic almsgiving.

Zoroaster, the founder of the Persian religion Zoroastria-nism.

Zoroastrian, an adherent of Zoroastrianism.

Zoroastrianism, a Persian religion founded by Zoroaster in the 6th or 7th century B.C.

Printed in the United States
64091LVS00003B/68

9 781597 810326